PRAISE FOR
Here for All the Reasons

"Critical essays take aim at [*The Bachelor*'s] stereotypical representations of contestants of color, its focus on heterosexual relationships, and its perpetuation of impossible standards for femininity. Other entries praise the franchise as a way to spend time with friends and connect over show-related gossip, an opportunity to escape from the complexities of real life, and a chronicle of genuine human moments, like the nonromantic relationships that arise between contestants. Offering intriguing arguments and passionate appraisals, [*Here For All the Reasons*] is a testament to the undeniable pull of a cultural touchstone."

—***Publishers Weekly***

"*The Bachelor* is a show that is regularly dismissed as trashy, disposable, and forgettable. *Here For All the Reasons*, a multi-faceted look at the show by its viewers—some long-time, some more recent, some who no longer watch—is a wonderful antidote to this dismissal, positioning *The Bachelor* as what it truly is: a rich text, through which we can see many of the social and political developments of the twenty-first century play out."

—**Dr. Jodi McAlister**, author of *Here for the Right Reasons*, *Can I Steal You for a Second?*, and *Not Here to Make Friends*

"As a longtime conflicted member of Bachelor Nation, this is the *Bachelor* book I've been waiting for. *Here For All the Reasons* is sharply observed, deeply interrogated, and fun as hell. It's the smartest watch party around."

—**Aubrey Gordon**, *New York Times* bestselling author of *"You Just Need to Lose Weight" and 19 Other Myths About Fat People* and cohost of *Maintenance Phase*

"Why do we keep coming back to *The Bachelor*? *Here for All the Reasons* demonstrates that while our reasons for tuning in are deeply personal, the show also reveals broad social dynamics like race, gender, sexuality, embodiment, community, politics, and religion. Alternately insightful and amusing, this engaging anthology will steal you for a second and show you that, amid the rose ceremonies and bedazzled evening gowns, *The Bachelor* is a rich site for textual analysis and cultural critique."

—**Danielle J. Lindemann**, sociologist and author of *True Story: What Reality TV Says About Us*

"Thoughtful, honest, and gloriously funny in all the right places, this anthology is a chorus of diverse voices studiously investigating reality TV, fantasy, and desire, while also telling moving stories of identity, belonging, and self-discovery. *Bachelor* franchise lovers and haters alike will discover something illuminating about how the show has defined a culture that can't seem to stop tuning in to love."

—**Eshani Surya**, author of the critically-acclaimed novel, *Ravishing*

"Reading this collection feels like having your smartest friends over for a holiday weekend when you've got a burning question on your mind. A highbrow examination of a lowbrow petri dish, these essays mix feminist criticism, sociology, reporting, and memoir with verve, energy, and humor in ways that break down that original binary and reveal *The Bachelor* to be a strangely profound and profoundly American text."

—**Emma Copley Eisenberg**, bestselling author of *Housemates*

Here for All the Reasons

Why We Watch THE BACHELOR

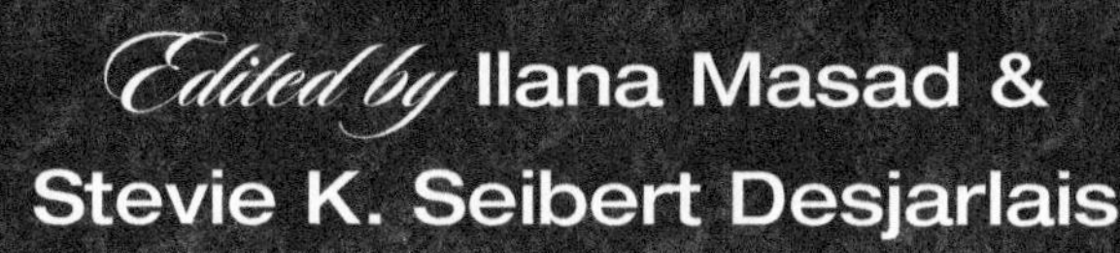

Edited by Ilana Masad & Stevie K. Seibert Desjarlais

TURNER
PUBLISHING COMPANY

Turner Publishing Company
Nashville, Tennessee
www.turnerpublishing.com

Here for All the Reasons: Why We Watch The Bachelor

Cover design by Kelli McAdams
Book design by Ashlyn Inman

Library of Congress Cataloging-in-Publication Data
Names: Masad, Ilana editor | Seibert Desjarlais, Stevie K. editor
Title: Here for all the reasons : Why we watch the bachelor / edited by Stevie K. Seibert Desjarlais and Ilana Masad.
Description: Nashville, Tennessee : Turner Publishing Company, 2026.
Identifiers: LCCN 2025019689 (print) | LCCN 2025019690 (ebook) | ISBN 9781684426119 paperback | ISBN 9781684426126 hardcover | ISBN 9781684426133 epub
Subjects: LCSH: Bachelor (Television program) | Reality television Programs—Social aspects—United States | Dating shows (Television programs)—Social aspect—United States | LCGFT: Television criticism and reviews
Classification: LCC PN1992.77.B245 H47 2026 (print) | LCC PN1992.77.B245 (ebook) | DDC 791.45/72—dc23/eng/20250623
LC record available at https://lccn.loc.gov/2025019689
LC ebook record available at https://lccn.loc.gov/2025019690

Printed in the United States of America

Contents

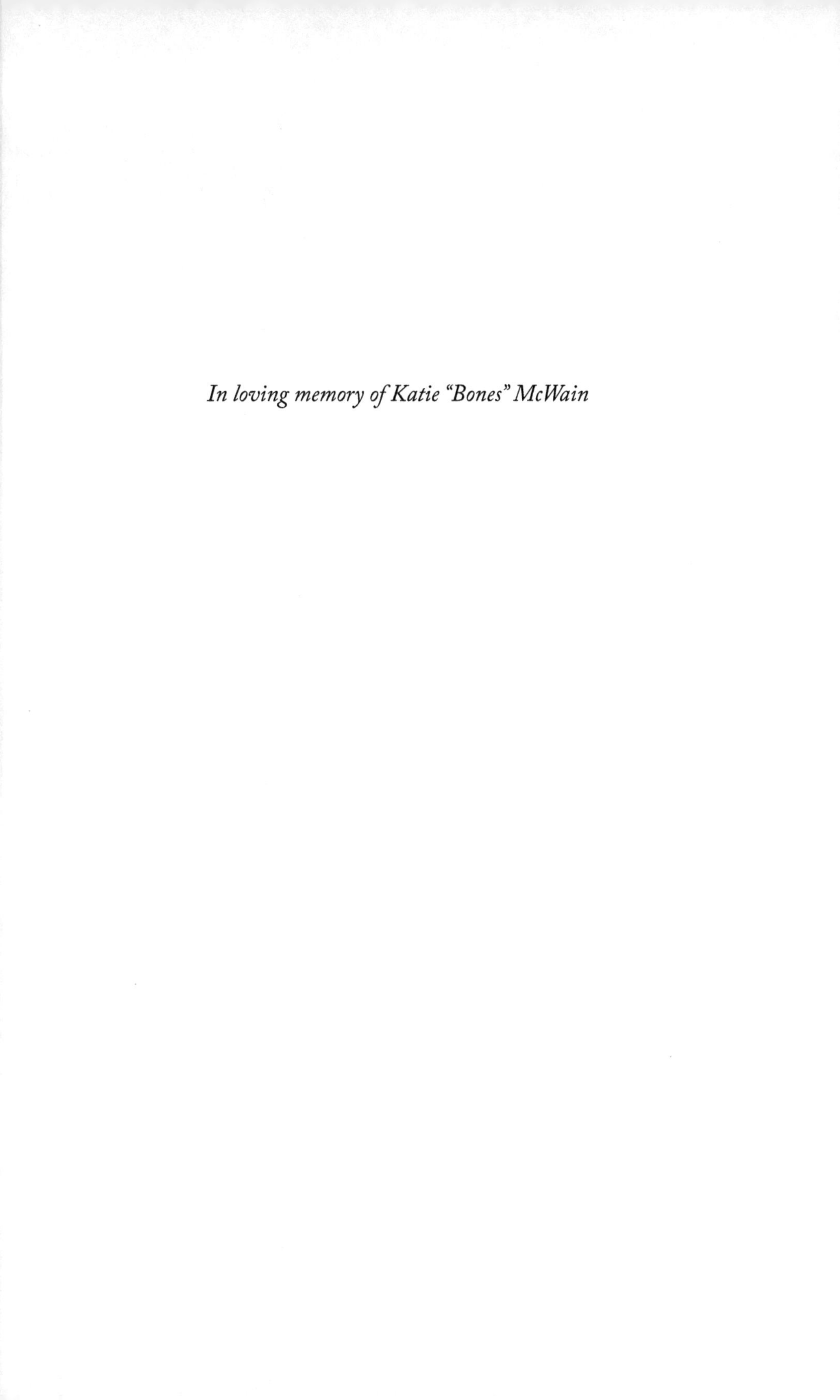

In loving memory of Katie "Bones" McWain

Editors' Introduction:

The First Impression Rose

You've likely heard of the reality TV show *The Bachelor*, even if you haven't watched a single episode, and you probably know, more or less, what it's about. A conventionally handsome man greets dozens of women in full glam—the contestants vying for his heart—and week by week, he whittles down the dating pool by handing out roses to a select few. By the end of each season, the Bachelor is expected to get down on one knee and propose to his one and only forever love. *The Bachelorette*? Same concept, gender-flipped, although the man still proposes. *Bachelor in Paradise*? A bunch of rejected contestants from previous seasons on a beach with an open bar, daily make outs and breakups and the occasional engagement to wrap up the drama with a dash of happily-ever-after. In all the shows, there is tension in the air between the expressed earnestness of finding love (and a spouse) and the bizarre construction of reality TV that is far from real.

Since *The Bachelor* first aired in 2002, the fans of the franchise have accompanied the eligible Bachelors, Bachelorettes, and contestants on their journeys to find love. We have laughed with and at them; cried along with their heartbreaks; tuned in again and again each season; and celebrated, alone and together, the love (or loveless) lives of perfect strangers on our television screens.

For many of us, watching with each other is a simple pleasure: couches, company, wine. But we're more than passive viewers. Think pieces, podcasts, and meme accounts abound in the community of Bachelor Nation, as fans of the franchise lovingly or begrudgingly call ourselves.[1] For decades, we have watched these formulaic reality television shows with one another and shared (publicly and privately) reactions to contestants, analyses of controversies, and thoughts on the elemental question of who on-screen is there for the "right reasons."

The Bachelor claims to be about finding love. However, most viewers know that the show is heavily edited, sometimes creating drama and plotlines where none existed in the first place. For most of its tenure, the majority of contestants and leads have been white, skinny and fit, and conventionally attractive. As you can see from the formula, there is no straying from a cisgender, heterosexual coupling at the end of any season. That each episode includes heavy product placement comes with the territory.

All that being said, we wonder, really, *why* do we keep coming back? The franchise needs us fans to survive; we produce the economy in which it thrives and provide discourse that keeps it relevant despite the increasingly irrelevant format and network television platform. The loyalty of Bachelor Nation's fandom is worth exploring.

Here for the Right, Wrong, and Complicated Reasons

What kind of person stands up and claims Bachelor Nation? All sorts, really. That's what we've come to realize and appreciate since the two of us began this journey together. Who are *we*, though? Let us introduce our relationship to Bachelor Nation:

In 2017, Ilana Masad was invited to visit the University of Nebraska-

1 Who belongs to Bachelor Nation is up for debate. Some believe the label includes only those who appear on the show, and others, like us, take the term to represent the fandom. Another faction sees it as an umbrella for viewers and contestants alike. ABC has co-opted the identification for promotional purposes, branding a website and utilizing the hashtag for show-sanctioned information.

Lincoln after being accepted to its English PhD program. Her host for the stay was Stevie Seibert Desjarlais, a third-year in the same program. It was the season of Rachel Lindsay as the lead on *The Bachelorette*, and Stevie hosted a regular watch party. Out of curiosity, Ilana—a snob with no interest in reality TV—decided to hang out in the living room with Stevie and other women from UNL. How was it that this group of graduate students, all clearly intelligent and intellectually motivated, watched this trash?

For Stevie, *The Bachelor* and *The Bachelorette* were part escape from the grind of graduate school and part continuation of her pop culture research in gender studies. She had seen the first season and tuned in sporadically over the years until becoming a much more dedicated viewer around 2011. The watch parties meant that she had to keep her house clean—sort of—but also that conversations among grad-school friends didn't always devolve into shoptalk. Not everyone who attended the watch parties was an avid fan of the franchise before meeting Stevie, but enthusiasm at the parties was contagious. The friends brought a bottle of wine, a bag of chips, or the odd baked good, and Stevie broke out the popcorn. Because of the weirdness of grad-school hours, the parties provided a neatly contained opportunity to socialize—the two-hour airtime of the show on network TV with commercial breaks muted for raucous debates and catch-up gossip sessions.

Ilana remembers that first night clearly: Natalie, Jess, Katie, and Stevie—plus Stevie's two cats and two dogs—gathered in the living room, crowding the couches and floor, digging into snacks and sipping wine. Over the course of the episode, she watched the women around her engage in the kind of conversation she most enjoyed—a mix of cultural criticism and gossip, commenting on gender dynamics and racial tensions on the show in one breath and discussing the Bachelorette's outfits in the next. As the episode wore on, Ilana began to ask questions, trying to understand how the show operated, how "real" it was, how the ridiculous format worked. As someone in a nonmonogamous relationship, she quickly realized there was something really strange going on in this show and its conservative definitions of what constituted love and commitment. Moreover, there was something to the way this group of brilliant women was discussing the show that made her want to join in next time.

The insightful banter of the watch parties was what made the effort to host worthwhile for Stevie. Her pop culture interests frequently led to small talk fodder on campus, especially with her students. When Stevie would ask her first-year English composition class what pop culture stuff they enjoyed, someone would inevitably bring up *The Bachelor*. But more than common ground to relate to students, Stevie encouraged them to develop critical media literacy skills and analyze what drew them to such phenomena. The most common answers from students for *why* they watched what they watched was simple: for entertainment, or more specifically, in the case of *The Bachelor*, the drama. While this is true for many viewers, including Stevie herself, media like reality TV yields more than just pleasure.

Spoiler: Ilana ended up attending UNL. She moved to Nebraska a few short months after her first time at Stevie's watch party and knew that she wanted to join again. Luckily, Stevie liked her—and the other women did too—and so she gained permanent entry to the space. Over the next couple of years, these watch parties were a lifeline amid the workaholic energy Ilana brought to grad school. Monday nights were sacred—a time to fully unwind, to gossip about the department and complain about the workload, but also to turn her brain to something entirely different. The world of *The Bachelor* franchise felt as foreign to her as another country, full of pretense and artifice that nevertheless yielded the occasional moment of true emotion. Before she knew it, Ilana had to admit: she was a fan.

Now, over the course of our nine years watching together, we've grown to appreciate the times when we react similarly to what we observe on-screen and in the fandom: the fact that positive masculine traits are rarely celebrated with as much verve as toxic masculine traits are called out; that the rapidity of intimacy among the contestants as friends is just as stark as the romantic ties between contestants and leads; and that the show's editing choices so accurately—though not intentionally—reflect real-world tensions regarding gendered and racial hierarchies and expectations. This isn't to say that we always notice the same things, though. We each bring unique perspectives. Stevie tends to fixate on human behaviors—reactions that folks have to one another and how they deal with conflict. Ilana tends to note those moments where the show accidentally breaks out of its straitjacket of cisheteronormativity.[2] Each of us is into different outfits. Our own intimacy as friends grew out of these conversations, the hours spent together, and the fervor with which we enjoyed analyzing the show.

Since everyone at Stevie's watch parties was affiliated with various graduate programs, the unavoidable reality of graduation and moving on from Lincoln loomed. Natalie moved to Kentucky; Katie ended up in Texas; Jess moved on to Indiana and later Washington; and then, Stevie moved to New York. Even with thousands of miles and multiple time zones between them, the group kept the spirit of Monday Night Bach (pronounced "batch") alive in the group chat. Live reactions were sometimes hard because there was the issue of spoilers given different airtimes, but there was always outrage at the newest disappointment at cut contestants and dating incompatibilities of the folks on-screen.

But life happens, and as our friends fell away from the ritual of discoursing over the franchise, we two remained and became ever more committed to it. When the beginning of the Covid-19 pandemic disrupted the filming of *The Bachelorette*, for instance, we missed our regular viewing so much that we found another reality TV show to share until Bach came back. When it did, we resumed our tandem-watching, and now that we live half a country apart from one another, we continue to live-text our reactions and thoughts. The screeds on our phones alone are proof of our

2 Cis or cisgender refers to a person whose gender expression matches their assigned sex at birth. Heteronormativity is the presumption that there is one normal and desirable sexual orientation (between one man and one woman), and this belief fuels homophobia and transphobia. Cisheteronormativity, therefore, refers to the cultural assumption that cis, straight couplings are the norm and thus more acceptable.

sometimes unhinged but always enthusiastic commitment to both loving and heavily critiquing the show.

As many other fans who have been long-time participants in Bachelor Nation can tell you, one of the seismic changes over the two decades of the franchise's existence has been the proliferation of online discourse. Social media accounts, podcasts, meme-ification of images and phrases from the show—all of this comes out of the viewership and our shared desire to talk about, react to, and digest the show *as a community.* We routinely send each other posts from Bachelor Nation fan accounts as shorthand for some of our own reactions to the show, but they also act as third, fourth, fifth, and beyond voices that challenge and expand our perspectives as we seek to understand what we've seen on a recent episode. When we see a smart take on a recent topic raised about the show—ranging from a heartfelt conversation that demonstrates emotional maturity (best case scenario) to the use of a racist dog whistle (worst case, but unfortunately common, scenario)—it feels as though we are part of a conversation that matters and that is larger than us. This ongoing online discourse is akin to a decentralized roundtable of experts, each of us using different analytical tools.

So why, with all the intelligent, funny, and critical discourse, is reality TV stereotypically considered to be trashy and for airheads? Well, technically, there's nothing wrong with trash TV *or* airheads. However, the fact is that millions of people engage with reality TV in meaningful and diverse ways. *The Bachelor* franchise, as one of the longest-running dating shows, has amassed fans from all corners of life who hold a plethora of identities and have a multitude of reasons for watching the show. For some of us, it's a way to shut off our brains for an evening; for others, it's about finding or participating in our online or IRL communities; still others enjoy the process of ripping to shreds the contestants, the shows' politics, the editing, or all of the above. In other words, *The Bachelor* franchise's fandom is a rich space for discourse on culture, race, sexuality, gender, human behavior, and community.

As such, we wondered: Why has there never been a collection of fan voices put forth to demonstrate the plurality of this widespread experience of reality TV fandom?

A *Dramatic* Anthology that has *Never* Been Done Before

Reality television in general has long been seen as fluffy entertainment, full of pandering celebrity wannabes whose trials and tribulations viewers are supposed to laugh at or mock. Yet, in the last couple of decades, reality TV franchises have become ubiquitous and include a growing number of sub-genres: long-standing game shows are arguably the OGs of reality TV; panel shows like *Ricki Lake* or *The Jerry Springer Show* use the veneer of reality to titillate their viewers; home-improvement shows, bake-offs, and talent competitions provide inspiration and aspiration; and let us not forget the more anthropological shows ranging from *The Kardashians* to *Duck Dynasty*. The genre is so broad at this point that it includes just as much edutainment as entertainment, raising the question of why dating shows like *The Bachelor* franchise are still seen as so especially egregious.

In a word: sexism.

Anyone who follows soap operas, is a fan of romance novels, or likes rom-com movies can tell you that romantic plotlines are explicitly associated with feminine audiences. As such, fandoms of these widely popular and oft-consumed genres are frequently diminished. If girls and women like it—or if the pop culture thing is even remotely associated with feminine desire or pleasure—there is an absence of seriousness or weightiness, and a perceived lack of intellectual or monetary value. All of this feels as though it shouldn't still be true in the third decade of the twenty-first century, and yet here we are. Millions of fans—of varied genders—can tune in to watch NFL games weekly without turning any heads, but a different kind of competition (less physically violent and somewhat less sponsor-driven) gets a wholly different treatment by the culture at large.

This anthology aims to correct that treatment and showcase the value and diversity of fan voices, experiences, and reasons for engaging with *The Bachelor* franchise.

Fans of Bachelor Nation are often presumed to look, sound, and think like the majority of contestants on-screen: white, cisgender, heterosexual, able-bodied, thin, and conventionally attractive. While there are plenty of viewers for whom this holds true, many fans of this franchise have very little to relate to while watching. Bachelor Nation includes people of color, queer and trans folks, people with disabilities, and fat and body-diverse individuals. These are just the most visible and obvious markers of difference. Digging deeper, there are also political, religious, and economic factors that are nearly always erased from the show but are openly discussed among viewers. The franchise largely fails to represent the diversity of humanity and human experiences. For these reasons, fans of the franchise have called out show creators for overly white casting, a lack of body diversity, and the unwillingness to discuss contestant controversy. As we pulled together our contributors for this anthology, we sought to explore these unexpected and underrepresented areas of Bachelor Nation.

No single media entity will ever represent all its viewers, nor is it expected to. Yet *The Bachelor* has been critiqued for lagging behind other, newer dating shows that try—at the very least—to cast more racially diverse contestants. So why does *The Bachelor* continue to have such a loyal fandom? Of course, those of us who watch *The Bachelor* do find relationship dynamics, plotlines, personalities, fantasies, and aesthetics we relate to or engage with. Some of the most critical fans of the franchise stick around season after season, and their critiques are a powerful form of engagement as well. Whether the franchise itself can or will change—and whether or not it purposefully courts outrage as engagement—there is value in the conversations we fans have surrounding this powerhouse cultural phenomenon. We use the show as a jumping off point to bigger issues: our conversations start with what we see on screen but quickly move beyond it to real-world systemic issues. Doesn't anyone want to hear our voices?

At face value—taking into account the longevity and popularity of the shows—*The Bachelor* franchise is a significant cultural artifact. Though it may be controversial to assert that it has the value or staying power of other canonized works that illustrate the human experience (for example, literature, music, film, and so on), reality television is here to stay. As such, it is fascinating to think about the enormous omission of fan voices explaining why we, as an audience, are consistently captivated by these shows. When we began this project, our research explored whether *any* pop-cultural audience or fan base had been given an opportunity to speak for itself in this way that we envisioned. Truthfully, no, it's never been done before. There are a few examples—such as a single *Harry Potter* fan anthology—but never something that focused on a fan base of an individual cultural artifact marketed primarily to women.

The fans in Bachelor Nation are legion, and as pop culture plays a significant role in most Americans' lives, and feeds or challenges our cultural ideologies and mythologies, this anthology reckons with these complexities. We invite you to join this journey.

Coming Up Next on *Here for All the Reasons*

The pieces in this anthology were all prompted by two simple questions: *Who are you?* and *Why do you watch?*

Our ~~contestants~~ contributors answer these questions in myriad ways, engaging with their personal and political identities, their community needs, their voyeurism or nostalgia, their praises and critiques, and their experiences as professional fans. With the shows' obvious and intentional leveraging of fantasy, our contributors grapple with the ways that desire is manufactured and what meaning producers create from the hundreds of hours of collected footage for each show's season. As fans writing to other fans, we wonder how our fascination with the show implicates us in the very controversy many of us would just as soon eradicate from the franchise. If we're being honest, our discourse does not exist in a vacuum, and our engagement in the show isn't always on ideological high ground; as we stated earlier, without an audience, there is no monetary value in continuing to make the show. All the same, our humanity is what makes this anthology interesting. We continue to grow and learn as we hold ourselves, each other, and the show as a cultural artifact accountable to what we believe is important.

Some contributors address the role of gender performance and sexuality in the franchise and its relationship to those of us on the other side of the screen; others examine the role of race as it pertains to both representation and fandom; personal traumas make appearances, as do moments of joy; and other voices relate the powerful sense of community involved in the shared experience of online and IRL simul-watching.

This anthology reflects an ongoing attempt by many of us in Bachelor Nation to make meaning of this thing that we love, love to hate, and hate to love. We hope you join us on this journey ~~to find love~~ of self-reflection, as we curiously, hilariously, and seriously try to figure out why we are Bachelor Nation.

How to Read This Book

At the start of every new season, there are usually some thirty contestants vying for the heart of the Bachelor or Bachelorette. They emerge from the limos one at a time or arrive in their own distinctive vehicle, and then they try to make an impression. They are there for the "right" reasons—to find the love of their life and get married—or not. They win us over or they don't. But they are all—each and every one of them—real people, with real families and friends and pets and neuroses and preferences and opinions and lives. Real people who really went through the bizarre and lengthy process of sending in an application, going through multiple rounds of interviews, signing contracts, packing a suitcase, and traveling to Bachelor Mansion.

This book, a little bit like a first night at the Mansion, contains twenty-nine unique contributions written by thirty people with their own families, friends, pets, neuroses, preferences, opinions, and lives. Each contribution is here for a different reason, and we consider them all to be, indeed, the *right* reasons. These writers each express something regarding their relationship to *The Bachelor* franchise, and each went through a lengthy process of pitching, signing contracts, thinking, writing, editing, and editing again.

In the following pages, you'll find a spectrum of current and past viewers sharing their thoughts: We've included folks who are still deeply dedicated to the shows' romantic plotlines; folks who have grown critical of how the shows depict love, people, and relationships; and folks who fall somewhere in between or completely outside of this framework because there are myriad ways to react to and engage with what we see on-screen.

If you read this book cover-to-cover, you will find that each consecutive piece is distinct from its neighbors. This mix of perspectives is intentional. We, Ilana and Stevie, wanted there to be separation between topics and moods, so that readers would be met with something that felt new and fresh at every turn. Yet even the pieces that might seem to be total opposites still start from the shared cultural text of this franchise.

In the early days of this anthology, when we tried to categorize the pieces strictly by topic, we found that we couldn't do so neatly—our writers often explore multiple ideas and aspects of their relationship with the shows within their pieces. We also don't want to tell you what you should take away from each piece, because we know that—much like the franchise we're all invested in, one way or another—readers will relate differently to our writers' identities, senses of humor, opinions, styles, and more.

While there isn't a single piece that goes through the entire chronological history of each and every season, you'll find that there is a healthy smattering of callbacks to the early days as well as think pieces about recently aired episodes. You will also find that our contributors don't agree on everything (nor would we want them to!), so you probably won't agree with all of their assessments of leads, contestants, dramas, representations, or other aspects of the franchise either. That's okay! If you find your favorite season, lead, contestant, or couple falls under someone's critical eye, it is an opportunity to continue the conversation—call up your watch party, drop some hot takes in the group chat, or post on the subreddit. You'll see that for many of our contributors, ongoing conversations about these shows *is* the point.

While the order of the pieces here was deliberately thought out, and we believe you could read the book straight through from front to back, we wanted to share some more context so that if you choose to go on a different journey, you may find your own path!

Starting Your Journey

We chose Claire Fallon and Emma Gray's essay (p. 17) to open the collection because they have been instrumental in mainstreaming the discourse of Bachelor Nation with their former *HuffPost* podcast, *Here to Make Friends*, and its follow up, *Love to See It*. Fallon and Gray include some foundational background information for the franchise's zeitgeist and its shifting cultural landscape. Regardless of where you go next in the anthology, this is a good place to start.

Other broader pieces that work as a first foray into the book include Ness Ilene Garza's comic (p. 56), which looks at how *The Bachelor* has become fodder for conversation and connection with their mother, and Ilana Masad's essay (p. 215) that walks through the fantasy of applying to join the show as a contestant. Alisa Ungar-Sargon's narrative (p. 81) is another good place to start; she walks through the simple pleasure of the shows' entertainment value while being well aware of its faults.

Choose Your Own Adventure

If you're a more critical viewer—or *were* a viewer and have left the show behind—and you're looking for kindred spirits, you'll want to read Prisca Dorcas Mojica Rodríguez's essay (p. 32) stat. When we reached out to her, we knew she would offer sharp, insightful criticism, and she more than delivered, focusing on the franchise's representations of Latine contestants, demanding that showrunners *do better*. Mojica Rodríguez certainly isn't alone in her critiques, and for each and every one of our contributors who takes issue with an aspect of the show, we stan their right to do so. Further contributors who take the franchise to task include Milo Muise (p. 183), whose tongue-in-cheek essay takes aim at the very heart of *The Bachelor*—its heterosexual relationships; Jeanna Kadlec (p. 89), who calls out the conservative, evangelical Christian gender norms not-so-subtly present in the shows; Jessica Masterson (p. 163), who considers the prevalence of trauma bonding during one-on-one dates; and Alana Hope Levinson (p. 118), who explores the shows' reliance on "pick-me girl" dynamics. (We should note that many other pieces include criticism as well—one of the great pleasures of being part of Bachelor Nation is complaining about the franchise's many flaws, missteps, and systemic issues—but, as you'll see, it's nestled in among other focal topics.)

Speaking of the franchise's issues being *fun*, many in Bachelor Nation use the shows as a jumping off point for conversation as well as an excuse to spend time with loved ones both near and far. Sophie Vershbow (p. 111) writes about how she took to Twitter (RIP) to share her takes and takedowns in real time while watching the show; Renée Reizman (p. 131) describes her long-standing Bach group chat as a bridge between show-related gossip and real-life friendships; and, for Erin Kayata (p. 176), her watch group uses the shows' social issues as a launch pad into conversations around religion, sexuality, and more—going deeper into human connection than the shows themselves.

If you still watch the shows for some possibility of romance—or at least can find something akin to true human connection on-screen—you will find plenty of company here too: Zainab Omaki (p. 73) writes tenderly about being introduced to *The Bachelorette* and watching a woman a little bit like her being the center of attention; Emma Rohloff (p. 49) shares her childhood perception of the shows and the princess-like qualities of being Bachelorette, which speak to the fantasy that many viewers still find appealing; Tamara MC (p. 97) outlines the chapters in her life alongside the journeys of love found and love lost on-screen; and Joy Alicia (p. 140) discusses the dynamics of watching, cheering for, and criticizing the Black Bachelorettes from her perspective as a Black woman.

If you're the type to find catharsis in witnessing other people's complicated feelings, then you need to check out our contributors who grapple with pain stirred up by the humanness that bubbles to the surface of reality TV despite heavy editing: Carolyn Huynh (p. 124) unpacks what it means to consider Jenn Tran—the first Vietnamese-American Bachelorette—a sister, and what it's like to see someone's shared cultural trauma play out on national TV; Shir Kehila (p. 156) frames the show as an over-the-top escape from the complexities of her own grounded romantic partnership; Samantha Page Rosen (p. 207) wasn't a fan of the franchise when it felt like the shows were a point of comparison for her own life, but grew to value the non-romantic relationships that emerge among contestants; Stevie K. Seibert Desjarlais (p. 169) holds onto the shows along with her grief for a lost friend; Samantha Allen (p. 26) explores coming to terms with the impossible standards of femininity demonstrated by women on the shows—and allows herself to let go of them; and Sophie Vershbow breaks up with the franchise when she moves beyond the idea that marriage is the only happily-ever-after.

This collection also offers cultural analyses that decenter purely American perspectives. Courtney Tenz (p. 68) describes her use of Germany's iteration of the franchise as a way to study dating norms as an expat; **AN** (p. 199) compares *The Bachelor/ette* to Indian reality TV and remarks upon the level of vulnerability and emotional turmoil shown on-screen; and Zainab Omaki (p. 73), hailing from Nigeria, describes why watching a Black lead was empowering after seeing the way racism affected her dating prospects once she'd moved to a predominantly white country.

Readers looking for outside-the-box takes on the franchise will find much to enjoy in Julia Moser's essay (p. 222) about bringing her hobby of birding into her viewing of *Bachelor in Paradise*; Chrissy Tolley's piece (p. 61) about performing psychic readings of the contestants for a dedicated Instagram following; and Milo Muise's hilarious (yet resonant!) diatribe (p. 183) about the imminent collapse of late-stage heterosexuality.

As mentioned in our introduction, we, the editors, met in academia, and we were thrilled to discover that we were far from alone in finding *The Bachelor* franchise rife for scholarly consideration. Iftin Abshir (p. 148) discusses the phenomenon of "spoiling" within Bachelor Nation and tries to figure out why so many viewers enjoy it. Adriane Stoner (p. 103) writes about the *Bachelor*-themed course she teaches at DePaul University and how willing and eager her students are to dig into the franchise's rhetorical choices. Serena Zets (p. 41), too, co-taught a course on *The Bachelor* franchise as an undergrad herself and describes its wild success. And, in a less traditional educational path, Sarah Gerard (p. 190) watches the dynamics between contestants through a forensic-interview lens while training to become a private investigator.

Happily Ever After

Whichever way you choose to read this book—straight through or via a meandering path—we hope that you'll find someone (or many someones!) that you connect with. We also hope that you find a perspective (or several!) that you hadn't yet considered. Most of all, we hope that your experience with this collection inspires additional thinking that you then carry with you as you continue watching this franchise (or others) and chat with your watch-party compatriots.

Remember, unlike *The Bachelor*'s final episode, you don't have to give out just one final rose; you don't have to choose one winner or loser, one good idea over another. We all contain multitudes, and we can walk off into the sunset together, all of us, the voices of Bachelor Nation.

1

How To Make Friends and Influence *The Bachelor*

Claire Fallon and Emma Gray

For a moment in the early to mid-2010s, it seemed everyone was writing them.

Roxane Gay wrote one. So did we—each of us, actually. *The Onion* even had a viral headline ("Woman Takes Short Half-Hour Break from Being Feminist to Enjoy TV Show") that nodded to the trend. *Vogue*, *Elle*, *Vox*, *Mic*, *Salon*, *HuffPost*, *The Guardian*, and *The New York Times* all dug into one looming question: Why were droves of smart, feminist women watching *The Bachelor*?

Over a decade after the franchise first premiered in 2002, the "Why Feminists Watch *The Bachelor*" genre became a staple of pop culture criticism. Suddenly, feminists were obsessed with writing about *why* feminists were so obsessed with this fundamentally conservative, schmaltzy show. It was a sort of coming-out party as women of a class who were usually assumed to prefer higher-brow entertainment—educated, middle- to upper-middle-class, professional women—bravely stepped forward to reveal their secret, guilty addiction to trashy reality TV about women behaving in stereotypical and unflattering ways. We were loud and proud *Bachelor* fans, and no, that did not negate our ability to pay attention to The Important Things, thank you very much.

As two white, college-educated, left-leaning women writers, we found ourselves right at the center of this particular discourse. We both worked at *HuffPost* in the heyday of the digital-media boom, cutting our proverbial teeth in a newsroom full of young, energized writers and homing in on the particular intersections of culture, gender, and politics. With the rise of Twitter and a dwindling number of shows that demanded live viewing, *The Bachelor* experienced a 2010s resurgence of cultural relevance. We found ourselves alternately captivated and horrified by this reality dating show, so much so that we launched a podcast about it in 2015—the first explicitly feminist podcast about the *Bachelor* franchise.

We were somewhat early to the "feminists love *The Bachelor*" discourse, or at least Emma was, but we were not out of step with the times. This was the era of asking every woman celebrity if they identify as a feminist and then shaming them if they misstepped in their answers, the era of *Lean In* and unironic #Girlboss-ing, the era of "male tears" merch and Princeton Mom and Dove's Real Beauty campaign and Barack Obama's second presidential term. The stakes of mainstream feminist discourse, while always fundamentally high, seemed less concrete and urgent than they do today after years of unsupported pandemic parenting and women being pushed out of the workforce en masse. And the center of that discourse was, for better or worse, pop culture.

Both devoted readers of *Jezebel* and *Feministing*, we already saw every cultural product we consumed—from Jonathan Franzen novels to subway ads—as ripe for feminist critique, bearing within it messages from the patriarchal society that produced it. We were also produced by that patriarchal society, and we bore those messages within ourselves. We grew up on Disney movies and old romantic comedies; we recognized that Jane Austen was a sharp satirist and also wrote some of the great love stories of the Western canon. Our souls thrilled to the idea of the perfect men kneeling before our ravishing figures clad in gowns and jewels, and we also didn't want to be limited to the role of a demure wife or mother. We wanted to be in *The Bachelor*, and we also wanted to deconstruct it brick by brick and destroy its foundation.

We loved the show—and we also loved to mock it. We wanted to point out the obvious flaws of this fundamentally conservative cultural product: the overemphasis on the necessity of marriage, the overwhelming whiteness and thinness of the cast, the underlying fundamentalist Christian ethos that seemed to run like an undercurrent through every episode, and the way the show gleefully seemed to set women against each other for the attention of a mediocre man. On Monday nights, we would live-tweet or blog about the show; on Tuesday mornings, we would discuss it ad nauseam with our similarly obsessed coworkers.

And so, when the newsroom was solicited for show pitches to help launch *HuffPost*'s podcast program, we knew exactly what topic we would want to opine about for an hour a week. What's more, we saw a gap in the public discourse about the franchise, which was either sappily romanticized, snidely mocking, or downright dismissive. What was missing? A show that neither dismissed nor embraced *The Bachelor*, but rather interrogated what we saw as its profound flaws alongside its appeal.

We saw *The Bachelor* as a Trojan horse for Feminist Theory 101—a way to use a lowest-common-denominator, pop culture product to spread the gospel of equality to the masses. And we weren't alone. At that moment in American culture, writers and commentators like us were announcing their affiliation with *The Bachelor*, and in the process, both normalizing the franchise—and other low-brow reality shows aimed at female audiences—as legitimate cultural texts primed for cultural critique and conversation, and also subjecting it to detailed, sustained scrutiny through a feminist lens.

This was at the tail end of the Obama years, when, for some naive and optimistic liberals like us, it seemed possible that the long arc of the moral universe would continue bending further and further toward justice. *The Bachelor* seemed, to us, like a relic of a dying breed of religious conservatism. We had both begun watching the show in the early 2010s, just as it was at peak whiteness and seemed to be dominated by evangelical Christianity. What we didn't realize at the time was that the latter trend was actually on the upswing; earlier seasons of the show had more of a cosmopolitan yuppie flavor (see first Bachelor Alex Michel riding a trolley to his consulting job in San Francisco during his introduction package). But in the 2010s, many of the franchise's leads—Jake Pavelka, Sean Lowe, Emily Maynard, Desiree Hartsock, Ben Higgins—professed strong Christian beliefs, which seemed to align well with the show's emphasis on heterosexual courtship and marriage (though perhaps less well with the indiscriminate kissing and sex-implied "fantasy suites").

In fact, *The Bachelor* wasn't a last bastion of outdated conservatism around gender roles in our steadily more progressive society. A backlash was brewing, and this show was shaping up to be a battleground between the two political forces on either side of the widening divide: anti-feminist and racist-revanchist conservatives, who coalesced into the Trumpian right, and liberal feminists. In the midst of the Obama era, the show became a pop-cultural vessel for this backlash—and also a vessel for pushing back on it.

The war for a less right-wing *Bachelor* began before our podcast launched. In 2012, two Black men filed a lawsuit against ABC and Warner Horizon Television,[1] alleging that the show violated racial discrimination laws by casting almost exclusively white leads and contestants. The lawsuit was dismissed, but production on Sean Lowe's season had begun in the interim. In 2013, for the first time in years, *The Bachelor* featured several Black contestants. Perhaps unwilling to court future lawsuits, the show continued to cast more men and women of color, though they rarely made it past the first few weeks on the show. Media outlets and fans continued to

1 "2 Black Men Sue 'The Bachelor' for Lack of Inclusion," CBS News, April 18, 2012, https://www.cbsnews.com/losangeles/news/2-black-men-sue-the-bachelor-for-lack-of-inclusion/.

scrutinize the shows' poor track record on diversity, and those "How Can a Feminist Watch *The Bachelor*?" essays began to pop up as women grappled with the problematic politics of one of their favorite guilty pleasures.

The show was, uneasily and reluctantly, diversifying. It was also catering more than ever to a viewership of white, conservative Christian women. And though feminist fans of the show were coming out of hiding, ready to live-tweet and gossip about their *Bachelor* opinions, they were taking notice.

When we launched *Here to Make Friends* in 2015, this is what we saw: women being shamed for having sexual intimacy on the show; men begging fathers for their blessing during hometown dates; Black and brown contestants who never made it past episode four; courtship rituals that virtually erased politics and religion, save for hints of the expected evangelical Christian beliefs; edits that framed cast members as sexist and often racist caricatures (virgins and whores, spicy Latinas and angry Black women, bimbos and nags); and casts containing mostly women in their early twenties meant to date men who were typically in their late twenties to late thirties. But we also saw an audience desperate for a way to harness their fury with this show—a show that, while just a reality TV series, was also a massive cultural institution and content machine unlike any feminist depiction of contemporary love and romance. We didn't want audiences to just passively consume all these toxic ideas about gender, race, and courtship—and many of them weren't. They were watching, but they were critiquing. They were ready to take the fight to ABC.

By the time JoJo Fletcher's season of *The Bachelorette* aired during the summer of 2016, in the immediate lead-up to the presidential election, the franchise's audience had gone into overdrive, trying to ascertain the political affiliations and attitudes of the cast members on our screens. There were Reddit threads with lists of suspected MAGA fans and deep dives into voter registration logs. It felt like every week we were being alerted via Instagram DM that another one of JoJo's Richard Spencer–looking bros had posed in front of a Trump flag. The season's supervillain, Chad

Johnson, was even branded by *Time* magazine as "the Donald Trump of Bachelor Nation."[2]

As the country's political polarization came into focus, so too did Bachelor Nation's. After Trump was elected president, it became increasingly impossible for the franchise to exist in the allegedly "apolitical" space it had long attempted to occupy. The show's core audience—white women—had fractured. (A 2020 YouGov survey found that 75 percent of people who had watched *The Bachelor* in the last year identified as white, and 77 percent were women.[3]) On one side were the viewers who earnestly enjoyed the shows' white, Christian, conservative hegemony. On the other side were the viewers like us—the snarky online critics who saw *The Bachelor* as an amalgam of cultural norms that desperately needed fixing. The franchise was our shared site of political struggle: a product onto which we could map the battle for cultural primacy, a battle that, at some point, one side had to win.

Things came to a head during the Covid-19 pandemic, when many *Bachelor* viewers were stuck at home, isolated—and thus had lots of time to aim their rage straight at their problematic fave reality dating show. In May 2020, George Floyd, a forty-six-year-old Black man, was murdered at the hands of white police officer Derek Chauvin. This set off a new wave of racial reckoning, which touched many parts of the entertainment and media industry, including *The Bachelor*. Progressive fans petitioned the show to cast a Black man to lead season 25,[4] and soon after, Matt James, who had never been on *The Bachelorette* but had ties to a popular white cast member, Tyler Cameron, was announced as the franchise's first Black male lead.

And then, in a depressingly predictable fashion, his season imploded. From the first episode, it was clear that James was going to be flattened

---

2 *Time* Staff, "Chad Johnson Is the Donald Trump of Bachelor Nation," *Time*, August 4, 2016, https://time.com/4436652/chad-donald-trump-villain-bachelor-nation/.

3 Linley Sanders, "What Type of Person Is Part of Bachelor Nation?" YouGov, November 16, 2020, https://today.yougov.com/entertainment/articles/33065-bachelor-nation-profile-poll.

4 Amy Kaufman, "18 Years. 40 Seasons. Just One Black Lead. These 'Bachelor' Fans Are Fed Up," *Los Angeles Times*, June 8, 2020, https://www.latimes.com/entertainment-arts/tv/story/2020-06-08/bachelor-diversity-campaign-bipoc-black-lives-matter-abc-warner-brothers.

into a caricature that would be deemed acceptable by a predominantly white audience. "In my conversion from person to prop, key pieces of me were left behind," James later wrote in his book *First Impressions: Off-Screen Conversations with a Bachelor on Race, Family, and Forgiveness.* By the time the season finale aired in March 2021, James and his winner Rachael Kirkconnell had (temporarily) broken up over her attendance at an antebellum-themed fraternity formal in 2018. Longtime host Chris Harrison was also ousted after a disastrous interview with first Black Bachelorette Rachel Lindsay in which he criticized the "woke police" of Bachelor Nation. (In the words of that *Euphoria* clip that frequently circulates on social media, *"Is this fucking play about us?"*)

Viewers on both sides of the political aisle vowed to abandon the franchise after season 25 of *The Bachelor*, and many did. But the dam had been irrevocably broken. The version of *The Bachelor* we naively thought always had and always would exist back in 2015 had buckled under the weight of collective critique. In 2023, *Bachelor* creator Mike Fleiss left the franchise after he was investigated for racial discrimination. If there was an ongoing battle for the soul of *The Bachelor*, it became clear that our side was winning, albeit partially, imperfectly, and perhaps temporarily. (In the nascent days of Trump 2.0, we are still waiting to see how far back the pendulum may swing.)

Back in the early 2010s, when we were writing feminist *Bachelor* viewer manifestos and telling snide men who asked us at parties why women like us who "seemed intelligent" would watch garbage like that, we had a relatively simple answer: *The Bachelor* is rife with sexism and racism, and it represents a deeply conservative view of romance. It is also a hugely popular, long-running show. For those reasons, it is an inviting target for critique, an easy way to discuss the pitfalls of dating men as women in a sexist society, and an obvious target for snark.

But in our youthful shortsightedness, we failed to account for something important. Reality shows are not fossilized in stone, nor are they the work of isolated auteurs. They are a mirror held up to an ever-changing society. Reality shows, like romance novels, are representations of exaggerated or idealized social relationships. By design, they react to changes in the audience's desires; they're constantly shifting and tacking to one side or the other as the shows' creators attempt to match the fairy-tale dreams of its audience. The hyper-conservative, uniformly white, and largely evangelical *Bachelor* that we came to as young adults was shaping itself in reaction to a growing conservative backlash against liberal elite values. But as a generation of women turned a critical eye on mainstream representations of the female experience and found them deeply wanting, *The Bachelor* had to choose whether to evolve in a different direction, to show them a vision of love and womanhood that did appeal.

As of this writing, far fewer people ask why feminists watch *The Bachelor*. After all, why would major publications bother wasting virtual ink tracking a phenomenon that has gone from subversive to mainstream? The recession of this question from mainstream discourse feels like an unanticipated win. When we started publicly talking about our favorite "frivolous" pop culture artifact, we saw *The Bachelor* as a stable, permanently retrograde product that we could use to position our own values against. But we ended up being part of a discourse that shifted the show, and in the years since, listeners have told us that our *Bachelor* podcast helped introduce them to feminism or even started them down a path away from long-held conservative political views.

Feminists watch *The Bachelor* for many reasons. We watch to be entertained. We watch to solidify our own politics and values in contrast to the ones shown on-screen. We watch, as men stereotypically do with sports, to have something to make small talk about. We watch to have an easy way to dissect and raise consciousness around the injustices of life under patriarchy. And now, the two of us have come to realize, we watch to have a voice in the conversation between show and viewer, *Bachelor* production and Bachelor Nation, about what the franchise will become.

Claire Fallon is a cohost of the award-winning *Bachelor* recap podcast *Love to See It* (previously *Here to Make Friends*) and coauthor of the culture newsletter and podcast *Rich Text*. She previously worked as a books and culture critic at HuffPost, and her work has also appeared in *Vice* and *Cosmopolitan*. She lives in Jersey City with her husband and two sons.

Emma Gray is a writer and award-winning podcaster. She cohosts the *Love to See It* podcast (previously *Here to Make Friends*), and coauthors a newsletter, *Rich Text*. She is the author of *A Girl's Guide to Joining the Resistance*. Her work, which focuses on gender, culture, and politics, can also be found in *The Washington Post*, *Elle*, *The Guardian*, *Vice*, *Cosmopolitan*, MSNBC, *Jezebel*, and *HuffPost*, where she was previously a senior reporter and editor. She lives in Brooklyn with her husband and plants.

2

Zeno's Blow Dryer

Samantha Allen

The day I learned about hair extensions, I felt like I had uncovered a vast conspiracy to make me feel bad about myself. But when you come to femininity late, much of its arcana remains obscured until someone says the obvious out loud: "She has clip-ins," "That's just contouring," "You haven't heard of filler?" As I transitioned from one gender to another in the 2010s, *The Bachelor* franchise became a sort of crash course in these secret rites and rituals. While my own thin, easily breakable hair slowly grew down to my shoulders, I watched in awe as waves of people my age pulled up in limousines with voluminous blowouts. Their makeup was perfect; mine was haphazard. To this day, I can't apply eyeliner without some kind of disastrous blinking event ruining my morning.

"Welcome to womanhood," many cisgender women joke when you first share your own feelings of inadequacy in the face of this unattainable ideal. It's patronizing. It's perhaps mildly transphobic, if perversely inclusive. But the longer I've been out, the more I've felt the deep exhaustion beneath the quip: *Yes, welcome to womanhood, where we are all dogs chasing cars we will never catch.* Or perhaps: *Welcome to gender itself, a simulation of a simulation only a few of us are even close to mastering.*

I came out in 2012 while in a women's, gender, and sexuality studies PhD program. Not only had I read Judith Butler, I had been the kind of undergraduate who helped other students understand *Gender Trouble*, translating the thesis out of academic-speak into plain language that sophomores who were just trying to check off a curriculum requirement could grok. But no amount of theoretical knowledge about the constructedness of gender—or sex itself, for that matter—can prepare you for the simple brutality of feeling like an ugly girl.

My first response to that blunt but wholly unoriginal sensation was to try to keep up with the *Bachelor* girls. I dyed my hair platinum blonde. I got my eyebrows threaded. I spent a small fortune—relative to my paltry grad school stipend—at Sephora. These were the parts of my appearance I could control. Hormones were doing their quiet, glacial work. My bottom surgery was on the calendar. In the meantime, I could clean makeup sponges, buy gallons of purple shampoo, and figure out my way around a flat iron. I wasn't very good at it. The handful of times I thought I looked "pretty" happened after other people did my hair and makeup for me. But I tried to get there the same way Zeno's arrow tries to reach its target.

Before long, I was taking a cathartic pleasure in those fleeting moments on *The Bachelor* and *The Bachelorette* when the tools of the trade peeked through the facade. Sometimes, women came downstairs in the morning without makeup on; they'd talk about their handsome suitor while daintily holding mugs of coffee or tea, and yes, they were still blessed in the bone structure department, but they at least looked *human*. Their eyelashes looked like eyelashes. Their skin had pores. After *Bachelor in Paradise* premiered in 2014, I freeze-framed the shots of their overflowing suitcases, with all their appliances and products spilling out onto the floor. I liked to spot the Dyson Airwraps.

It was only in Sayulita that the labor of looking like a Clare Crawley or an Ashley Iaconetti became clear to me. Battling the elements without the benefit of air conditioning, many women seemed to step onto the sand with lofty aspirations: They were going to look as good as they did at the cocktail parties back at the Mansion, heat and humidity be damned. Only a few days later—or "weeks," in the parlance of the show—the women started giving into the inevitable. Their hair got pulled back into ponytails. They pared back on the cosmetics. They even got zits. It felt almost cruel for production to send a wave of "new girls" to the beach just when the original cast was beginning to melt, but that was probably the point. Like *Love Island* after it, *Paradise* figured out how to create a cross-generational dynamic in miniature: the recent arrivals, ferried to Playa Escondida in climate-controlled black SUVs, seemed so much "fresher" than the women who had surrendered their losing battle to remain pristine. They were all still gorgeous, and almost exclusively in their twenties, but suddenly half of them were made to feel like old maids by comparison.

Gender dysphoria is a hell of a thing. If I could turn back the clock and undo my first puberty, I could have avoided having a squarer jaw than I do. Maybe then well-meaning Boomer women would stop telling me I look like Daryl Hannah when I don't; she's just their only cultural reference point for a famous woman whose chin *doesn't* taper off to a Disney princess–like point. I could have been a few inches shorter. I might not have to search so long for shoes in size ten and a half. To be trans is to live with the intractable. But at some point over the last decade and change, the rarer form of dissatisfaction I feel with my body dovetailed with, and then became indistinguishable from, the banal grief of lost beauty. Gravity had its way with my face. Lines got deeper. Lips got thinner. I got older watching *The Bachelor* while the women on the show stayed forever twenty-five. Time moved frustratingly forward.

By 2020, when I was watching the pandemic-era "bubble" seasons of *The Bachelor* on an iPad in my pajamas, I waved my own white flag. My makeup first went into a junk drawer, then the garbage. I gave up on being as blonde as the day I was born. I bought scrunchies. In ways, I was relieved to stop caring. Simply making it past thirty as a trans woman feels like a miracle in itself. So why, then, couldn't I shake the deep envy I had developed for these reality TV influencers, who could make a living in the "beauty and lifestyle space," as Tayshia Adams so memorably described it? I was embarrassed by my childishness: I wanted to be like the popular girls, even as I made fun of them. But maybe this too was another consequence of delayed adolescence: At thirty-three, I was finally experiencing the torment of comparison that most of my peers have endured since middle school.

I wish I could report that I have since overcome that jealousy, especially when I'm enshrining this admission in print. There are so many tempting ways to try to intellectualize it away: I could take a second-wave feminist route and tally up all the billions of dollars spent trying to stop wrinkles from forming on our faces. A dash of third-wave attitude could be fun; I'd probably feel hotter if I played the guitar in a riot grrrl group. And, of course, there's always the old PhD to fall back on: I could dust off my queer theory monographs and remind myself that gender is both a function of discourse and a prerequisite for participating in it, an ouroboros that encircles us all. It doesn't take too much thinking to realize that the economy of appearance upheld by *The Bachelor* is pegged to a false currency.

But I've come to accept there's no choice but to sit with the plainness of it. After all, I once used similar tactics to try to talk myself out of transitioning: I thought it would be silly to change my whole life based on a gut feeling, as powerful as it was inarticulable, so I stayed in the closet for years. When I started coming out and told people I wanted to start hormones, some of them seemed to expect a logical explanation, like gender was algebra and my solution would be invalid unless I "showed my work." If I had tried to satisfy them before taking any steps, I never would have found the sense of correctness transition has brought me. Brains can sometimes get in the way of our needs. Which is why I'm trying to just let myself feel what I need to feel about approaching forty.

I stopped watching *The Bachelor* in 2023, though I still keep tabs on the Nation. Call it harm reduction: just because I'm allowing myself to experience the sorrow of lost youth doesn't mean I need to exacerbate it. I'll return to the show one day, when the subject is less sore. I aspire to be one of those fifty-and-over women at a watch party somewhere in the Midwest, enjoying the show at a comfortable remove with friends who have also escaped the gauntlet of life's first half. We'll laugh. We'll make some snide comments. We'll say we're thankful we're no longer twenty-five, and for the first time, we'll actually kind of mean it. For now, though, I need to get through the awkward dissonance of being proximate to, but painfully far from, the last time I felt beautiful.

I did *try* recently, for a work event. I got my eyebrows waxed for thirty dollars and a haircut for a hundred. I purchased a cocktail dress, shoes, and all sorts of skincare nonsense with product copy I didn't understand but that apparently meant it could be four times as expensive as Cetaphil. On the night of the company party, I got my hair and makeup done professionally by a trans twentysomething who told me sweet lies about my "good skin." I was a literal Mastercard commercial, dropping an obscene amount of money to try to generate something "priceless." Did it work? Measured by the metric of whether I felt like an ogre or not, I suppose, though if I had to stand next to Susie Evans, I might not have even cleared that bar. The five-dollar slice of pizza I had in my hotel room at 1:00 a.m., after subsisting on a couple of canapés the entire night, gave me more joy than all the other things I had bought combined.

And in a way, how wonderful it is to go through something so pedestrian. Back in 2012, my then sixty-one-year-old mother—perhaps my favorite well-meaning Boomer—asked whether I really wanted to become an "old woman" one day. The concern was genuine, even if the intent was likely to dissuade me from transitioning. On paper, she had a point: There's a reason Jesse Palmer can host *The Bachelor* while Kaitlyn Bristowe had to deal with a deluge of vile comments about her appearance while she was still in her thirties. But being trans is not the product of some cost-benefit analysis. No pros, cons, or calculators are involved. People who have never experienced dysphoria themselves may never understand it, but you can't argue with a raw, crushing need throbbing in your skull. My choice was being an old woman or being dead.

For the first few years after I came out, my friends and I spoke across a sometimes-invalidating divide. They were curious about "the surgery" or "growing boobs," and I wanted to know all the mysterious knowledge I had missed by not being out until I was twenty-five. At best, I was a willing participant in a generous cultural exchange; at worst, I was an alien making first contact. Trans women are women, but *The Bachelor* will probably be taken off the air before a doll ever gets a rose. Our experiences are still decades away from being accepted by mainstream society as women's, full stop.

Interpersonally, though, time has proved to be a humbling equalizer. My friends and I don't talk about our differences so much anymore as we talk about our similarities: our slowing metabolism, our fading cultural relevance, and our need to only ever be photographed from a high angle. Seriously, please stop kneeling down to take group pictures of elder Millennials. I may have lost the novelty I once held for a cis audience, but I've also never felt a more boring sense of belonging among them. I'm just another Samantha they know who's not the girl she used to be. Welcome to womanhood, I guess, where aging is gender-affirming care.

Samantha Allen is the author of *Patricia Wants to Cuddle*, *Roland Rogers Isn't Dead Yet*, and *Real Queer America: LGBT Stories from Red States*.

3

Latinidad on *The Bachelor/ette* Franchise: Proximity to Whiteness Preferred

Prisca Dorcas Mojica Rodríguez

I started watching *The Bachelorette* in 2009, when Jillian Harris was the Bachelorette. This was when I was still in undergrad and streaming it on Hulu, which was still a free service. I did not watch *The Bachelorette*, and later *The Bachelor*, to feel represented. I did not view the women on that show as versions of myself or anyone I even remotely knew. Initially, I watched with curiosity what felt like a once-in-a-lifetime glimpse of women reveling in choices and whittling down a cast of men to their perfect match. I was raised in a hyper-conservative and Christian household, and while Christianity seemed to be an undertone of the show, it felt like it did not dominate the women's lives like it did mine. The show felt like a fantasy.

And yes, it felt very white; that detail never escaped me. Seeing these white people on my screen gave me a glimpse into a world I was not a part of as someone who is not white. I am an immigrant from Central America, Nicaragua specifically. And I was raised in the capital of Latin

America: Miami. Latinidad is not a racial category, which means Latines can sometimes be white people. I have blond-haired, blue-eyed friends who hail from Latin America. This is not uncommon. I, however, am not white and have never passed for white. I am racialized as other, mixed, with indigenous and Black ancestry, with the spattering of colonizer/Spaniard along the way. In my country and here in the US, I am not white—and I have understood that about myself for a very long time.

My interactions with white America when I began watching *The Bachelorette* were minimal. In 2011, when I moved to Nashville, Tennessee, to attend graduate school, I began to experience white American culture more personally. I began understanding the ways that white people saw me and people "like" me. I began to see something I had not experienced before because, while I knew white Latines, we shared similar cultural history and had an understanding of our experiences—but white Americans moved differently. They expected me to be like them, and they saw my differences as something to ridicule and belittle—with little to no curiosity involved. It is what we now know to call white privilege, microaggressions, and xenophobia, but even when I lacked the language to name it all, I knew to clock it.

I saw the ways I was accepted within white American spaces when I mirrored their culture back to them or was interesting enough for their investment. This is when the few and far between Latine people on *The Bachelor/ette* became my new focus. Through *The Bachelor* franchise, I started seeing the ways Latinas were portrayed for a white American audience. The experiences I was having in Nashville began to fall into place when I investigated these reality television personalities through my own interactions with this type of whiteness.

I have felt the pangs of being the butt of white Americans' jokes for not dressing like one of them. There is a uniform I see on my TV screen, a pageant-adjacent aesthetic that we are not naming for what it is—a class signifier—and casting a wider array of contestants means casting across class lines as well. I am intimately aware of the injury of not having the same sense of humor, a thing white Americans even in the most progressive spaces seem to not understand as part of the experience of being othered.

I have even felt the dehumanizing gaze of white Americans as I dated in Nashville and experienced first-hand the consequences of having my humanity stripped from me. All this because of the irresponsible ways that white American media reduces me to something to be consumed through years of reducing Latines to narrowly-defined stereotypes.

Jessenia Cruz has openly discussed the death threats she received and racism she was subjected to when competing against a white woman for a man on *Bachelor in Paradise*. I remember when the *Chatty Broads* podcast referred to a male castmate as a "hot Latin man" and the fantasy of it all. I became furious because viewing people as types takes their humanities away from them. These are well-documented phenomena that started before *The Bachelor* franchise even began and are still present for Latines represented in media today. And *The Bachelor* franchise explicitly plays into this awful history of using Latines as pawns, not stars.

> In the 1940s, when [Carmen Miranda] appeared on American movie screens, the tempo quickened. Dressed in her deliberately outrageous costumes, her head topped by hats featuring bananas and other tropical fruits, Carmen Miranda sang and danced her way to Hollywood stardom. She was rarely cast as the romantic lead. Instead, directors made the most of her feisty comic performances. She added wit and energy to any film. But Carmen Miranda also played a part in a serious political drama: the realignment of American power in the Western Hemisphere. Her 1940s movies helped make Latin America safe for the American banana companies at a time when U.S. imperialism was coming under wider regional criticism.
>
> —Cynthia Enloe, *Bananas, Beaches and Bases: Making Feminist Sense of International Politics*[1]

1 Cynthia Enloe, *Bananas, Beaches and Bases: Making Feminist Sense of International Politics*, 2nd ed. (University of California Press, 2014), 213.

Season 18 was the first time we were gifted with a Latino as the lead in *The Bachelor* franchise. It was 2014, and his name was Juan Pablo Galavis. Born in the US but raised in Venezuela, Juan Pablo had been a soccer star in his college days and later went on to play for the Miami FC—the now-dissolved Fort Lauderdale Strikers. He is known by fans deep in the pit as the most hated Bachelor because the franchise put him on a stake and fried him, even while they were still very willing to exoticize him for his accent. The franchise's use of him let me know that I, and people like me, existed only for their amusement—and even that had its limits. The unwillingness to accompany our cultural differences with genuine interest or curiosity told me that white Americans were here to patrol me at every turn.

And I am not even that invested in personally defending any man, but it was hard to not separate the man from the culture. He felt familiar to me, more familiar than a lot of the Latines did on the show. He, like me, is an immigrant navigating white American culture.

I understood what he meant, as someone who was the primary translator for my parents at doctors' offices, as they tried to get out of tickets with cops with jokes and appealing to their morality, or with judges trying to sort out big adult things. His apparent crassness came from his obvious ESL limitations; my parents are also blunt when trying to speak English. They lack the colloquial niceties often accompanying any directive because that is what fluency teaches you. I knew intimately what he did and did not mean, and I understood the ways men are treated in Latine spaces. I saw the ways that production and the audience interpreted him, misinterpreted him, and doubled down on it. Production did not like that they could not manipulate him, something analysts of the show like Chad Kultgen from *Game of Roses* continually emphasize. They did not understand his stubbornness, his decisiveness, as a response to wanting/needing to be taken seriously in another country. They did not understand that pride is sometimes the only capital immigrants have, and they will cling onto it with bloodied knuckles, at every cost.

Instead, they made him into a joke, they ridiculed him, and did not protect him like they were known to do with their leads up to this point. And no one even thought to stop and think: Maybe we do not understand him culturally and need to bring someone to translate this person to us with some cultural sensitivities. No, they made him into a spectacle—when the fact of the matter is that Juan Pablo was still a foreigner on American soil. The injury done to someone who is navigating otherness was made worse because the optics were off, and no one stopped to think about that.

Every once in a while, I would catch Latine last names that made me interested to see how we were represented. Names like Martinez, Galavis, Pepin, Cruz, and similar. They were versions of Latinidad that catered to the white gaze. Like Mariela Pepin, who was a teen beauty-pageant winner and Miss Maryland, contests that historically prefer proximity to whiteness and seldom allow non-whiteness to be rewarded. Yet, every time Mari came onto my screen, they played salsa music, sometimes even flamenco music. It felt like she was packaged for a white audience to consume her into their sensibilities. She had a successful match and is married to someone from the show. She was one of the "good" ones of us, and they made sure to let us know that, but still, they made her into a Latin beauty—a thing to play with but not humanize fully. She was spicy and hot-headed, and they let us sit in that when they had her throw Kenny Braasch's birthday cake into the ocean on *Paradise*.

Or Jessenia Cruz, who literally was walking perfection, a model Latina—and they erased her completely. On *Paradise*, she had no love story, she did not create drama, and instead she attempted to be demure, so she became a figment of the show. Not a star, but a toy to be played with and put down as needed. The messaging felt clear: Play nice and we will use you as needed. Don't obey, like Juan Pablo, and we will destroy you.

You are either 1) acceptable enough to still be made a spectacle like a Mari Pepin; 2) not respectable and discarded like a Juan Pablo; or 3) white enough to have your Latinidad completely erased like Bekah Martinez or Gabby Windey, two of the more successful Latinas from the show based off social media numbers. Two Latinas whose entire Latinidad could be erased; Latinas white people could and would willingly fall in love with.

> Becoming white meant gaining access to a whole set of public and private privileges that materially and permanently guaranteed basic subsistence needs and, therefore, survival. Becoming white increased the possibility of controlling critical aspects of one's life rather than being the object of other's domination.
> —Cheryl I. Harris, "Whiteness as Property" in *Critical Race Theory: The Key Writings that Formed the Movement* [2]

This is where it all goes beyond being some silly show a portion of Americans consumes. This show has ripple effects because it plays into old tropes. The shows lay out our choices as Latin American and Caribbean peoples, it shows us the consequences of falling out of line and points us toward the benefits of erasing ourselves. And I believed it—somewhere along the way the subliminal messaging began to make sense in my body. It took me years of decolonial pedagogies to realize what had happened, and that is when I stopped watching the show.

It was during Matt James's season that I knew to divest. So many people asked for this type of representation, petitions were started, and the show, much to everyone's surprise, gave it to us. But the franchise fumbled it. They did not know how to roll out the red carpet for him, they did not cast intentionally for a Black man, they did not treat him with the respect owed after years of pretending the show did not have a race problem. I tried to watch the *Paradise* season that followed, but could not engage like I used to. And slowly and yet somehow quickly, I fell off. The initial and lightly empowering motives for watching this show were no longer present because we as a society have evolved, and seeing a woman have choices

2 Cheryl I. Harris, "Whiteness as Property," in *Critical Race Theory: The Key Writings that Formed the Movement*, ed. Kimberlé Crenshaw, Neil Gotanda, Gary Peller, and Kendall Thomas (The New Press, 1996), 277.

cannot be the only thing luring in viewers, especially non-white viewers. We have choices now in what we can consume, and seeing Black, Indigenous, and People of Color represented better in alternate dating shows means that we, too, can move on from this franchise that seems to talk a lot about improving on their previous racist practices but seldom shows us much of that commitment.

I have come to a place of understanding that what I am watching is what the show wants me to consume. I have heard the horribly frankenbitten sentences. I have heard contestants rail against a lead that we were told was Prince Charming. Like Gerry Turner, the first senior Bachelor, who talked about his large shoe size (penis) ad nauseam, but we never saw that because they packaged him to be our hero. I have hardened and grown bitter because of what I am being fed, and I know better than to tear these contestants apart. And yet I still watch, peripherally, through my favorite podcasts. I do not give the network my streaming numbers, but I give my more progressive podcast hosts my numbers. I have chosen how I will consume a show I find amusing without feeling like I am contributing to the problem.

Ultimately, the onus falls on the franchise. The onus falls on those making the most money from editing and cutting these clips into the show. The onus falls on casting, the onus falls on the network.

To expect contestants to take off from work past the allotted paid-time-off of most companies is to expect a certain type of candidate with a certain amount of personal or family wealth, or one who is young enough to not have to worry about that. Because the show does not pay contestants to be there, and they barely want to even pay their leads to be there.

Being equitable means leveling the playing field. Taking equity seriously means understanding how oppression works, it means doing what you can to fill the voids with as much of a diverse cast as possible—and paying those contestants who cannot afford the luxury of unpaid time off. This cannot possibly be that hard to do, especially knowing how many millions these shows have made the network. This is how you level the playing field, with an anti-racist lens that invites a wider range of contestants, and thus viewers. The responsibility is on the entire entertainment industry to do better—if they mean to do what they said they would do back in 2019 and 2020.

I am a Latina who loved the franchise until it began to give me a bad taste in my mouth. I am an immigrant from the Global South who has felt too intimately my disposability through white American politics, personal interactions, and television. I am a brown person who has been dehumanized, and I know exactly what that looks, feels, and sounds like, and when I watch *The Bachelor/ette*, I find a complicit perpetrator, not a love story. I have done all the things I have needed to do to avoid being othered and have seen the fruits of my labor rot the second I am not perfectly palatable to a white American gaze. To buy into any of the whitewashing the franchise does to their palatable contestants is to set them up to fail.

Do better.

Prisca Dorcas Mojica Rodríguez was born in Managua, Nicaragua, but calls Nashville, Tennessee, home. She is a feminist, theologian, storyteller, and advocate.

Mojica Rodríguez got her Master of Divinity from Vanderbilt University's Divinity School in the spring of 2015. She is a respected storyteller who has traveled across the US telling stories to countless college and university students. Mojica Rodríguez merges storytelling with pedagogy to help folks understand the larger forces at play, also known as systemic oppression.

As a first-generation student and immigrant, her passion is in naming the experiences of first-generation students navigating systems not built for them. As the oldest immigrant daughter, she explores the ways that sexism impedes the development of girls and women. As a graduate from a white-serving institution, she names systemic racism as a roadblock for success and decolonizes western notions of said success. Mojica Rodríguez also explores the relationship between religious trauma through Christianity and white supremacy within the US empire, which is where her theological training really shines.

To date she has participated in the Young Adult anthology *Nevertheless, We Persisted.* Recently Mojica Rodríguez also participated in an anthology edited by Lynda Lopez titled *AOC: The Fearless Rise and Powerful Resonance of Alexandria Ocasio-Cortez.*

She started the platform Latina Rebels in 2013, and currently it boasts over 300,000 organic followers online. She has been featured in Telemundo, Univision, Mitú, *HuffPost Latino Voices*, *Guerrilla Feminism*, *Latina Mag*, NBC, MTV, *Cosmopolitan*, *Everyday Feminism*, *PopSugar*, and the list goes on. Because of Mojica Rodríguez's extensive body of work, she has also worked with the United Methodist Church, National Endowment for the Arts, Smithsonian, National Association of Latino Arts and Cultures, and Planned Parenthood, and she was even invited to the Obama White House in 2016.

She is unapologetic, angry, and uncompromising about protecting and upholding the stories of Latinx communities. *Que viva la gente!*

Currently, she has two full-length books published through Seal Press, a subsidiary of Hachette Book Group.

4

What Teaching *The Bachelor* Taught Me

Serena Zets

Like many viewers, I first came to *The Bachelor* seeking escape. I was a college student tired of the drama of dating at my tiny liberal arts school, and I wanted to watch someone removed from my world fumble through its trials instead.

I was well aware of the show's pop-cultural dominance, and many of my friends had tried for years to convince me to watch it. I found myself reading stories about successful (and unsuccessful) *Bachelor* couples in tabloids at the supermarket, or later on social media and gossip sites like RealitySteve. I knew about the shows' scandals long before I ever watched it, which is proof of concept for the reality television machine. *The Bachelor* drives a national conversation that millions are forced to participate in, whether they want to or not.

I finally caved and joined my friend Marisa to watch the premiere of Colton Underwood's fraught season. I was hooked from the second twenty-three-year-old Demi Burnett walked out of the limo and proclaimed she hadn't dated a virgin since she was twelve. At the time I, and the rest of the country, didn't know that Demi would go on to become a Bachelor Nation mainstay, changing the franchise forever when she came out as bisexual and became half of the franchise's first onscreen queer couple. (In hindsight, maybe she's why I enjoyed Colton's premiere so much.)

As we continued watching the premiere in a dorm common area, I was fascinated to see the famously straight show portray what was functionally non-monogamy for an audience dominated by straight, white, Christian female viewers (a demographic I don't fall into). Questions like *What did it mean to expose this audience to nontraditional dating models? How could it be that the show's structure resembled my own messy queer dating life? Who was* The Bachelor *actually for?* interested me far more than *Who will Colton end up with?*

Marisa, also an Asian American woman, related to components of the show too. Both political science majors, and writers and critics in our free time, we spent our days working, thinking, and analyzing. For some, reality television like *The Bachelor* can be an opportunity to turn your brain off, but for us, watching became another conduit for analysis. Watching Colton's season and debriefing episode by episode became an unlikely way to deepen our friendship and understanding of ourselves. We wondered: *Was anyone else, particularly queer people of color, unexpectedly relating to the show?* And more specifically, *Was anyone else on our campus watching and relating to the show?* Even though the student body's main shared pastimes were hating and rejecting the mainstream, we figured we couldn't be alone.

As social scientists, we wanted to conduct an experiment to help answer our questions.

The quirks of our liberal arts curriculum provided the perfect research method: a class. Our school had a department fully run and taught by students and community members to supplement the college's traditional curriculum. The Experimental College was a rare way for students to try their hand at teaching and dive deeper into subjects the faculty weren't experts in. Each proposed course has to undergo an accreditation process, and students who teach in the department are supported with pedagogical resources and training and can get extracurricular credit too. We decided to develop an analytical class about *The Bachelor* where we could further study, explore, and interrogate the topics we had thus far only talked about amongst ourselves on a larger scale.

Marisa and I spent weekend afternoons that spring hunched over laptops in our favorite coffee shop, intellectualizing our discussions into a syllabus that would earn accreditation. We exchanged topic ideas, readings to provide, specific moments to clip, discourse to unpack, and more, as we sipped lattes and giggled like kids who had been handed the keys to the kingdom. In many ways, that's exactly what we were. What nineteen-year-olds are granted the opportunity to not only pose an absurd question but also use institutional resources and time to find out the answer? The luck we had wasn't lost on us.

In the fall of 2019, we were approved to teach our class—BachCo: A Critical and Cultural Analysis of *The Bachelor* Franchise.

We created an exhaustive Google Form for interested students that asked essential questions including: *If you have watched, what is your perception of* The Bachelor *shows you've viewed? If you haven't, what's stopped you from watching? What do you perceive as* The Bachelor *franchise's role in the reality television and pop culture landscapes?* And most importantly, *How would you make your limo entrance if you were a contestant?*

We curated our ideal class by bringing in students with a range of perspectives and backgrounds and striking a balance between students very familiar with the show (like Marisa) and students skeptical and new to its world (like me).

In our first class, as we introduced ourselves and our experience with the franchise, it became clear that our group didn't look like the stereotype of Bachelor Nation: Our class was racially diverse and full of students watching the show through a queer lens. Many students shared that they were drawn to the class because they didn't have anyone with similar identities or politics to discuss the show with. We had all ended up in that classroom because we were seeking community and an outlet. Marisa and I were hopeful we could find it together.

Every class began with a lecture and presentation followed by an open discussion around a set of core questions; it was a formalized version of the weekly conversations Marisa and I had shared the previous season. Our syllabus stated: "We want to resist the idea that *The Bachelor* and *Bachelorette* are merely a 'guilty pleasure' reality show and rather investigate why it remains so popular when it contradicts the notion of progress our society claims to be moving towards." We covered the shows' structural elements including rhetoric, tropes, spin-offs, international franchises, and the role of production as well as the shows' specific cultural depictions of sex, sexuality and gender, race, orientalism, colonialism, and international travel.

About a month into our semester, we were thrown a pedagogical curveball. A student who wasn't in our class informed us that they had close ties to the franchise: They were the child of an executive producer, and our syllabus had piqued the interest of the production team. Would we and our students like to observe the filming of an episode of *The Bachelor* (Peter "Pilot Pete" Weber's season) when the show came to Cleveland?

We jumped at the chance; this class, already Marisa's and my greatest sociological adventure yet, had just gotten more interesting. The details of the observation took shape: A producer would shadow one of our classes and partake in a Q&A, our students would be extras during the filming of a one-on-one date, and our class would observe the ABC control room for the filming of a rose ceremony. It felt like a site visit at the end of a long research period, as if we'd been unknowingly preparing our students to enter the belly of the reality television beast.

The producer visited our class in Birkenstocks and a plaid shirt, looking more like one of our students than a Los Angeles executive. Despite his presence, our students were as candid and critical as usual. Other lessons had required our students to read and watch producer interviews, so we were all prepared for a heavily media-trained session that wouldn't reveal too much new information. But what ensued was a very honest conversation where he acknowledged, and even reciprocated, the vulnerability our students displayed. The class asked him why fan favorite Mike Johnson, a Black contestant from Hannah Brown's *Bachelorette* season, had been passed over for Pilot Pete, that season's lead. This question prompted a conversation about race and racism on the show that demonstrated that production was thinking critically about these topics behind the scenes, even if their public statements left much to be desired. The producer's candor humanized what had always felt like an impenetrable part of the show: production's psyches.

Next, it was time to attend the filming. *The Bachelor* team had taken over a museum in Cleveland's University Circle neighborhood to serve as that episode's makeshift mansion, and rooms were set up for the cocktail party, informal chats, confessionals, the rose ceremony, and, of course, the production room making everything else happen. Upon entering that sacred space, we noticed it was built much like a war room. The stakes felt that high. Monitors of all sizes lined the walls, long tables had been set up to accommodate equipment, and producers hustled through the space screaming into walkie-talkies. Our class watched as the team produced the standard cocktail party and rose ceremony, two scenes we had long studied from a distance but were now unfolding directly in front of our eyes. We were enthralled.

From watching and studying the show, we conceptually understood how involved the producers always are, but seeing it in real-time was entirely different. The familiarity and comfort between the in-house producers and the contestants and lead were palpable. In the production room, we witnessed producers responding to unfolding plotlines and updating documents to mark where the season might go, almost like novelists mapping out possible outcomes for their characters. Some producers entered the set occasionally to calm cast members down, lend them a listening ear, or pull them into the confessional room to capture reactions in the moment.

The process was fatiguing, which was the greatest shock of seeing it all up close. The episode we observed was the fourth in a twelve-episode season and the contestants already seemed exhausted. They were fighting and crying, seemingly not that smitten with Peter, the man they were all vying for. It got late, and everyone was drained, cast and producers alike.

Our class was just witnessing, not competing or working, yet our students were worn out by the experience too. We would get to leave and return to our campus, but the cast and staff were stuck there for as long as filming took. Then they would catch a few hours of sleep before hopping on a flight to their next destination. The contestants were undoubtedly beautiful and powerful, but I did not envy them. In lulls between filming, some of our bored students in the control room swiped on Tinder and whispered about crushes, reminding us of our own mundane and fraught dating landscape, but we got to endure it on our terms. The contestants didn't have that luxury. They were in this world until their journey concluded and their NDAs ended.

Watching the filming disrupted the illusion of envy and desire that I knew the show was meant to provoke. Rather than wishing I was one of the women, I merely wished that they all got a good night's sleep. Beyond finding love, I hoped they left the season with their energy and sense of self intact.

In the five years since teaching our class and that unexpected visit to *The Bachelor* universe, the world has changed dramatically while the show has remained consistent. While reading think pieces and listening to podcasts about the racial reckoning and demise of the show, I've often thought of those women from years prior and wondered how they were feeling about the show's evolution. Were they surprised? Still exhausted? Resigned? Hopeful for change? I wanted to know.

It seems *The Bachelor* has become aware of its failings yet keeps setting itself up for continued future failure. Like all good reality television, it's a train wreck you can't look away from. But Jenn's "train wreck" felt too cruel[1]; the show had gone too far. I missed the insights of my students and wished we could come back together to analyze what had just happened. What could our lessons on rhetoric and the design of the show teach us about this disappointing moment? How would this group of primarily progressive queer people of color understand and make sense of this?

I no longer live on that rural college campus and now call Washington, DC, my home. In the years I've lived here, the story of BachCo has become my favorite party anecdote. Saying "I've been to *The Bachelor* Mansion" comes in handy when playing two truths and a lie. I watch people's responses closely to gauge if they understand *The Bachelor* as the ripe and nuanced subject I now see or if they've written it off like I once did.

The question I'm most often incredulously asked is "What do you mean *you* taught a class on *The Bachelor*?" I get to ask them, "Why couldn't a person like me be interested in *The Bachelor*?" Queer and trans people, people of color, and progressive people watch and analyze the franchise. I continue to meet some of my favorite people through these conversations and bonding over the complexities of reality television, the same way Marisa and I did. My time in DC has proven our theory on a much larger and more varied scale than our twenty-person class: People of all backgrounds watch, and love, *The Bachelor*—even if it doesn't necessarily love them back.

The Bachelor tries to live within and portray a world that doesn't truly exist, a world where race, gender, sex, class, global pandemics, political elections, and more integral facets of daily American life don't matter when dating. For those of us watching, the show forces us to look into a distorted mirror and see our greatest flaws, embarrassments, and triumphs portrayed through people we've never met and initially share little in common with.

1 Editor's note: For more on Jenn Tran's tumultuous season of *The Bachelorette* in 2024, see 16: "How *Not* to Project Your Own Traumas onto the First Vietnamese Bachelorette," by Carolyn Huynh, on page 124.

Yet by coming together to dissect the show, we find that there is some shared experience at the core of love and heartbreak, regardless of who you are.

To me, the greatest lesson of the show and the class is that *The Bachelor* forces us to find communion and empathy with those we detest, an act that feels particularly challenging right now. *The Bachelor* is not made for me, and yet I remain loyal to the show. The core of my gratitude for it resides in the fact that it brought me, Marisa, and our students closer together through deep analysis and a once-in-a-lifetime experience. The show continues to disappoint me, but that capacity for surprise and flicker of camaraderie, whether with those on-screen or off, is what keeps me in Bachelor Nation. That empathy remaining possible even in the least likely of circumstances is what keeps me alive.

Serena Zets is a creative nonfiction writer and journalist based in Washington, DC, by way of Appalachia, whose writing focuses on the intersection of social movements and queer arts and culture. Serena *is* here to make friends.

5

American Princess

Emma Rohloff

The second I found out who the Bachelorette was, I wanted to be one.

Being "the most eligible bachelorette in America" was no joke to Little Emma. My media diet had enough glossy magazine covers and princess movies to recognize what it meant to be one. It meant pretty dresses, travel to wondrous locales, and national fame. It meant respect.

This was my perspective when I sat down for my first-ever episode of *The Bachelorette*. I was nine years old, sitting in a plush armchair next to my grandmother. To introduce me to the show, she even created a game for us to play during its run time. A grocery store bouquet of roses laid on her glass table, with clear instructions: throw petals in joy, throw the rose in anger. Cute guys? Petals. Betrayal? Rose. My grandmother was a casual fan who enjoyed the cast and the mystery of each season. It took some time to convince both her and my parents that I was ready to watch it, but I was insistent. My curiosity, born from hearing secondhand drama, won out in the end.

Before watching the actual show, I gleaned most of my information from conversations with adults and *Yahoo! News* headlines. I expected that the Bachelorette would be going on one-on-one dates with all the guys individually, so she could get a chance to know them and make an informed decision. I was incredibly confused by how the Mansion worked with the travel that I knew would happen. How could there be a famous *Bachelor* Mansion, but a *Bachelor* engagement in Mexico every year? Other than these minor gaps, I understood the basic structure of the show and knew its lead from magazine covers.

My first impressions of Emily Maynard were incredibly positive. I was told that she was (in this order) a single mom, a fashion icon, and a sweetheart. When she was on-screen, all these things became real to me. Wide eyes captured the praise lavished on her, and just when I was getting jealous, she shared her story. Tragically losing her fiancé and finding out that she was pregnant right after was an unimaginable tragedy. In the wake of my heartache, my hope for her to find love grew, and I was hooked.

I felt that she deserved to be the Bachelorette because she was a good person. She made the role seem more expansive than just being the prettiest in the room. I saw the way she acted with her daughter, the care she treated the men with, and believed in all of it. As far as I was concerned, Emily Maynard was Cinderella.

I looked up to her like she was an American princess. She was the holder of an official post that made her the ambassador for American femininity.

Despite my deep respect for Maynard at the time, I'll confess that I didn't watch the entirety of her season. I was still nine years old, so I got bored with two-hour run times, but I managed to tune into the finale. When her breakup with Jef Holm was announced a while after, I asked if she was going to have another season. Upon hearing "probably not," I decided to give the franchise a break.

If you told a young Emma that the Bachelorette herself was often subject to a mountain of criticism, I would have been confused. Who was so confident that they could take shots at the designated "most desirable single person in America"? Since then, I've become more familiar with the judgmental nature of social media commentary and the resulting disrespect that gets cast on each lead, but I'd argue that respect and power remain a major part of Bachelor/ette-hood. Nearly every season of *The Bachelorette* will have a moment where the lead will lay down the law in front of the men to remind the audience that, yea verily, she does deserve to be regarded specially. These moments often become especially resonant in their seasons, like Hannah Brown moving the podium or Ali Fedotowsky giving a cheater a dressing-down in front of all the other guys.

As a kid, I would have expected that being named the Bachelorette would shield you from having to do this. These women had already proven themselves to be worthy, right? The Bachelorette needs to be so sweet that she can break up with someone every week and still look like a hero. She needs to be pretty like a model (and skinny and usually white, but that nuance was lost on me until I was older), eloquent like a politician, and up for adventure. She must be willing to date multiple people, but unsure about whether she can fall for more than one person at a time. She has to be the cream of the cream, hand-selected from the elite *Bachelor* contestants, and beloved by audiences.

I saw Emily Maynard as a role model. She was proof of the American Dream. Yes, you too can be plucked from your small town and become a national star; all it takes is virtue, looks, and good luck. As a girl, I heard the message clearly. A certain kind of woman is desirable, and if you are lovable enough, desire becomes respect. It becomes renown. Skinny blonde girls who are patient and sweet have a shot at this position, and at age nine, all those things looked achievable.

As a country without a monarchy, Americans have a habit of creating pseudo royalty. Our exported princesses, like Grace Kelly and Meghan Markle, become the source of fascination and regard. We'll occasionally get swept up in the grandeur of foreign princesses, like that memorable year when Kate Middleton married into the British royal family. Though we greeted her with interest, the warmth faded quickly, because she wasn't *ours*. She, and others like her, aren't able to inspire national pride the way American princesses do.

The public seems to have an itch for unmarried, beautiful, and virtuous American women to publicly adore. It's one of the reasons why Miss USA gets a crown every year to rapturous applause. In the absence of a divine claim to the throne, we settle for a meritocracy, like *The Bachelor* franchise. There are two winners of every *Bachelor* season: the one who gets the ring from the lead; and the one who gets the crown from the producers, the *Bachelorette* gig, which signifies special levels of poise and desirability.

Far from just being the *face* of American femininity of that year, the exposure of national television can allow them to become a voice for it as well. There's even a chance that, like Rachel Lindsay, they'll go on to speaking careers where they will shape the minds of young people. Lindsay was an especially notable case in the pantheon of Bachelorettes, because she was the first Black woman to take on the position. This was in 2017, after fifteen years of *The Bachelor* franchise airing. Despite being long overdue, the decision still brought unfathomable backlash.

Princess-hood is defined by its exclusivity, so anytime there's a "first" Bachelorette, it means something. The crown comes with provisions (it's temporary, the public can still turn on you, and you need to play ball with producers), but it's still a bestowal of power. Bachelorettes are still chosen to be role models, even if the roles being modeled have shifted over the show's two-decade run.

I returned to the series in my late teens, beginning with retro seasons on Hulu. I started tuning into the live broadcasts during Katie Thurston's season. By then, my outlook had shifted drastically. I was on the other side of a lot of struggles with my body image, based on standards I had internalized at a young age of what pretty looked like. *The Bachelor* franchise was not the only influence on me in this space, but it was one of the voices in the choir.

When producers were selecting their cast, I doubt they considered the effect that their definition of "most desirable woman in America" would have on the girls in its audience. It affected me all the same. When I saw the type of woman who was desirable, I noticed the ways I couldn't measure up. By the time I was old enough to apply to be on the show, I could point out how much I didn't look like the average contestant. Even if I never expected to be on the show, it still stung to imagine that I wasn't pretty/thin/feminine enough to get in if I wanted to.

By the time I was watching again, I was resolved not to let the beautiful women on my screen stoke insecurity. I consider myself lucky to have stumbled back into *The Bachelorette* party for Thurston's season because she reminded me so much of myself. As a comedically-minded Capricorn who was against bullying, we had some key things in common. I saw someone like me on the screen at a time when I felt worlds away from the desirability implied by Thurston's casting.

The maturation of *The Bachelor* franchise, though not complete, has been a welcome parallel to my own. As my definition of "beautiful" grew to include more types of people, so too did the franchise. Age also let me see how looks alone don't land you the gig. It takes a strength of character and charisma to succeed in such a high-pressure environment.

A younger me didn't appreciate the fact that most Bachelorettes start by being brutally and publicly dumped. Because of that, Little Emma certainly couldn't appreciate how most Bachelorette narratives are about the strength that it takes to fall short and then try again.

As a college-aged woman experiencing romantic pitfalls, however? The message was vital. Post-Katie Thurston, I started dipping further into throwback seasons and saw old drama through matured eyes. Imagine how it felt watching Arie Luyendyk Jr.'s season on Hulu, watching Becca Kufrin get through a heartrending breakup in its nauseating entirety. A groundswell of support rose behind her, including Venmo donations to "get her a drink."[1] On live TV, she announced that she would be donating all $6,000 of the fund to Stand Up to Cancer. That donation was matched by the show and Katie Couric, and Becca Kufrin received an offer to become

1 Emily Wang, "Becca from 'The Bachelor' Is Getting Sent Wine Money by Strangers on Venmo," *Glamour*, March 6, 2018, https://www.glamour.com/story/becca-from-the-bachelor-venmo.

the next Bachelorette.[2] Being pretty and fit wasn't what turned her into an American princess; it was the resilience she showed when she turned a brutal breakup into an $18,000 philanthropic pursuit. *The Bachelor* producers decided that was worth admiring.

Who do we put on the pedestal? Who becomes the source of admiration? Who gets to be a princess?

It dawned on me that as beautiful as Kufrin was, her looks weren't why I actually admired her. I wanted to emulate her strength, not her killer makeup. A few weeks after seeing the Luyendyk finale, in the midst of my own heartbreak (I don't remember the cause of it, but I remember the pep talk I gave myself), I used this as a source of inspiration. *Becca Kufrin got dumped on national television, and she turned out fine. She got through it and became an American princess, and you can too.*

I am now the target audience for the fantasy. ABC wasn't selling the show to me as a kid, but they are now. I am now the age that many women are when they first send in applications to be on the show. With that in mind, I have a confession about my own particular *Bachelor* fantasy.

When I said that I wanted to be the Bachelorette as a kid, it was a bit of a lie. I certainly fantasized about it a few times, but I had a slightly different dream. As I proudly announced to my grandma after watching a few episodes, I wanted to be the first girl to self-eliminate from the show. (I had assumed that it had never happened before.)

I have an honest respect for the women who get to the Bachelorette position, because I see it as a heavy responsibility. But I thought the only thing more gratifying than winning was to get in and then leave of your own accord. To look around and say, "I've had my fun, but I don't need this guy, or those producers, to be what I want to be."

---

2 Mike Vulpo, "*The Bachelor*'s Becca Kufrin Donating Her $6,000 Venmo Donations to Stand up to Cancer," *E! Online,* March 7, 2018, https://www.eonline.com/news/918965/the-bachelor-s-becca-kufrin-set-to-donate-her-6-000-venmo-donations-to-stand-up-to-cancer.

Emma Rohloff is a writer and graduate from Rochester Institute of Technology. Based in Austin, Texas, she writes pop culture commentary, fiction, and comedy.

6

NONE OF THESE WOMEN TOLD ROMANTIC FAIRY TALES ABOUT FALLING IN LOVE.

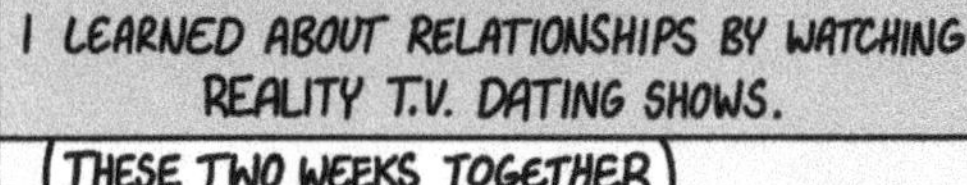

WITH A STRICT EIGHT O'CLOCK BEDTIME, I HAD TO SNEAK INTO THE LIVING ROOM TO CATCH SNIDBITS OF THIS NEW TELEVISED COURTING RITUAL.

MY GRANDMA MIGHT'VE BEEN RIGHT TO STOP ME FROM WATCHING THE "NASTY MAN," BECAUSE THE BACHELOR ENTERED MY SUBCONSCIOUS MIND. FOR THE NEXT FIVE YEARS I HAD A RECURRING NIGHTMARE ABOUT A FACELESS MAN IN A TUXEDO PICKING WIVES OFF A CONVEYOR BELT.
NO! NO! NO!
THAT ONE.
I DON'T WANNA BE A WIFE!

THE BACHELOR REENTERED MY LIFE WHEN I MOVED BACK HOME AFTER COLLEGE.
I ACCEPT THIS ROSE... I GUESS.
ART SUPPLIES
MY MOTHER AND I HAD A STRAINED RELATIONSHIP. WE HARDLY SPOKE AND HAD NOTHING IN COMMON. THE ONLY ACTIVITY WE DID TOGETHER WAS WATCH T.V.
OUR VIEWERSHIP WAS LIMITED BY OUR DIGITIAL ANTENNA'S RECEPTION.
WHO USES AN ANTENNA IN 2015?!
WHAT ARE YOU WATCHING?
THE BACHELOR.
WOW. THAT SHOW IS SO TRASHY.
ABC IS THE ONLY CLEAR CHANNEL.
WATCHING A SHOW BASED ON DATING AND FINDING LOVE WITH MY MOM MADE MY SKIN CRAWL. THESE TOPICS WERE STILL SO TABOO BETWEEN US THAT I COULDN'T HAVE ANTICIPATED HER REACTIONS.
SHE WAS INVESTED.
THESE WOMEN ARE CRYING OVER A FARMER?! THIS IS GONNA BE A HOT MESS.

BACHELOR 19, CHRIS SOULES, WOULD HELP MEND OUR MOTHER-DAUGHTER RELATIONSHIP AND DEMYSTIFY MY MOTHER'S THOUGHTS ON ROMANTIC RELATIONSHIPS.

THIS GUY IS ATTRACTIVE?

I THINK...
I'M JUST HAVING...
A PANIC ATTACK.

GIRL...
YOU'RE GONNA THROW YOURSELF ON THE FLOOR...
OVER A MAN?!

YOU THINK THAT BRITT WANTS THE LIFESTYLE LIKE SERIOUSLY?

JUST STOP YOUR CRYING AND GO USE YOUR MASTER'S DEGREE. YOU WERE NEVER GOING TO MILK COWS OR WHATEVER.

Ness Ilene Garza is an autobiographical comic artist from Riverside, CA.

7

Reality TV Psychic

Chrissy Tolley

I'd already been working as a psychic for four years at the start of Michelle Young's season. Four years seems like a long time in my industry because every internet baddie started reading cards during the pandemic. But for career psychics, the ones still giving readings in their seventies, four years is child's play. By October of 2021, I felt nervous about how bored I was of the work already. Not unfulfilled, but bored. I wasn't an excellent psychic by year four, but I'd finally become a good one. I'd gotten just good enough to no longer be overwhelmed by it, and the boredom in me craved chaos. I'd spent well over a decade in talk therapy and on psych meds and long ago discovered that the least damaging way to experience chaos was by watching reality television. I wasn't always able to blow up my life, but I could watch someone else blow up theirs.

My intake of reality TV doubled when I forfeited my office at the start of the pandemic. The night of Michelle's premiere, I closed my MacBook after wrapping up a Zoom session with a client, *didn't* meditate, and wandered into the living room to start the show. After fifteen minutes of poorly produced antics (hosts Tayshia and Kaitlyn find a contestant's incriminating document!), Michelle stood in front of the resort entrance, radiant in the softest metallic green. The first limo pulled up and all six feet and eight inches of Nayte Olukoya bounded out. I responded to his energy the way I do every new character I'm introduced to in a reality series. I felt into it. I felt, "Nayte: Flaky, weird relationship with Mom?, performer." In that second, an idea emerged that a part of me regrets to this day. I grabbed my phone, opened Instagram, and started filming my own TV screen. In my Instagram stories, I caught fifteen seconds of Nayte and Michelle lighting each other up. I captioned my story with ugly typewriter font: "NAYTE, FIRST OUT OF LIMO: FLAKY, WEIRD RELATIONSHIP WITH MOM?, PERFORMER" and dragged the text toward Nayte's head. I posted it before I could think the choice through. I'd signed up to spend the next several hours creating tiny videos describing my psychic takes on twenty-nine more men. I'd never be bored again.

Even with my middling Instagram following, a surprising number of people cared about my takes on the season premiere. A few hundred people had watched my stories all the way through and nearly fifty messaged me with responses. The following Monday, I unpacked Michelle's pull toward men she couldn't possibly settle down with, pausing the show every five to ten minutes to figure out which fifteen seconds I should rewind back to and film on my phone. Where did Joe Coleman's palpable fear come from? Why did Michelle carry such a similar demand for (and unconscious rebellion against) "perfection"? The similarity spoke to growing up in that region as mixed kids playing basketball at a competitive level, but was it a karmic thing? Why would both of those souls choose that similar of a childhood, and why bring those souls together right now? For the first time outside of a one-to-one session, people were witnessing how my brain works, how I parse through energy. Most of them seemed less interested in whether I was "right" and more interested in how bizarre it was that I was doing it at all, unannounced and sans context. Some loved *The Bachelor* and were clients of mine and longtime fans of the show. More had never seen it, or never cared about it, but were entertained enough by how brazen the conceit was to stick with me.

It felt freeing to talk about something trivial, to be silly again and let myself experiment with something fun. Still, if I'd understood that this fifteen-second video would result in an undertaking that would last four seasons, I'm not sure I would have done it. I would have texted a friend, "The guy dressed as a table looks dead behind the eyes," and gone on with my life. But I don't see that much of my own future. Most psychics don't. Especially when they're ignoring it on purpose for attention.

I always struggled to explain to the internet what I do for a living. False bravado sustained me when I started in 2017, and word of mouth managed to keep me afloat after that. I felt insecure the entire time, debilitatingly so at times, but I wasn't allowed to admit that. Girlbossing forbids uncertainty. But I could talk about *The Bachelor*, and I mentioned reality TV so often that it had inadvertently become a part of my brand. Something about my identity including a universal and trivial element seemed to make people less scared of me. Sessions with clients would wrap up before launching into a quick debrief on *Love Island*. Combining my work more formally with reality television made me feel like I had coworkers again—actual people to talk to about my job in ways they understood. Had I been truly observing my own energy, I would have clocked the boredom as loneliness from the beginning. It certainly wasn't the first time I'd made a wild choice in public; one could make that argument about my entire business, really.

Halfway through Michelle's season, I made a separate Instagram account: @reality.tv.psychic was the closest handle available that made any sense. The name stuck.

Because I didn't know why I started Reality TV Psychic, I honestly didn't know what I was teaching. I just knew that anyone who uses their free time to watch relational chaos happen to real people is someone whose body remembers relational chaos. There's a theory that service-based practitioners tend to attract versions of themselves, which might be why nearly all Reality TV Psychic viewers were neurodivergent people with childhood trauma who liked gossip. Most were raised in high-control religions and cultures, and almost all of them had grown up with a parent they couldn't trust. Their childhoods trained them to ignore their feelings and stole their ability to define their own reality, so they seemed to respond well to a silly, low-stakes way to practice doing so.

The premise of Reality TV Psychic stayed pretty simple: teach people to notice and validate their instincts, collect data about behavior over time to see if their instincts were correct, and identify which of their own biases informed their instincts and in what ways. I did it by modeling it, no matter how vulnerable or wrong I needed to be to model it well. *The Bachelor* presented dozens of people at a time for me to energetically assess all while observing a lead forced to energetically assess right alongside me. The point wasn't to accurately predict the winner, though it was exciting when it happened. The point was to intentionally push back against what counted as legitimate data using whatever veneer of legitimacy my role afforded me. My clients considered my initial instincts "data," but didn't trust their own first instinct about someone in the same way. I knew I could push them to validate themselves with practice.

For my more naive clients, the kind who said, "I'm probably just being judgmental" about dangerous behavior, Reality TV Psychic allowed them to practice discernment without any real consequences. You don't like that guy the second you see him? Good, that matters. Who does he remind you of? What do you notice your body do in response to his energy? Can you find your gut instinct somewhere in there without suppressing it? For the overly defensive, it exposed bias. What triggered you initially? What wound have you not integrated that warped your interpretation of that person's vibration? Can you see that pattern? Can you notice it repeatedly over time until you have objectivity around that bias in order to change it? I pushed people to stop wondering if they were allowed to have feelings about people, places, and things while still honoring the discipline it takes to catch ingrained layers of prejudice, preference, and preconception. Navigating the pendulum swings from naive to guarded and from self-doubt to self-trust is the path of trauma survivors, one that contestants on the show famously demonstrate while surviving the trauma that is the experience of the show itself.

Clayton Echard's season may have been my best work. Clayton carried no vibrations of malice or deceit outright, but his desperation to be "good" translated to unconsciously deceitful behavior throughout his season. Production primed Clayton to see himself as unworthy of the lead, and they tugged on his unworthiness repeatedly throughout the production schedule. It destabilized his energy considerably and made him incapable of connecting with his own truth when he most needed it. He shocked Bachelor Nation and his final three contestants—Susie Evans, Gabby Windey, and Rachel Recchia—by announcing that he loved all three of them and had slept with two of them. Their responses to him, all very different, were examples of how to navigate this type of energy: walk away, negotiate, or fawn, respectively. Everyone had either dated a Clayton or behaved like a Clayton at some point, and I couldn't keep up with the number of messages people were sending me via DM.

Between filming episodes, creating content, and juggling conversations, I started to spend about eight hours a week on Reality TV Psychic. There was a photoshoot, a part-time virtual assistant, and awkward attempts at TikTok. I launched a Patreon and corresponding Discord chat server. Once gathered in a chat room, the people who had been talking to me about their intuition were suddenly talking to each other. Gabby and Rachel's season struggled, but my weird little community solidified. I started hosting watch parties, psychic group readings, and a weekly meet-up. A client earnestly messaged me, "I really think this is the spiritual community I was always looking for," at the exact moment I typed, "Can someone tell me why the fuck *Bachelor in Paradise* is still airing *THROUGH THANKSGIVING??!!!!*" I couldn't tell if we were watching TV together or forming a coven. Is there a difference?

By the end of that year's season of *Bachelor in Paradise*, I finally came clean. I could no longer deny that using reality TV to not blow up my life had still resulted in using reality TV to blow up my life. With the core desire for connection now filled through the community, filming Reality TV Psychic as content became exhausting, pointless even. The whole idea remained pedagogically unsound. After four seasons, I had to admit that *The Bachelor* continued to be a limited instructional medium, and that so many attempts to diagnose energy dissolved into assessing the tactics of production and the franchise itself. I stopped wanting to promote it. The dynamic of the group I'd already cultivated felt too precious for me to shake up with new people I didn't know, especially people who didn't already trust me or understand my brand.

As a full-time self-employed person, the effect of Reality TV Psychic on my bottom line felt obvious to me all at once. I could have spent thousands of hours over the past year doing anything else. Of all the things I could have invested time in—a podcast, a side hustle, volunteering with children, for God's sake—I chose psychic performance art about *The Bachelor*? Reality TV Psychic was morphing into an embarrassing rudderless flop, but I finally understood my own energy pattern. I kept making wild, public choices just to not feel alone. What does it mean to be a person who compulsively opens themselves up to other people in ways no one should? Why can't I be someone who learns things quietly?

Reality TV Psychic ended in early 2023. I still feel a little stupid about it sometimes, but I take comfort in knowing that my behavior is in line with some of the franchise's recent greats. Gabby Windey realized she was gay. Gerry Turner needed to stay at the lake house, apparently. Jenn Tran just wasn't done learning about her childhood. They're all in better places for it at this point. Making the wrong choices teaches us important things we don't learn in other ways and leads us to people we wouldn't connect with otherwise. I can't really regret Reality TV Psychic when it gave me my community. We still meet weekly for energetic check-ins and connect daily on Discord. Members have formed life-long friendships all on the basis of trusting me and liking the project. In the years we've spent together, I've watched this group transform from insecure agnostics to literal witches who can channel and counsel at my same level. We still watch reality television too. After all, psychics are multifaceted. A lot of them love *The Bachelor*.

Chrissy Tolley has worked as a professional psychic since 2017. She writes regularly on her Substack, *Ask Your Psychic*, a monthly advice column. Before starting full-time metaphysical work, she was a public school teacher and received her master's in education from the University of Arizona. She lives in Tucson, AZ, with her husband and their two cats, and can be found online at www.chrissytolley.com and @chrissytolley.

8

The Bachelor auf Deutsch

Courtney Tenz

"Love?" my dentist asked expectantly. "Did you come here for love?"

She held my lips back with a tiny mirror, her face closer to mine than any had been in ages. Her hands hovered over my cheeks, a tiny tartar scraper poised over my teeth. *Small talk? At a time like this?* I wanted to ask. Saliva pooling beneath my tongue, I resisted the urge to laugh and instead shook my head slightly.

Germans are known for their directness; my students used to scoff when I tried to teach them polite entries into conversation, would make fun of the Americanness of it all. Brits, at least, spoke of the weather, the never-ending rain. But we Americans were superficial with our niceties—*How's it going*, after all, asks for a nod in reply, not a list of the recipient's ongoing ailments. A *How you doin'*, Joey-from-*Friends*-style, is not to be interpreted as a request for a truthful answer, and the Germans I met often had trouble recognizing this. They thought our disinterest in the details of their terrible-horrible-no-good-very-bad-days rude. My dentist's straightforward question, however, still caught me off guard.

"It's just that no one really comes here except for love. Or a job," she continued, moving her hands away from my face for a moment so I could swallow. "And since you're a woman..."

"You are too?" I laughed, though I understood. Most of the expat women I had met were stay-at-home moms or trailing spouses, their days filled with long lunches and day trips to Paris. "Anyway, I came to Germany to do research. And now we're divorced."

"Oh wow." She smiled. "No wonder. German men don't really like that."

"Like what?" I asked, not bothering to tell her that my ex, like me, wasn't culturally German.

"Independence," she said, sticking her hands back into my mouth before I could respond.

I had only been single for a year at that point, but I was finding pieces of that truth everywhere. At job interviews, where future bosses asked who would look after my toddler while I worked (daycare in Germany is heavily subsidized). While flat hunting, where prospective landlords asked where my income would come from (aforementioned job). Even when I lifted weights at my gym, men expressed their concern about my going at it alone.

Yet there was no other option but to be independent. The divorce had been my idea and there was no new love affair waiting in the wings. Friends would ask when I planned to get back in the game, and I would joke about the need for Prince Charming to teleport into my living room. After all, I couldn't afford a babysitter to spend my evenings out at concerts or art exhibitions in the hopes of meeting someone. And though I'd been chatted up on occasion, it never moved past a fun, flirtatious conversation.

A (happily married) friend told me this was the German way. Feminism, she said, meant that women had to take the lead. If I wanted a man, I'd have to go after him. Men would no longer hold the door open for women, she said, as we might find the gesture insulting. Nor would they ask for a phone number or invite a woman out to dinner; extending an invitation in German culture also means paying for the meal, and most are too frugal for that. "My own husband didn't invite me out until we were engaged," she joked.

At the heart of all the many ways that Germany continued to surprise me after years of living there lay this misreading of gender imbalances and the firm hold traditional culture had on the population. Despite having a female chancellor who fought for gender parity in her appointments, women—especially those with children—worked outside the home full-time less frequently than in other countries; it also still has one of the largest gender pay gaps in the industrialized world. Yet, socially, men thought of equity as never offering to pay for pasta and wine on a night out.

The culture was so confounding that I realized I would have to study up on the mating rituals of the Germans before entering the dating market. Besides, Germans are notoriously protective of their privacy, especially in the digital world, and a quick scroll on the apps revealed few options—most available men were either in an open marriage or the ex of a friend.

So I did what any seasoned researcher would do when the subject pool is small: I sought out the cultural phenomenon that might offer the best insight from which to theorize and found *Der Bachelor*, the American television franchise that had been newly readapted.

Entirely new to me, even if by 2012 it already had a loyal following in the States, *Der Bachelor* recast the unscripted series according to local norms instead of dubbing or subtitling the US show. Airing on the private broadcaster RTL, colloquially known as Reality Trash Live, they cast a semiprofessional footballer as the first hunk to schmooze two dozen women with promises of a rose and/or engagement. For my controls, I reasoned that live-tweeting would help me connect with the broader culture: *Is this normal in Germany?* I would ask the then–less than 1 percent of the population who came together on the microblogging platform to critique women's appearances and cringe at their desire for a red rose.

I learned quickly that the show was difficult for some to talk about—quite literally. Not only are hard r's difficult for Germans to pronounce, but also the Anglicized title confused more than one person; reforms to the university system were in full swing and all the talk of "Bachelor's" centered on college degrees, not unmarried men, for whom the überDeutsch title of *Junggesell* (literally: young fellow) already existed. I liked, then, to imagine a group of intellectuals tuning into the weekly series in hopes of watching smart young women compete to see who would be first to pass their exams and grab a BA that would propel them on to law school or set them on the path to a career in medicine instead of peacocking for the affection of a man.

What I got instead was a lesson in cattiness. Settling into the sofa every Thursday night after tucking the toddler tightly into bed, I turned on the TV and waited for Germany's most eligible bachelor—a blonde northerner who appeared to fancy himself the next David Beckham—to enter the scene. With his shaggy slicked-back hair and tightly tailored suits, our man from Hamburg was the quintessential *Hochdeutsch* dreamboat; he knew his angles and was very clearly enthralled by his own good luck in getting to "date" a number of the German-speaking world's finest twentysomethings. So enthralled that he could hardly bring himself to speak most episodes, a quality that made me question whether he was holding his cards too close to his chest thanks to all the cameras or if the crisp Baltic air of Germany's north country had blown into his ear, emptying his head of anything worth saying.

Though I had commenced my *Bachelor* watching convinced that indulging in the show would surely sharpen my language comprehension better than any evening course at the adult education center, I ended up wondering whether my linguistic skills had caused me to miss the depths of the dialogue or misunderstand innuendos. There really was no other explanation for just how boring the show was and how unmemorable its characters were otherwise. Despite attempts at suspense to keep us returning after every commercial break, the scripted dramas often amounted to behind-the-scenes footage sprinkled with acts of sabotage and superficiality: "Oh was that your curling iron I switched off? Sorry! Your hair looks great straight anyway!"

As the women filed into solo sit-down interviews, instead of expressing their excitement to the cameras that they might gain a precious few seconds of our Hamburger's time, they were often throwing digs at each other. Though I couldn't always parse their words' meaning, most frequently I found myself confused because I couldn't tell the women or their voices apart: they all spoke in a well-practiced hush previously reserved for toddlers and cats (and which we've now come to associate with Instamums). These solo interviews stood in sharp contrast to the group scenes, where some harsh southern German accents slipped out and vulgar slang peppered their speech. A few bottles of wine in, their evening gatherings on the veranda often switched from superficial lovefests into judgmental revelations of each other's flaws; the women clearly saw one another as competition to be cut down.

Far from the cultural lesson in dating in Germany that I had anticipated, *Der Bachelor* revealed itself to be a microcosm of female relationships. How women can work against each other in order to curry favor with invisible audiences—or worse, for the audience of one undeserving man. It revealed how men can be opaque about their desires and unfathomably fickle yet still hold the upper hand in relationships. And it highlighted how we've monetized voyeurism, prizing asocial behavior in the quest to reach a place where the gender gap is yawning: marriage.

Instead of learning about German courtship rituals, I undertook a study in socialization, understanding finally why men were so reluctant to hand me a job I was well qualified for or allow me to sign a lease on a new home. As a woman, I only existed in competition for their affection and attention; they, even in all their aloofness, held the power. It was a lesson that solidified that my own interests in dating and relationships lay in me first. German men may not have been apt to invite me to dinner, but I knew that I would not wait around or compete for a solitary rose.

Courtney Tenz writes about European arts, culture, and travel. Her work has appeared in *The Cut*, *Harper's Bazaar*, *The Guardian*, and more.

9

I, Michelle

Zainab Omaki

It's the summer of 2022. I am in Toronto, Canada, crammed into my best friend's small room in a shared house while on break from my doctoral program. Thus far, in the five days since I have been here, we have wandered the streets of downtown Toronto, savoring sweet, crunchy churros while window shopping outside towering stone buildings. We have taken a road trip to Montreal, where we spent a night at a sad club that only had a handful of people speckled across its disco ball–lit dance floor. We have pretended to be giants across the winding floors of Little Canada, a tourist attraction of Canada's greatest highlights in miniature. We have hung out on a mutual friend's balcony, trying Canada's legal weed for the first time, the blanket of stars above us dulled by the glaring lights of the gas station next door. Both introverts, my best friend, M, and I have exhausted our social batteries. The exterior masks that we slip on when we leave the house, which allow us to face the outside world with some energy, need recharging. It is how we end up stretched out on her double bed, idly scrolling for something to watch, with curtains drawn to block out all signs of life but our own.

"Ou!" M squeals when she comes across *The Bachelor*'s thumbnail on one of them. "Have you ever watched this?"

I scoff. "No."

She gives me a slanted look. "Ahn ahn, too good for it?"

"Thirty women competing for one man? Yes."

"That is a lot of criticism for something you have not even seen, my girl."

"And I stand by it."

She rolls her eyes. "Just watch it. You might be surprised."

She scrolls through the seasons for the ones that she likes, settling on season 18, Michelle Young's.

"You'll like this one," she promises. "And it's *The Bachelorette*, not *The Bachelor*. The power dynamic is all flipped."

I am still crotchety as she puts it on. The opening scenes are Michelle in her classroom, teaching her students fractions. Then, she's with her family, talking about her hopes for the future, followed quickly by snippets of the men she will be meeting soon who all seem overjoyed to be meeting her. They use words like "beautiful," "strong," and "genuine." When it's finally arrivals day at Bachelor Mansion, she looks like all those things in a sparkly, silver dress that brushes her heels. Each man who comes out of the limo emerges with an over-the-top, often corny line and overture designed to make himself stand out and sweep her off her feet in one breath. One man speaks French. Another shows up in a restaurant serving cart, selling himself as the meal. A third appears in a fire truck. I don't want to be hooked, but I am. What it must feel like to have all those men want and vie for you.

Three years prior, in 2019, I left Nigeria for the United Kingdom. I was in the country to pursue a master's degree in creative writing at a university in Norwich. The weather was mostly pale and cloudy. The chill was unfamiliar to my tropical body. The people were nice and polite, but I would quickly learn that was a facade. It didn't really mean anything.

At the time, I was also going through a breakup. For seven years, since I was the doe-eyed age of twenty-two, I had been in a relationship with a man eleven years older than me. In the beginning, it was fun. We bonded over our love for fantasy television, books, and a lust for the world beyond our borders. But time had rubbed the shine off the relationship with the discovery that he was averse to the commitment that I craved, and I was too codependent or anxiously attached (whatever psychological term applies) to end things with him. Leaving for school made it, at last, easy to do. With distance came the questions of what would become of us. With his inability to answer those questions came the end of the relationship. With the end of the relationship came rather lonely and somewhat sad initial months in Norwich.

I wrote and mourned, mourned and wrote. It felt like I would never dig myself out of the depressing, dreary space that I was in; then one day, I started to wonder what it would be like to date other people. I had, up until this time, only been in a relationship with my previous boyfriend. I had never shared a meal with another romantic interest. Never bopped at a concert with one. The prospect was exciting to me. Heady.

I wrote of this excitement to my friends, several of whom were in countries scattered across the Western world. M, in Canada, wrote back with a *Yay! Finally!* Anatasia, in America, joked, *I'm so glad you've been liberated from that mess.* Neither of them had particularly liked my ex-boyfriend. They were relieved to see me trying to move on. M was also full of warnings. *I'm really happy that you want to put yourself out there,* she wrote in a chat regarding online dating, *but I want you to temper your expectations. Dating in this part of the world isn't the same as dating back home.*

What do you mean? I asked. The bubbles appeared and disappeared, appeared and disappeared. *I mean, it's just different. You're dating here as a black woman, and men aren't checking for you the way they are other races. I don't want you to be overly disappointed or anything (and maybe I'm wrong sef) but just lower your expectations.*

I didn't fully understand what she meant, but I said I would. I downloaded the app, nervously made my profile. Before I could be on there very long though, Covid hit. Lockdown went into effect. Masks were everywhere. The prospect of meeting a stranger even for a socially-distanced walk was abhorrent. I deleted the app and focused on work. Somewhere along the line, my ex-boyfriend and I rekindled things. I forgot all about my friend's warnings, her appeals.

Michelle goes on a group date in the second episode of her season. It's at a basketball court to honor her past as a Division One basketball player. She's at the court first. When the men arrive, they whoop and holler at the sight of her. They all run up, energetic puppies determined to hug and kiss her.

By this time, a night has passed, and M and I have opted to stay home and watch more episodes rather than go out. We gobble up burgers that we had DoorDashed to us while watching Michelle tell the men that she wants to introduce them to her first love—basketball. The men play for her affection and time. Joe Coleman, the reserved, handsome Minnesota basketball player, and Michelle have the sweetest interaction, reminiscent of the 2000 film *Love and Basketball.* I am not aware that I am smiling through it until I turn and find M smirking at me.

"You're enjoying it, aren't you?"

I throw a pillow at her. "Get out. Stop watching me."

"Just admit it."

I am enjoying it, it's true. The entire scene reads like a fairy tale, like an unabashed fantasy after my last few months. Women, black women, in this part of the world don't get this. Or maybe that's a generalization. *Many* black women in this part of the world don't get this. But watching it makes me feel like we do.

I, MICHELLE

In 2021, after graduating with my master's in the UK, participating in a writing residency in Germany, and breaking up with my boyfriend again, I ended up in America, where I began a doctoral degree in the Midwest. It was my first time in this part of the country. My previous visits to America when I was much, much younger, were to New York and Washington where my father had worked. In the Midwest, I faced adjustments to the severe flip-flopping of the weather—cold in the morning, hot in the afternoon, and vice versa—and to the Midwestern politeness, which was not so different from the British politeness, to the flatness of the prairie land, and to the whiteness of the space outside the university program.

Single, with my heart on the mend from my breakup, which I had taken so much better than the previous one, I was once again excited about the prospect of dating, of that too-used phrase "putting myself out there."

I was wary of dating apps now. The last two years had given me the daydream of meeting someone "in the wild," which kept me from immediately going on them. Instead, I allowed myself the opportunity to meet someone organically. As I went through my daily life—meeting up with friends, going to the grocery store, going to bookshops and poetry readings, sitting in coffee shops and wandering through exhibitions at the only real museum in town—I nursed the hope of a meet-cute. Perhaps, I would find myself in front of an oil painting at said museum that drew the attention of a handsome stranger, sparking a conversation between us. Perhaps, I would lend someone a charger at a coffee shop, and we would bond over fall drink selections. I don't know. Something.

It didn't happen that way, though. Not only did I not meet anyone, I began to notice that I moved through the world here differently than I did back home. Men didn't really look at me in this part of the world. When I crossed paths with them at the stores, I was see-through. In cafés and event spaces, I might as well have been a ghost that one could walk through. It was a disorienting feeling. I wasn't gorgeous by any measure of the word, but back home, at least, I'd felt tangible to the opposite sex. Here, I was as good as invisible.

I sent M a tentative message about this, asking, *This is what you meant back then, right? Or am I going mad?*

She sent back a tired emoji. *No, you're not mad. This is what I meant.*

Like me, M had been in a relationship before leaving Nigeria, and, like mine, hers had ended. In her new hemisphere, she had tried dating unsuccessfully. A private person, she had kept her thoughts close to her vest, but now she explained to me: *It took me a while to really get it. At first, I thought it was like a cultural thing, you know? Like men here had a different way of interacting with women. Then I started going out with my friends of other races and realized, no; we're just not considered attractive in the same way.*

That takes me by surprise. Of course, I had heard the statistics of black women being the least sought after demographic among all races in many Western countries, but I had not really considered it. Growing up in Nigeria, a predominantly black nation, I hadn't been raised to see myself as black—I had been raised to see myself primarily as a Nigerian citizen. Although I had known the statistics, it simply hadn't occurred to me that they applied to me.

I wanted to believe that it wouldn't be so bad. Eternal optimist that I am, I told myself that you experience what you believe, and I finally downloaded a dating app. If in-person meetings were not happening, perhaps I would have better luck there.

On Hinge, my matches were abysmal. And I don't merely mean the quantity, but the quality. Of the few men that I did match with, many were monosyllabic terrors that didn't seem interested in pursuing any real conversation—not uncommon, perhaps. Others were overtly and subtly racist; *your skin is so sexy to me*, one wrote. A few I met up with had eyes that glazed over me as though I was not there. *Maybe I am doing something wrong*, I thought to myself. *Maybe it is* me, *not my race*. But I had black friend after black friend who had suffered similar experiences, which made me question whether it wasn't both. Sure, there were people who simply had no interest in me as a person, but there were also many others who had no interest in me because of my skin.

Month after month, I continued to try, though. I moved from Hinge to Bumble to Coffee Meets Bagel to OkCupid, then cycled back around again. I tried to be funnier and perkier in my prompts. I tried to select better pictures. Soon, I grew tired of all that effort. There is only so much you can do when society feels stacked against you.

By the time the summer came and I headed across the border, I was a husk in need of filling; I was a person desperate for some hope.

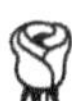

In the third episode of Michelle's season, she goes on another group date to an air museum. By this time, I have fully bought into the show. I am not pretending to be on the fence about it. I am not pretending I don't enjoy it. Although M and I leave the house to sightsee, I am excited about coming back to continue from where we stopped.

Michelle is joined by the cast of *Top Gun: Maverick* at the museum, where they put the men through athletic and emotional challenges—they do some pushups, they're stuck in a spinning wheel and have to tell her how they feel about her. I cannot come to terms with how excited they all are to take part in these challenges, to share their budding emotions for her. It's silly, but at some point I begin to superimpose myself into the picture. Instead of the gorgeous, smart, accomplished woman on the screen, I am suddenly the one on the receiving end of all that adoration. As she listens to the men belt out their regard for her, I am the one listening to them. When she watches the men compete in a dog fight for her, crowing loudly, I am the one watching and crowing. There is something healing about this. After all this time of being invisible, I am no longer invisible. After all this time of feeling like someone with my skin in the part of the world I now inhabit has fewer romantic opportunities, I'm suddenly confronted with an abundance of opportunities. I want to stay in this place for as long as possible. I want everyone I know with similar experiences to come into this place with me.

This is the beauty of *The Bachelorette*, I come to realize later. Of course, there are a million reasons to watch it. It's fun. It's easy. It can be gamified if you choose the right phrases to watch for—*my person, here for the right reasons, the most shocking season ever*—but it also has the power to center bodies that are typically on the periphery. Though the franchise doesn't do this as often as it ought to, the times that it does, it gives a host of marginalized women someone to see themselves in.

M and I finish watching the season before I leave, and, when I return to America, I tuck into the other seasons on my own. I cycle on and off dating apps for a while, still searching for a romantic connection. My prospects don't improve significantly. But *The Bachelorette* becomes a place that I can go in order to self-soothe. When I need the thrill of being the first pick and not the last, I go there. When I need convincing that there is an alternate reality of America where I am sought after, prized and valued, I go there too. I return to Michelle's season, in particular, over and over. Through her, I can access that reality. Somewhere, in a plane just out of my line of sight, I am her, and I am standing in front of a glamorous mansion in a sparkly dress, or on a basketball court, or at the entrance to a museum. Thirty men vie and clamor for me. For a moment, I am gloriously seen.

Zainab Omaki is a Nigerian writer who holds a PhD in creative writing from the University of Nebraska- Lincoln. She has a master's degree in creative writing from the University of East Anglia, where she received the Miles Morland African Writers' Award. Her essays, fiction, and literary criticism have been featured in *Callaloo*, *Five Points*, *The Los Angeles Review*, *Passages North*, *Transition Magazine*, *The Rumpus*, and more. Her novel-in-progress has received support from the University of Bayreuth in Germany, the Jan Michalski Foundation in Switzerland, and the Nebraska Arts Council.

10

I Miss Being Single... And Then I Watch *The Bachelor*

Alisa Ungar-Sargon

Watching *The Bachelor* these days is such a meta experience. When it first aired, *The Bachelor* was merely a story of boy meets many girls, drama ensues, and a beautiful love story commences. Now, decades later, the show has evolved to keep our attention, and we viewers have risen to become Bachelor Nation. Watching now is a whole conversation—one where everyone is shouting over each other at the same time, on multiple channels, but in a (mostly) fun, sisterhood-y kind of way.

A *Bachelor* episode airs, and before it's finished, you can peruse thousands of live-tweets with hot takes and memes and declarations of love or hatred. The next day, you've got recaps, multitudes of them, some delivered by former contestants who were once themselves scrutinized by other recappers. Reddit fills up with conversations and screenshots of DMs from contestants that prove they are terrible people with sus dating histories and that they should have been disqualified long before night one at the Mansion.

And into this fray wade the players themselves! On social media accounts of varying levels of curation, we get our leads apologizing for not ousting the house bully soon enough, contestants blaming their bad behavior on the producers' invisible hands controlling the edit, and other contestants sharing blithely optimistic photos of themselves with their friends. Oodles and oodles of sponcon.

This is Bachelor Nation.

And I love it.

I started watching as a single lady, hoping to get a bit of vicarious love and adventure. Now I'm married with children, with my husband stumbling into the room while I'm watching *Bachelor in Paradise* to say things like "That was such an alpha move!" about Noah Erb, and all I can do is stare at him in disgust because everyone who isn't my husband knows how Noah acted like such a child on Tayshia's season. (Turns out he was right though.)

I love the drama of Bachelor Nation, and I love the conversation. I search for the Twitter recap posts on Reddit as soon as I finish an episode. I love Ali Barthwell's hysterical recaps for *Vulture*, even when she's sick of writing them and just wants to go back to winning Emmys #thankyouverymuch. I loved the *Roses and Rosé* YouTube recap series with a fiery, theater-kid passion.

> (Sidebar: Where is my Chris Harrison and Lauren Zima rise-and-fall Lifetime Movie Network romantic docudrama?)

I love finding out that the most annoying contestant has a history of being mean to women. I almost love the tea more than the show itself.

I joined Bachelor Nation gradually. At first, the brilliant, scripted TV show *UnREAL* made me curious about its source material. I was 100 percent part of the anti-*Bachelor* brigade before this. I thought of *The Bachelor* as an affront to feminism, making women compete for the same man. I thought *The Bachelorette* gave men the opportunity to band together and judge a single woman in a hostile space. Whenever I recommended the movie *Bachelorette* (2012), I made it VERY CLEAR that I was *not* talking about the TV show.

Kaitlyn Bristowe's season didn't really do it for me, but I likely wasn't giving it a proper chance. The pacing felt slow, and I just couldn't get into the idea of competing for an engagement the same way other shows positioned prizes—a show at Fashion Week on *Project Runway* or an acting role like on *The Glee Project* and *Legally Blonde: The Musical: The Search for Elle Woods.*

But *Bachelor in Paradise*—now *there* is a show that has pacing! It used to air at the height of summer when there was nothing else on TV, and I fell hard and fast for it. The sweat and the sunburns; the make out sessions and the love triangles; the desperate moves in the eleventh hour to secure a rose from someone you can barely tolerate. I loved how sloppy and raw it was.

But the editors do a really bad job of providing context for *Paradise* players! I want a highlight reel of bad behavior! I want to know why Chris Randone is in such high demand, despite having the personality of a Mickey Mouse pancake! I want to know if there were signs that Dean Unglert and Blake Horstmann were gonna turn out to be such f-boys, or if Shanae Ankney was really all that crazy because on *Paradise* she just seems a little competitive. I want to know why they thought Colton Underwood had such main character energy that they had to convince Bibiana Julian to give him a friendship rose to keep him around long enough to have a *Paradise* arc so that he could then become the Bachelor. Mysteries abound!

When I was single and dating, my reasons for watching *Bachelor in Paradise* were purely voyeuristic. Much like the WWE, it was for cheering on the hero and witnessing the downfall of the villain. I wanted drama, and I wanted to watch mean people get their comeuppance. I wanted the guy at the tip of the love triangle to realize he wanted the wifey (but he always chose the hot one).

> (See Dean Unglert choosing Danielle Lombard over Kristina Schulman.)

I wanted the woman in the love triangle to realize she wanted the sweet golden retriever (but she always chose the one she wanted to sleep with).

> (See Amanda Stanton choosing Josh Murray over Nick Viall.)
>
> (I do need you to reach back in your memory for just how good of an edit Nick had on *BIP* S3.)
>
> (Also, shoutout to Hannah Godwin for choosing Dylan Barbour over Blake Horstmann's shtick.)

I found pleasure in the archetypes and in guessing what would happen next.

It wasn't until the pandemic and the Clare/Tayshia season that I became a regular viewer of the main shows, and that was, again, because there wasn't much else to watch at the time. By then, I was married and had just given birth. There was some good dramatic irony in *The Bachelorette* that season, because Clare's portion was intentionally spoilered from the start.[1] There was fun and drama. But it also helped me slow down and appreciate some of the things I was starting to take for granted.

Now, a couple of kids later, I'm still watching.

The things I miss about being single that the show conjures up for

1 Editor's note: Season 16 of *The Bachelorette* in fall 2020 was filmed during the first year of the Covid-19 pandemic, and filming took place under strict isolation protocols. When the first lead, Clare Crawley, decided to become engaged to her preferred contestant, Dale Moss, early in filming, production recruited Tayshia Adams as the new Bachelorette, and she began dating Clare's cast. Due to the time lag between filming and airing the show, the franchise was able to tease the change in leads prior to the season's premiere, and many viewers figured out that Clare would be leaving early. For more on spoiling, see 19: "Will You Accept This Spoiler?" by Iftin Abshir on page 148.

me—the mystery, the excitement, the unpredictability, the *time*, god, the TIME it would take to go for a dip in a hot tub or attend a tantric yoga class or fly to Australia or get rip-roaring drunk and be hungover for a day or three—are outweighed by the schadenfreude I feel watching the pure mess of the contestants on my TV.

How is it possible that I am most grateful for a stable, reliable marriage, for having a consistent home base waiting for me whenever I leave, for chasing after toddlers so they'll wash their damn hands, while I'm watching *The Bachelor*? How is it possible that this show—where women wear cut out dresses without a single back roll, where men reveal abs to rival a Renaissance-painting Jesus, where camera angles are trying their best to fool me into thinking I'm watching a nineties rom-com and not real people—is the one thing to make me think: *Yeah, I'm good. I'll stick with my own baggage, thanks.*

I do miss the mess. I miss putting on foundation and wearing high heels, the thrill of knowing someone new is into me. I miss meeting new people! I miss the world opening up in a limitless way and TV shows being designed specifically for my demographic. I miss seeking out new experiences. I miss being awed on a regular basis. I miss the potential of not knowing what's going to happen next.

Right now, I feel like the mindless slogging of routines is massively outweighing the joy. Though there is joy, don't get me wrong. When my oldest was a little over one year old, he used to open and close the tray on an old DVD player without knowing what it was. One day, my husband got a CD and the necessary five thousand cables together to plug it into a soundbar. When the music started playing, my son was so surprised and so filled with delight that he started spinning around with his arms out. Over and over again, dancing to the music and then stopping to watch the room sway around him. There was so much joy in him that it produced a physical response, propelling him around like a tiny, mischievous helicopter.

That made me grateful. His joy transmitted something visceral to me, something I had been missing since I'd given birth. Maybe I didn't expect having kids to be *that* hard. Maybe I thought there'd be more payoff. I don't know. But I cried. I didn't feel his joy myself, but a little bit of it reached me, watching him.

And yet. And yet, I don't miss any of my singleness enough to wish I was twenty-three again. Twenty-three was about learning to work a full-time job and not knowing who I could trust. Twenty-three was about feeling fat and being a socialist and so much inadequacy and being so anxious that I developed acne for the first time in my life.

And *The Bachelor* is a great reminder of that.

Not of the acne, of course. None of the contestants have acne. But of the awkwardness of not knowing where my priorities should lie.

The disagreement on Joey's season between Madina Alam and Lea Cayanan is such a great encapsulation of that. Madina, a contestant in her thirties, had expressed insecurities about being one of the oldest women in the house. This set off a maelstrom of accusations: Sydney Gordon and others accused Maria Georgas of bullying. Sydney, who was a friend of Lea and Madina, was sent home because of the misunderstanding (or not).[2] After that, Madina kind of chilled out and was friendly to Maria. Lea, a woman very clearly working her way through her early twenties, took it PERSONALLY. She was mad that Madina was betraying Sydney and couldn't believe she would fraternize with the enemy. How dare she laugh at Maria's jokes! And Madina was just…baffled. She'd thought the drama was over. And she couldn't understand why Lea was yelling at her.

That, in a nutshell, is a case study of how a woman's priorities can change from decade to decade. For Lea, #squadgoals is the most important aspect of her life. Her friends are better than everyone else's friends.

2 Editor's note: You may be wondering, if you didn't watch that season, how does one woman expressing insecurities about her age lead to two other women accusing a fourth of something completely different? You'd be right to wonder, but the interpersonal dynamics of a couple dozen people living together and vying for the same romantic interest tend to be messy—and that's before you take into account how production edits and presents events to the audience. Briefly: Madina mentioned her insecurities about her age; Maria, upon hearing about this, responded that Madina (31) wasn't that old and that following her logic, Maria (29) should be worried about her own age as well. Sydney, Madina's friend, decided to tell Madina about this, leading to Madina feeling her insecurities were being dismissed. From there, things devolved further. Maybe just watch the season.

They're more important than the reality competition show she's on, and they're certainly more important than some himbo she's "dating" with twenty other women. Madina, on the other hand, knows that it doesn't matter if your friends are cool or not. You can like Beyoncé *and* Taylor Swift. You can be friends with Maria *and* Sydney. Why limit yourself? Madina's insecurities about her age aside, she seemed so much more settled and connected to herself as a person throughout this conflict.

I wouldn't say my own thirties are a shining example of self-actualization (who has time for that when you have to schedule playdates?), but I absolutely love that I don't hate my body anymore. I've figured out the kind of work I enjoy, and I aim to do that when I can. I have a loving, supportive husband who wants us to grow together.

This show makes me thankful that I don't have to discover someone's true hidden nature anymore or find out that their politics or religion are incompatible with mine (**cough** Becca Kufrin and Garrett Yrigoyen **cough** Tayshia Adams and Ivan Hall **cough**). I don't have to wait around and find out if they think someone else is hotter than me or will put out more or less than me (**cough** Demi Burnett and Kenny Braasch **cough**). I'm not going to find out (again) that the guy I kissed is going around kissing every other girl I know.

> (See John Graham, a.k.a. Venmo John—but I can't even hold it against him, the women all seemed happy about it.)

Sometimes I'll try to share parts of the show with my husband—you know, the parts that really get a rise out of me, parts from which even a layman might glean something. Hannah Brown and Luke Parker's utter lack of communication on their final date is such mind-blowingly good television. And then she seals it with that exit line: "I *have* had sex...and Jesus still loves me." I MEAN!!! Then there's that one-on-one date from Clare's season, the kerfuffle not-kiss with Zach Jackson where he ends up panicking and grabbing her neck. It was so bad that Chris Harrison sent him home early before the evening date. And I still relish my husband's shock when I correctly anticipated Tayshia's top four, in order, as she called them out at the rose ceremony. He doesn't always get it, but he appreciates that I do.

I watch *The Bachelor* because it reminds me to swim out of the undertow of my daily routine and take a look around. It's a weekly reminder, in the trenches of parenthood, that there's beauty in being steadfast. Unlike so much of modern pop culture, which tends to celebrate what's new and young and stylish, *The Bachelor* makes me grateful for stability.

And I can't wait to talk about who's up next.

Alisa Ungar-Sargon received her MFA from Northwestern University. Her writing on pop culture often focuses on storytelling, including the different techniques used in reality television. For more information, visit her website at https://www.alisaus.com/.

11

White Picket Cage

Jeanna Kadlec

I was a latecomer to Bachelor Nation. This is surprising given how much of my early adult life aligned with the traditional, conservative values at the heart of the franchise. I was a devout evangelical Christian who married the first man who seemed like a viable candidate; I believed that marriage was not only for life, but that it was also God's plan for me. But the lived reality of having a conservative, evangelical husband who wanted to control my bodily autonomy had me filing for divorce by the time I was twenty-five. I didn't just leave my marriage, but the church and an entire community and way of life. I also came out as queer, and it wasn't until my late twenties—living in Park Slope with my then-girlfriend—that I was properly introduced to *The Bachelor* franchise via Nick Viall's season.

Watching that first night of limousine arrivals and catfighting over cocktails, I had a strange out-of-body sort of experience, like I was watching an alternative version of my former life. I was stunned at how Christian-coded the show was in its treatment of gender roles and relationship expectations, and how hypocritical; for example, the show is belligerently insistent on ignoring the fact that contestants are in an open relationship with the lead while professing traditional values. But due to equal parts horror and fascination with this Frankensteined monster of conservatism, I couldn't look away. It wasn't just a bunch of flirty, sexy singles competing for screen time and dates in order to get post-show product endorsements, à la the UK's *Love Island*. No, a lot of these women seemed to truly, *genuinely* prioritize marriage as the great life goal they were moving toward. They believed in "the process" and that "everything happens for a reason," and they were there "for the right reasons." For many of these women, *The Bachelor* is their shot at an überpublic American fairytale—one that happens to be built on traditional, conservative, evangelical-coded values around gender and sexuality.

My then-partner was shocked I took Viall's season (and then the devoutly Catholic Rachel Lindsay's following *Bachelorette* cycle) so seriously. She insisted that *The Bachelor* properties were just mindless entertainment—but she didn't grow up in the church, and she didn't see what I saw. To me, the show was a not-so-covertly disguised promotion of heteronormative values. When female contestants talked about wanting a husband who was traditionally strong and assertive, when both contestants and leads talked about wanting a partner who had "family values" (a classic evangelical euphemism in mass media), all I heard was an implicit commitment to biblical womanhood—all the more insidious for its ability to go unrecognized by nonevangelicals like my girlfriend.

"Biblical manhood and womanhood" is a phrase invented in 1987 by evangelical heavyweights John Piper and Wayne Grudem, the latter of whom was on the translation committee for one of the most popular conservative Bibles (the English Standard Version). Per the Council on Biblical Manhood and Womanhood, this ideology rests on two essential principles: first, that the two sexes—and there are only two—are "separate but equal." Second, that "Distinctions in masculine and feminine roles are ordained by God as part of the created order..."[1] These ideas are further

1 Council on Biblical Manhood and Womanhood, "The Danvers Statement on Biblical Manhood and Womanhood," accessed April 26, 2025, http://grbc.net/wp-content/uploads/2015/09/The-Danvers-Statement-on-Biblical-Manhood-and-Womanhood.pdf.

grounded in the Bible's strictest admonitions to women, such as Ephesians 5:22–24 (NIV): "Wives, submit to your own husbands as you do to the Lord. For the husband is the head of the wife as Christ is the head of the church…" Other verses that are part of the so-called "household codes" include 1 Timothy 2:12 (KJV), which states "But I suffer not a woman to teach, nor to usurp authority over the man, but to be in silence." Essentially, biblical womanhood builds upon heteronormativity and traditional gender roles in the way that it positions them as *God-ordained*. God's will. God's plan. Within evangelical logic, any understanding of gender roles (say, around gender expansiveness), same-sex relationships, or queerness, generally, isn't just threatening to the social order, but to God's plan and arguably to the Christian God himself. Heavy stakes.

The Bachelor is, of course, not *explicitly* Christian. However, the franchise is a product of what is still a highly puritanical culture here in the US. In its presentation and preservation of heteronormative values, the show is positioned as a safe haven for the white moms of Middle America. When a viewer understands *The Bachelor* franchise in its context—that it debuted in the United States in the wake of 9/11 during the decidedly conservative and evangelical Bush years, and also on the heels of '90s and '00s purity culture (pledges to wait until marriage for sex demonstrated through purity rings, purity balls, the *I Kissed Dating Goodbye* movement)—the show's underpinnings become more clear.

The *Bachelor* franchise became a sensation, rising in ratings as the racist, conservative, and deeply evangelical Tea Party movement—the forerunner to MAGA—emerged in opposition to President Barack Obama in 2009. In 2015, Trump became a serious contender for the presidency, and for the next few years, the number of devout and practicing Christian leads on the flagship shows skyrocketed, with prayers and discussions of faith being featured on air in a way that was visibly more prominent. Leads Ben Higgins (winter 2016), Rachel Lindsay (summer 2017), Becca Kufrin (summer 2018), Hannah Brown (summer 2019), Colton Underwood (winter 2019), Peter Weber (winter 2020), Tayshia Adams (fall 2020), and Matt James (winter 2021) were *all* devout, practicing Christians.

While Bachelorette sex educator Katie Thurston was a break from that trend in summer 2021, she still had devout Christian men competing on her season, including one who was waiting until marriage for sex. On a season with an explicitly sex positive lead, he was clearly just cast for the drama—and to be the evangelical voice of that group of viewers. Even recent leads who profess other faiths—like Bachelorette Jenn Tran, who is Buddhist—still aspire (at least publicly) to marriage, motherhood, and the "family values" of the conservative right. The franchise peddles a conservative fantasy and tokenizes contestants and leads (like those who are not white, who are not straight) who would disrupt that. Participation in the show is predicated on a belief in, or willingness to front for, the heteropatriarchy.

It is especially notable that leads and contestants who diverge from the white, hetero norm—think Black leads Rachel Lindsay, Matt James, and Tayshia Adams, and *Bachelor in Paradise* queer couple Demi Burnett and Kristian Haggerty—tend to be *devoutly* Christian. (Kristian, Demi's ex-fiancée, for example, has been extremely outspoken about her faith; as of this writing, she has deleted her Instagram, but numerous posts had referenced scripture and Christ, and her bio included the phrase "Jesus First.") Their divergence from the *Bachelor* standard, whether through race or sexuality, is then mediated through Christianity; in this, viewers are assured: this person does not look like you or act like you, but they love the same God as you. In a particularly prominent moment, James offered a word of prayer to open the first cocktail party on night one: "Dear Heavenly Father, thank you for bringing us all together healthy. Give these women the courage to get through these next few months. You say that you work all things for the good of those who love you and are called according to your purpose, Father God. And I feel like that's why I'm here, and I feel like that's why these women are here, Lord."[2] Even beyond the content of his prayer (which includes references to scripture), there is, in his action, an underlying practice of biblical manhood: that the man is the leader of faith in the relationship and should act accordingly; that men should pray for protection over their women and safeguard them spiritually. James's prayer was straight out of a co-ed adult Bible study, which was clocked (and applauded) by other Christians in the room. On the flip side, a conservative Christian woman generally wouldn't pray over a group of men, so Tayshia Adams didn't do that in her season, although she did very explicitly eliminate contestants who did not share her commitment to her faith. It is very clear that the franchise uses religion to make Black and queer contestants more palatable to white, conservative, Middle American audiences.

They might pray together or read the Bible together (as my ex-husband and I did), but leads and contestants of faith tend to be defined by one characteristic: their attitude toward sex before marriage. While my own past self's reasons for not having sex until my wedding night are, in hindsight, obvious (being a lesbian sure will make it easy to not have sex with a man), I had grown up in the straitjacket of purity culture and understood the mindset of contestants who waited, although I was fascinated that such strictly devout folks would go on a sex-saturated show in the first place.

And then there is the misogyny that underlies so much of purity culture: the belief that while women may owe a man fidelity and purity, the feeling is not mutual. For all that Bachelorette Hannah Brown famously declared "I've had sex, and Jesus still loves me," the only reason that she said that in the first place was that one of her men, Luke Parker, was steeped in the misogyny of purity culture and was giving her ultimatums about sex. In the leadup to the Fantasy Suites, Luke said that if she had sexual relations with another contestant, then she would not be "pure"—at least,

2 Ariana Romero, "Matt James Explains That Unprecedented *Bachelor* Premiere Prayer Moment," *Refinery29*, January 4, 2021, https://www.refinery29.com/en-us/2021/01/10248034/bachelor-matt-james-christian-prayer-scene-interview.

not enough for him—and he'd go home. He also offered to forgive her for her former sexual "slip-ups." Brown eviscerated him but used the language of faith: "You know the story in the Bible when the woman was called out for adultery, and she was stoned in the village, and Jesus said, 'He that is without sin among you, let him first cast a stone at her.' You're holding your stone up at me and asking me what I've done."[3]

It's easy to cheer for her when watching that breakup scene—she delivers epic one-liners and kicks an entitled man to the curb to boot—but there is a blink-and-you'll-miss-it framing that she uses that affirms the traditional Christian values she holds. When Luke opened by saying he expected her to not have sex with other men ("I don't believe that's something that you should be doing"), she came back with, "Why do you have the right to do that? Because you're not my husband."[4] The implication being that her *husband* could tell her what and what not to do, thus still adhering to biblical womanhood. Even in celebrating her sexuality, Brown modulated her response through the framework of biblical marriage.

I go through seasons of watching *The Bachelor* (and *The Bachelorette* and *Bachelor in Paradise*) before inevitably needing a break from the values being promoted that so deeply misalign with my own life. On this show, as in the church, double standards about men and women's sexuality are commonplace. Even the structure of the show promotes a more traditional type of path: Fantasy Suites (a.k.a. Final Three), the first time that contestants and leads can be alone together without cameras, comes only *after* Hometowns (Final Four), when contestants have introduced the lead to their families and, hopefully, gotten their approval.

The Bachelor franchise embodies and perpetuates the mythos of the (one mom, one dad) natal family: In this world, adult children are close to and emulate their adult parents and will either repeat or rectify their

3 Devon Ivie, "A Compendium of Hannah's Scorched-Earth *Bachelorette* Breakup Quotes to Luke," *Vulture*, July 15, 2019, https://www.vulture.com/2019/07/the-bachelorette-hannah-brown-luke-parker-break-up.html.

4 Bachelor Nation, "Hannah Sends Luke P Home After Fantasy Suite Warning! | *The Bachelorette* US," July 15, 2019, YouTube, 7 min., 59 sec., https://www.youtube.com/watch?v=V67eThktn-Mw&ab.channel=BachelorNation.

parents' example; where there *is* estrangement, there is cause for suspicion (and painful, production-forced confrontations, such as with Matt James and his father). In this world, men are men and women are women and there is no such thing as trans or nonbinary people. In this world, sex—if it happens—is had between consenting adults, and so there is no need to talk about sexual assault or abortion (even though the show, in spite of purported precautions, has still cast *multiple* men with records—including Jenn Tran's final pick, Devin Strader, who had a 2017 restraining order from an ex-girlfriend,[5] and earlier, Bachelor Colton Underwood stalked his final pick after the finale[6]). Leads who *do* talk about these issues (such as Katie Thurston) are punished by production with both difficult edits and difficult casts.

I've come to treat *The Bachelor* properties as a temperature check of where the white evangelical movement is, and I take heart that, while reactionary Trump policies are flourishing, this show and others like it are dying. To be fair, most of network TV is suffering, but this show has had a steady decline in viewership since the late 2010s (incidentally, when producers were the most in love with having a devoutly Christian lead). In 2002, the show's viewership peaked at nearly twenty-six million; these days, the show is lucky to bring in three (season 27 averaged 2.9 million[7]). *The Bachelor*'s death knell is reminiscent of those of a particular kind of white American evangelicalism, which is *also* losing its audience by the droves—indicative, perhaps, of the ways in which evangelicalism, so subsumed by Trumpian policies, has become more of a rallying cry against the Other, more focused on the perception of "fixing" external problems, than a faith that serves to inculcate embodied and internalized puritanical values.

---

5 Charmaine Patterson, Liza Esquibias, and Danielle Bacher, "*Bachelorette's* Devin Strader Violated Ex's Alleged Previous Restraining Order, Was Arrested for Trespassing in 2017: Affidavit," *People*, September 17, 2024, https://people.com/bachelorette-finalist-devin-strader-violated-ex-alleged-previous-restraining-order-was-arrested-trespassing-8713702.

6 Mckenna Aiello, "Colton Underwood's Alleged Texts to Cassie Randolph Revealed in Restraining Order Filing," *E! News*, September 15, 2020, https://www.eonline.com/news/1187870/colton-underwoods-alleged-texts-to-cassie-randolph-revealed-in-restraining-order-filing.

7 Jamie Burton, "'The Bachelor' Franchise's Painful Decline," *Newsweek*, July 4, 2023, https://www.newsweek.com/bachelor-bachelorette-franchise-painful-decline-1809593.

I was once a closeted person really trying to win at heteronormativity, at evangelicalism—or, if not win, then at least pass within successfully. Life was so much easier with a husband. I was depressed and suicidal, sure, but I got to go through my days as a married white lady. It conferred a kind of respect. I never had to question whether it was safe to hold his hand if we were out after dark. I didn't have to be aware of every single person in the room and whose attention was on us, because usually, it wasn't. With a husband, no one at church said shit to me—about my clothes, my language, my behavior—like they did to the single women, because I had a husband who was the one to "check" me. If he was okay with what I did, then, by the Word of God, they had to be too. Because of all this, I understand the appeal of living within that system. It feels safe. It feels secure. There is an agreed-upon life path, rather like what *The Bachelor* offers in condensed form—meet-cute, dates, more dates, hometown, fantasy suite, engagement, marriage. It requires very, very little self-reflection. In this world, "the right reasons" are the societally approved reasons: desire for marriage, for children, for a white picket fence.

Jeanna Kadlec is the author of *Heretic: A Queer Revolt Against Evangelicalism, Empire, and the Lies We Are Sold* and the forthcoming *Astrology for Artists*. She lives in New York City with her wife.

12

My Journey with *The Bachelor*: From Young Mother to Golden Age

Tamara MC

When *The Bachelor* first premiered in March 2002, I was a thirty-year-old mother of two boys, ages five and seven. The show was like looking into a mirror of possibility—contestants searching for what I'd already found. I watched Alex Michel, a thirty-one-year-old, dating twenty-five women in hopes of finding the kind of love I was living. Six weeks of group dates, romantic one-on-ones, and rose ceremonies built to a dramatic finale, while I sat content in my own love story, nine years into what would be a seventeen-year marriage.

I've always been drawn to love stories, starting with *Cinderella* and graduating to the stolen Harlequin romance novels my sister would bring home from the library. I'd scan them eagerly for the romantic parts. Later, when friends would share their dating stories, I'd listen with rapt attention, collecting these real-life romance narratives with the same enthusiasm I had for those borrowed novels. So, when *The Bachelor* debuted, I was thrilled to have another romance story unfold before my eyes.

I was twenty-one when I first spotted my future husband at university—he had a class right before mine, and we'd pass each other in the hallway. I barely dated; I just met him and fell in love. We married in the Sonoran Desert, where we'd spent our college years. Our university friends gathered as witnesses to our love, with towering saguaro cacti standing against the purple mountains. After the ceremony, we celebrated under strings of twinkling lights swaying in the warm desert breeze, surrounded by blooming ocotillo and paloverde trees. The evening unfolded with a feast of Mexican food—a buffet laden with cheese enchiladas, warm flour tortillas, and creamy refried beans. Two years later, we welcomed our first son, and two years after that, our second son arrived, making our family complete.

When *The Bachelor* began, our beautiful home echoed with my boys' voices—playful arguments over Nintendo games and excited chatter about Pokémon cards drifting through the halls. My boys were navigating elementary school, their days a whirlwind of homework and after-school activities, while I cherished every moment of being their mom. Without DVR technology back then, I'd race to settle into our living room sofa at 8:00 p.m. sharp, determined not to miss a moment of the show, though sometimes mothering young children meant missing episodes.

After the success of *The Bachelor*'s first season, ABC took a chance on reversing the format. Trista Rehn, who had won viewers' hearts as the runner-up on *The Bachelor*, became the first Bachelorette in 2003. The nation watched as she chose Ryan Sutter, a Colorado firefighter, and their televised wedding in December 2003 drew over twenty-six million viewers. Their love story offered hope that this unlikely format could lead to real connection.

My husband's career began requiring extensive travel—five to six days a week away from home, so I was mostly there alone with the boys. Then, in 2006, I found my dream house and threw myself into fixing it up, making it the perfect home for my boys to grow up in. I treated myself to the ultimate luxury: a Kingsdown mattress that felt like sleeping on a cloud.

The boys were in middle school by then, and technology had evolved. With a DVR, I could finally record my shows, creating my own evening ritual after homework was done and sports practices were over.

Then one ordinary evening in 2010, my world fell apart. I was propped up against the pillows on my Kingsdown mattress when my husband walked into our bedroom. I can still picture every detail: the soft glow of the bedroom lamp, the familiar weight of my chihuahua curled at my feet, the sound of the TV playing softly in the background. He lay down beside me on our bed, where we'd shared so many family moments, where I'd spent countless nights waiting for his return from business trips. "I want a divorce," he said. His reasons echoed through the room—he'd gotten married too young and wanted to experience being single.

That night, the woman I saw in my mirror became a stranger. The marriage I'd built my life around was ending. The bedroom that had been my retreat would soon belong to someone else. The weeks that followed passed in a blur. Every mirror in our house seemed to reflect a different woman than the one who had decorated these walls, hung family photos, built what I thought would be a perfect life.

Eventually, we foreclosed on my dream house, and I moved into a much smaller place. I had to put that king-size Kingsdown in storage—it was too big for my new space, like my old life no longer fit. Everything I had dreamed of and achieved—the marriage I thought would be my forever-after, the home we'd made together, the life we'd built—had to be packed away or divided up.

Reality TV took on a different meaning then. *The Bachelor*'s carefully orchestrated journey to love seemed like a fantasy I could no longer embrace, a reminder that even the most picture-perfect love stories could crumble without warning. The fairy-tale endings I once believed in had lost their magic, yet somewhere deep inside, my heart still held onto romance—those borrowed Harlequin novels and cherished love stories remained a part of who I was, even as my own marriage ended.

Raising teenagers as a single mom was my own reality show without the glitz and glamour. My ex still traveled for work, which meant most of the caregiving remained with me, now coupled with the need to fully support myself. Between shuttling my boys to wrestling matches and football games, pursuing my PhD, and keeping our household running, I barely had time to breathe, let alone watch TV, let alone watch *The Bachelor*.

In 2011, dating became my new reality—something I never imagined having to do again in my life. Despite my shattered fairy tale, that eternal romantic in me, the one who'd always believed in love stories, pushed me forward into this new chapter. When online dating was still relatively new, I created profiles on Match.com and eHarmony. There were fewer people online then, which made the experience less overwhelming. But each coffee date and dinner out felt like my own personal dating show—complete with awkward silences, stilted conversations, and the occasional ghosting long before that term even existed.

The years flowed by, and then accelerated. My boys had grown into young men before my eyes, and suddenly, I found myself an empty nester. First, I had lost my marriage, and now the daily rhythms of motherhood—the heart of my identity for so long—had transformed into something new. What I had loved most—being needed, being present, being "Mom" in all its loud, messy, beautiful moments—had shifted into something quieter.

Fast-forward to September 2023. I was fifty-one, and my mother, in her late seventies, surprised me with her own confession: she'd become hooked on reality TV. She kept insisting I watch *The Golden Bachelor*, ABC's groundbreaking spin-off featuring seniors looking for love. For the first time in the franchise's history, the show centered on contestants in their sixties and seventies who carried decades of life experience—widows, divorcées, grandparents, all seeking another chance at romance. At first, I resisted. Why would I want to watch *The Bachelor* again? After years of breakups, my life was completely different now.

Finally, I gave in. By this time, I'd bought my first place since the divorce and retrieved my things from storage, and the Kingsdown mattress had come out and into my new bedroom—the first bedroom that was truly mine alone. After all those years, the mattress felt familiar but different, just as I was different. The woman who once lay there watching *The Bachelor* while happily married had become someone who understood both loss and independence. Since I didn't have cable TV, I'd watch each episode on Hulu the day after it aired, creating new routines in my own space, on my terms.

Mom would patiently wait for me to watch before calling to discuss. We'd talk about Gerry Turner, a seventy-two-year-old widower who brought something new to the franchise—a leading man who cried. And boy, did he cry. He cried remembering his late wife. He cried giving out roses. He cried sending women home. He cried telling stories about his grandchildren. We'd laugh together as we recounted each episode, just enjoying the simple pleasure of dissecting reality TV drama.

The Golden Bachelor revealed something special in the sisterhood that blossomed among the contestants. Unlike the competitive atmosphere of traditional seasons, these women seemed to form genuine bonds. Their support for each other became central to the show—from celebrating each other's successful dates to comforting those sent home. Even during rose ceremonies, they'd hold hands and whisper encouragement.

Building on the success and lessons of *The Golden Bachelor*, ABC launched *The Golden Bachelorette* in 2024. The show chose sixty-one-year-old Joan Vassos as its lead, who viewers remembered from her brief appearance on *The Golden Bachelor*, where she left in week three due to a family emergency. Joan emerged as a sweet presence, a pretty, thin blonde who always seemed to say the right things—perfectly cast for the franchise. Like Gerry, she was a widow with a seemingly perfect marriage behind her—thirty years with her high school sweetheart before cancer took him too soon.

The men of this season brought their own dynamic to the franchise. They demonstrated something unprecedented in *Bachelor* history—the depth of male friendship at this age. Their brotherly bonds rivaled any romantic connection, offering a new model of mature masculinity.

When Trista Sutter made a cameo on *The Golden Bachelorette*, I realized something surprising—we were about the same age. I'd never done the math before. While she was beginning her journey on the first season of *The Bachelorette*, I was already deep in motherhood. I'd found love earlier, had my children sooner. Now, here we both were at fifty-one—though I might be a year older—at similar life stages but different places. Her twenty-year marriage to Ryan has lasted longer than mine did, and while she's raising kids who are still in their teens, my boys are grown. These days, as she speaks publicly about her experiences with menopause and hair loss, I find myself relating to her honesty about midlife changes.

My boys are now almost thirty, and our relationship has blossomed into something more beautiful than I could have imagined. My younger son has been living his own fairy-tale romance, having found his person in high school and nurturing that relationship for over a decade. My older son—handsome, successful, and single—is building his own path. Though he'd make a perfect *Bachelor* contestant, he'd never consider it; reality TV attention is the last thing he'd want, though he finds my enduring love of these shows endearingly amusing. And no, he has never watched a single episode with me—I'm pretty sure he'd rather watch paint dry than join me for a rose ceremony.

Still, as proud as I am of the men they've become, there's an ache that lingers in their absence—a bittersweetness. I miss being a mother more than anything. Not the role itself, which never ends, but the daily presence of my children. What I miss most about my old life isn't my marriage but my children in the house with me—their laughter echoing through the rooms. Being their mother has been my greatest accomplishment, my truest love story.

Looking in the mirror now, I see a different kind of contentment reflected back. Love has grown richer and more complex with time. While the contestants search for romantic partnership, I've found new fulfillment in my writing career, cycling adventures, and shared passions with my mother. She's been a pickleball player for almost fifteen years—an OG of the sport—and now I've joined her on the courts, adding another layer to our relationship.

The Bachelor franchise has been more than just television for me—it's been a mirror reflecting the changing seasons of my life. From those early days when it reflected my own perfect love story; through the years when that reflection twisted like a fun house mirror, distorting everything I thought I knew about love; to now, when it shows a broader truth about connection and contentment in what is the beginning of my own golden years.

This season finds me contentedly single, curled up on my Kingsdown mattress with Hallmark movies playing in the background. My love for fairy tales and rom-coms has always been part of who I am—from *Cinderella* to modern romantic comedies, these stories remind me why I still believe in love's possibilities. I've quietly dreamed of writing romance novels myself, so who knows? Maybe one day I'll become the next Nora Roberts.

And if Bachelor Nation ever decides to cast women in their fifties, I might just leave my beloved Kingsdown behind for a chance at my own rose ceremony. This mattress, now eighteen years old, has outlasted my seventeen-year marriage and carried me through countless nights of dreaming, imagining, and rediscovering. But let's be honest—it's time to let it go. In this second half of my life, I'm ready for something new—maybe even a Tempur-Pedic.

Tamara MC, PhD, is a poet, writer, and scholar with a PhD in applied linguistics, specializing in the Middle East. Her work explores themes of identity, exile, coercive control, and survival, often blurring the boundaries between language, memory, and resistance. Her writing has appeared in *The New York Times*, *Newsweek*, *HuffPost*, and over eighty other publications. She has received fellowships and residencies from Bread Loaf, Sewanee, Virginia Center for the Creative Arts, Ragdale, and more. Learn more about her at www.tamaramc.com.

13

Professing *The Bachelor*

Adriane Stoner

I've long described myself as a conflicted fan, but it wasn't always that complicated.

The Bachelor franchise didn't come into my life until I was in graduate school. I was first exposed after accepting an invitation to watch an episode at a friend's house, and if I'm being completely honest, I had only accepted to be polite. I distinctly remember being aghast upon realizing that the episode was TWO HOURS LONG. An important thing to note is that this was before streaming and before most people had DVRs. At this point in time, "appointment TV" more or less dictated your schedule, and you had no choice but to sit through the episode in its entirety—including its forty or so minutes of commercials—which is exactly what we did.

This particular episode happened to be mid-season, and my initial exposure left me underwhelmed. It wasn't until I got to work the next day and started complaining about the experience that I realized a coworker had also watched it. Before I knew it, we were having a lively conversation about the lead, Ali Fedotowsky, the remaining contestants, and how we thought things might play out. This motivated me to give the show another shot, and the following week when I sat down to watch, the same coworker and I texted snarky commentary back and forth. "No way is she going to end up with HIM!" "What a waste of a trip to Tahiti!" All the while I'm thinking, "This is pretty entertaining."

It didn't take long for me to realize the show's potential to create and solidify social ties between those who watched it. And it did so in a way that was of particular interest to me—via analysis of the interpersonal dynamics between the constants and the leads. I have been a loyal viewer ever since.

Fast-forward a few years. I had finished my PhD in communication and started teaching full-time at DePaul University in Chicago. The classes I taught ranged from media communication to interpersonal communication. After I had some experience under my belt, I was given the opportunity to create new courses that fell within my areas of expertise, and I pitched the idea of a *Bachelor* class to my program chair.

Course description: *The Bachelor* aired its first season in 2002 and has become one of the most commercially successful shows in reality television history—boasting several spin-offs and an ardent fan base. This course will explore content from *The Bachelor* franchise (and related fandom) through the critical examination of themes including courtship, gender, race, heteronormativity, monogamy, and romantic relationship dynamics.

The course was quickly given the green light, and before I knew it, I was prepping a 300-level communication special-topics course. I had no idea what I was getting into, but I was very excited to get started. As I began to build the syllabus, pulling together readings and crafting assignments, I was very curious to find out what kinds of students would be enrolling in the course. I assumed that the average student would be a *Bachelor* fan and started to become concerned that these students might not be willing (or able) to examine the franchise through a critical lens. In my experience, *The Bachelor* was not regularly the site of serious academic analysis, which was the tone I was hoping to set right off the bat.

Tapping into my background in media studies, I decided to begin the class with an assignment designed to tell me more about the students' "uses and gratifications" when it came to consuming *Bachelor* content. Uses and gratifications theory was developed in the mid-twentieth century as a way to examine what media consumers find gratifying as well as the ways in which media content can serve to fulfill social and psychological needs of those who consume it.[1] These social and psychological needs can range from information seeking to entertainment, companionship to escapism. In the early days of media studies as a formal academic discipline, uses and gratifications theory was used as a vehicle for scholars to go beyond questions of "How much?" to more nuanced questions of "Why?" I was certainly interested in "how much" my students watched *The Bachelor/ette*, but I also wanted to get them thinking and reflecting on the "why."

So, in their first assignment I asked students to complete both a viewer profile and a self-analysis. In their viewer profile they were asked questions like: "How often do you watch?" (e.g., *occasionally* or *I never miss an episode*); "*How* do you watch? (e.g., solo, with friends, family); and "Do you/have you ever participated in a *Bachelor*-fandom community?" In the self-analysis portion, students were asked to reflect on their experience watching the show by responding to two questions: "Why do you think the show is so popular?" and "Why do you watch?"

But before writing out their responses to these two questions, I asked that they do some self-reflection. To help guide their self-reflection, I included a list of questions for them to ponder, including "What is the question you're most afraid to be asked?" and "If you didn't care what anyone thought, what is your most deeply held aspiration?" Without realizing it, I was asking the students to wax philosophical on the question that is, and will forever be, at the crux of the *Bachelor* universe: What *are* the "right reasons"? Maybe throwing them into the deep end on the first day of class wasn't the best idea, but hey, I was forging uncharted territory.

As soon as enrollment opened, the class quickly reached capacity. I had

1 Thomas E. Ruggiero, "Uses and gratifications theory in the 21st century," *Mass communication and Society* 3, no. 1 (2000), 3–37, https://www.tandfonline.com/doi/abs/10.1207/S15327825MCS0301_02.

finished putting the final touches on the syllabus, and I was ready to get started, but all this was occurring in March of 2020—and we all know how the story goes from there.

The official announcement that all courses would move to online instruction soon came. It seemed, as if overnight, daily life as we knew it had disappeared, and along with it, any excitement or enthusiasm I had about teaching the class.

During those first few weeks of lockdown, teachers everywhere were scrambling to convert their in-person classes to online ones. Memes circulated likening teachers to the musicians playing as the ship sank, and it certainly felt that way. I cobbled together an online version of the course and just kept on playing.

The term and the class began as scheduled, albeit online. During the first week, the class met via Zoom, and the vibe was a strange mix of uncertainty and despondency. I answered the typical questions about assignments, readings, and deadlines. Before signing off, I got one last question: "Can we get people from the franchise to Zoom with us?" My response was something to the effect of "knock yourself out," adding that they were free to reach out to anyone and to keep me posted. We all signed off and went about the business of trying to make sense of this new world in which we were living. Later that evening, I opened my inbox to find an email from one of my students, Olivia. Subject line: Chris Harrison. I came to find out that shortly after our class earlier that day, Olivia had sent a DM to Harrison. The exchange went as follows:

> **Olivia**: Hey Chris! :) my name is Olivia and I am a student at DePaul University in Chicago. My class is called "Examining Bachelor Nation" and we would love if you could zoom into one of our meetings! :)
>
> **Harrison**: Ok is this really a legit college course?

After Olivia reassured him, he agreed. Upon hearing the news, I was shocked and excited, but also skeptical. In the days that followed, we agreed on a date, and I had Olivia send along the class link. At the appointed time, I was holding my breath as my students began populating the screen and then, lo and behold, Zoom informed me that "Chris Harrison entered the waiting room."

We chatted for a good thirty minutes. Chris seemed genuinely enthusiastic to be chatting with us, and we came to find out that he too was a communication major in college. My students came prepared with excellent questions about the franchise's role in popular culture and how he navigated his role as host. But they didn't stick to softball questions; they also pressed him about the lack of diverse representation within the franchise. He listened closely to the students' questions and acknowledged their points while still staying within his role as the mouthpiece of the franchise. I observed in awe as the conversation played out. I thanked Harrison for joining us, and he signed off, after which one student remarked, "That was exhilarating!"

As it turned out, the class greatly benefitted from the lockdown in that many of the franchise's biggest stars went from having jam-packed schedules to just sitting at home like the rest of us. Over the course of the term, we Zoomed with some of the biggest names in Bachelor Nation including Rachel Lindsay, Nick Viall, Ben Higgins, Tayshia Adams...the list goes on. In these Zooms, which were mostly off the record, we learned about the experiences and aftereffects of being part of the franchise—some positive, some negative, but all life-changing in some capacity. Outside of just talking about the franchise, we chatted about everything from social activism and political aspirations to dating advice and natural deodorant. Halfway through the term, *The Chicago Tribune* contacted me to do a feature on the course.[2] What had started off feeling like a sinking ship now felt like a rocket to the moon.

2 Tracy Swartz, "A DePaul Class on 'The Bachelor' Went Online Because of the Coronavirus. Chris Harrison, 'Grocery Store Joe' and Other Alumni Have Joined In," *The Chicago Tribune*, May 11, 2020, https://www.chicagotribune.com/2020/05/11/a-depaul-class-on-the-bachelor-went-online-because-of-the-coronavirus-chris-harrison-grocery-store-joe-and-other-alumni-have-joined-in/.

Each week we examined the franchise through a different lens. What role do gender stereotypes play? What messages are sent about expressions of sexuality? How, if at all, are different races and ethnicities represented? Does the show acknowledge the intersectionality of any of these identities? As the students made their way through the syllabus, reading histories and critiques of the franchise, we engaged in deeper and deeper levels of critical analysis. Through our discussions, we also found the space to explore and dissect the ethical issues that plague the broader reality television industry.

With each week that passed, I was more and more impressed with my students' ability to intellectualize *The Bachelor*. Getting the amazing opportunity to ask questions and learn about the perspectives of some of those who experienced it firsthand was the cherry on top.

Along the way, most of us came to realize that our relationships with the *Bachelor* franchise were complicated, and that even after ten weeks of attempting to unpack all that was embedded into the franchise, we had just scratched the surface. I think this is evident to anyone who takes the time to really think about the messages sent and reinforced by the franchise and the implications this has not only for the individual viewer but for society as a whole.

As our whirlwind of a term was coming to an end, a student posed a question to the class that has always stuck with me: "Why do I love a show that I know I am supposed to hate?" I have wrestled with this ever since that first class, and the question will always give me pause in its simplicity and elegance. To me, it reflects the paradox inherent to the show. This paradox does not present itself to every viewer, but for those that it does, I would argue that it has an intoxicating effect. It represents something that we actively want to dismantle (e.g., the patriarchy, heteronormativity, misrepresentation and lack of representation of marginalized groups), all while allowing us to indulge in "toxic" structures that are still deeply embedded into society.

It never takes long for our class discussions to take on the topic of feminism as represented in the franchise, and I usually pose certain questions to the class in an attempt to apply conceptions of feminism more generally. When prompted with a question such as "When it comes to a proposal of marriage (in a heterosexual relationship) which partner should do the proposing?" almost all students will say either partner. But when this question is followed up by "How many of the heterosexual women here see themselves proposing marriage to a partner?" very few hands are raised, if any. I will certainly acknowledge that the needle has moved slightly over the years, but I still think many (including Gen Z) struggle with identity, especially when it comes to adhering to and pushing back against traditional gender roles. From my perspective, *The Bachelor/ette* and its related fandom have become spaces where we can exist in that paradox by indulging in and critiquing these powerful social constructs simultaneously.

Today the *Bachelor* class is one of my favorites to teach; each year brings with it more content to analyze and a longer legacy to unpack. Even though it is indeed a legit college course—and, in my opinion, very much worthy of serious academic analysis—I still get my fair share of eye rolls when I tell people that I teach a class on *The Bachelor*, and some are better at masking their contempt than others.

Is *The Bachelor/ette*—or, for that matter, all reality TV—trash? Sure. Call it what you will, but that "trash" can reveal a lot about us and the powerful social structures that shape our behavior—for better and for worse. It is much easier to dismiss the cultural significance of *The Bachelor* franchise than it is to critically engage and reflect on the impact of its legacy.

Let me put it this way: Taking a class on *The Bachelor* is a lot like falling in love. You might not take it seriously at first, but if you're willing to let your walls down, you are in for a wild ride.

Adriane Stoner is an instructor in the College of Communication at DePaul University. In addition to developing and teaching a course on *The Bachelor* franchise, Adriane teaches courses on interpersonal communication and digital communication.

14

Falling Out of Love with *The Bachelor*

Sophie Vershbow

Sean Lowe was my first.

It was the beginning of 2013, and I was working as a publicity assistant at Simon & Schuster, dealing with visceral post-college ennui made worse by the fact that I'd just broken up with my long-distance boyfriend for the second time since graduation. After four years living on campus at a small liberal arts college in the middle of nowhere, I was desperate for community in any form it found me. So, at the insistence of my first work wife, I decided to tune in to watch a born-again virgin—apparently a thing in Texas—try to find his actual wife in a sea of generically beautiful women in tight sequin dresses.

Despite what you might expect from bookworms, *The Bachelor* runs deep in the veins of the staff at every publishing house I've worked at, and it didn't take long for me to join their club. Suddenly, I couldn't wait to get to the office on Tuesday mornings. Even though I didn't care about Sean Lowe or Catherine Giudici, and I *really* didn't care about Lindsay Yenter, all I wanted was to huddle in someone's cubicle to dissect the previous night's viewing. Although little action took place each episode, it seemed that endless group discussion could be milked from recounting even the dullest moments. Wasn't it weird that Lindsey showed up in a wedding dress on the first night? Why did Sean really send Sarah Herron home? What happened in the sexless Fantasy Suites? Should Sean have given Tierra LiCausi the first impression rose? Is Tierra here for the right reasons? Am *I*?!

While bonding with my coworkers over our mutual obsession, I also started to post my *Bachelor* hot takes on Twitter (never X), where show discourse reliably spread like wildfire on Monday nights (and Tuesday nights when ABC demanded four hours of us in one week). Despite having few followers, live-posting under #TheBachelor hashtag made me feel as if I was watching the show with a group of friends instead of alone on the thirty-first floor of a divorced-dad-filled Financial District high-rise that swayed like a wooden ship when it stormed. That desire for shared monoculture is what fueled my love of *The Bachelor* and its many spin-offs for nearly a decade. The inside jokes and deep-cut references that could only be gleaned from watching season after season made me feel like a part of something at a time in my life when I often felt unmoored, in search of something or someone to steady me.

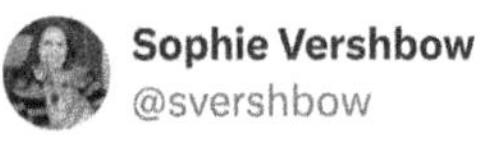

My newsfeed is full of tweets about stupid football players. I guess this is how people feel when I live-tweet #TheBachelor every Monday.

3:41 PM · Mar 9, 2017

After changing jobs and leaving my beloved publishing coworkers behind for an ill-fated attempt to work at a startup, Twitter was the main reason that I kept tuning in through not one but four Nick Viall seasons. If I couldn't watch the show live while firing off tweets, poking fun at everything from Neil Lane's garish diamond rings to the overtaxed parents who just wanted their kid to join Match.com, I couldn't see the point of watching it at all. With all due respect to those who produce it, *The Bachelor* is not an action-packed show 90 percent of the time. Most of the episodes are stuffed to the gills with filler scenes, and there's practically as many commercials as there is actual airtime. I wasn't racing home on Monday nights to watch a Canadian dance instructor get engaged to a jealous personal trainer because their love story kept me glued to the TV for two hours. I was racing home because I couldn't wait to make jokes with my new friends on the internet.

Dear Recent Followers,
I live-tweet #TheBachelor every Monday night. It makes me very happy. Please don't yuck my yum. If you can't handle it, then goodbye & thanks for the memories.

xoxo
Sophie
28, Former NBA Dancer

6:29 PM · Jan 1, 2018

And while Chris Harrison was usually lying when he claimed, "This is the most dramatic rose ceremony ever," there was no shortage of things to comment on each episode. I've never been someone at a loss for words, but the hilarious minutes of a show like *The Bachelor* or *Bachelor in Paradise* is a breeding ground for my hyperactive brain that can turn anything into a joke. Juan Pablo saying, "It's OK," over and over again to a glaring Andi Dorfman. Chad Johnson chain-eating cold cuts in the background of JoJo Fletcher's cocktail party. Hannah Brown telling Luke Parker that Jesus still loves her even though she had sex with Peter Weber four times in a Greek windmill. Chris Harrison searching for Colton Underwood in the dark after he jumped over a fence when Cassie Randolph left. Every botched rose ceremony and blatant display of terrible judgment, I gleefully tweeted through it all—then listened to multiple podcasts recapping the exact same events in order to extend the time I could spend each week engaging with Bachelor Nation in lieu of thinking about my own life.

ABC is giving us back to back 2 on 1 dates to help deal with Trump's America, and I'm totally into it. #TheBachelor

8:25 PM · Feb 6, 2017

But as my twenties stretched into my thirties, *The Bachelor* and *The Bachelorette* started to leave a bad taste in my mouth. Déjà vu moments on the show like a twenty-two-year-old crying because she'll never find love or two men fighting over a woman like she's a piece of property stopped making me want to laugh and started making me want to cry.

It wasn't just that the girls seemed younger—and they did—but from the emotional and financial safety of my early thirties, I could barely recognize the husk of myself I'd been back when Sean Lowe's season first aired. At twenty-three, my life had been fueled by anxiety as I crawled out from the last grasps of the eating disorder that had swallowed me whole since high school. The energy I didn't expend bingeing and purging was divided between an assistant job that paid $30,000 a year in New York City, worrying that all my friends were hanging out without me, and managing a low-level Ambien addiction. I sought men's validation as a way to drown out the screaming in my head, redirecting those voices to obsess about someone other than myself for as long as possible. So every time a relationship or situationship fell apart, so did I, because being on any other planet was better than the one I inhabited alone. I was desperate to be saved from my own life, and so I understood why a young girl with her entire future ahead of her might sob in the back of a limo about a guy she's known for two weeks. I would have too.

It wasn't just my insecurity that made me sympathize with their desperation. My *Bachelor* Era overlapped with the span of time in which I attended three or (significantly) more weddings a year. Starting at twenty-six, it felt like all my friends talked about was who was going to get engaged next or whether to hire a wedding planner. Weekends became a stream of interchangeable bridal showers and bachelorette parties that left me broke, exhausted, and feeling terrifyingly behind on my own path to adulthood. At the same time, my man-child of an older boyfriend was making it abundantly clear that he wasn't ready to join them at Crate & Barrel to register for flatware. Attending wedding after wedding with a boyfriend who wouldn't—or couldn't—commit to me, lost in the blinding sparkle of my friends' engagement rings, I didn't consider anything that comes after "I do." I wanted a man to choose me so my life could begin, even if that man was so obviously the wrong one.

If I went on #TheBachelor I'd use it as an opportunity to re-wear all the hideous bridesmaids gowns I was forced to buy in my 20s.

8:48 PM · Jan 22, 2018

Ironically, it felt like my life began the moment I walked out of the cramped apartment I shared with that noncommittal boyfriend in Alphabet City, choosing to rebuild my life instead of sleeping one more night next to him with a knot in my stomach. The well-worn sentiment that being in the wrong relationship is lonelier than being alone has proved true to me every day since, but I've never shaken the understanding that, had he proposed earlier, I'd have stuck around to claim what I then saw as a prize. I now see that prize for what it really was: a dangerous mirage resulting from a culture that still declares "happily ever after" at the altar, as if a wedding day is the last chapter in your love story, not the first. A culture that made me desperate to work things out with someone incapable of treating me well for four years because starting over so close to thirty seemed more daunting than getting married to the wrong person.

Thank you #TheBachelor for finally giving me a reason to be happy about my breakup. Tonight, I'm reclaiming my three hours of uninterrupted reality television without someone telling me how stupid it is.

7:00 PM · Jan 7, 2019

What is *The Bachelor* if not a franchise peddling the uninvestigated marriage fantasy, often among people too young to have fully-formed prefrontal cortexes? This is a show that has two-hour-long fairy-tale wedding specials and encourages the cast members to say they're falling in love as soon as humanly possible, sometimes as early as the first night. In *The Bachelor* universe, being alone is considered a fate worse than death and divorced people are treated like pariahs. We know from interviews that the final couples spend fewer than twenty-four hours together before getting engaged, and we rarely see them on camera discussing anything of value to two people trying to determine their compatibility, like how many kids they want, where they'll settle down, or who will be the primary parent, etc. These are people who want to get married, not who want to marry each other as an expression of their love, which is the only kind of marriage I now have any desire for.

I only got to see how full my adult life could be without a romantic partner because circumstance gave me the time and space needed to build a happy life on my own, and I'm often left thinking of all the women whose circumstances turned those bad relationships into worse marriages that stole far more than four years from them. The women who go on *The Bachelor* shows seem primed for the latter, and I find it too depressing to watch them be so eager to secure their own handcuffs without really investigating who they're giving the key to. Every once in a while, a couple cuts through the haze with a genuine connection, but I can't devote so much time to a franchise promoting a marriage mindset I escaped from by the skin of my teeth.

I don't judge anyone for their reality TV viewing habits—after all, I continue to ingest an alarming quantity of Bravo—but *The Bachelor* now triggers me in the bad way, not the way that made me want to write little jokes on Twitter. When a twenty-three-year-old calls a thirty-six-year-old man she met a couple of weeks ago "her best friend," I want to scream, not laugh, then hug her actual best friend at home who must be thinking, "What the fuck?" When a thirty-two-year-old gets sent home and acts like her life is over because this was her last chance to find love, I want to poke my eyes out then remind her how lucky she is not to be divorced and coparenting with an asshole. That she is free to do whatever she wants now that she can stop pretending that Cleveland is the perfect place to fall in love with a pilot.

I hate-watched the show all through 2020 because quarantine wasn't the time to abandon a lengthy weekly television commitment. During that period of profound loneliness, I craved the online chatter each Monday more than ever, but at the same time, I resented having to watch something I enjoyed so little just to participate. I was no longer that husk of a person who relished the two-hour distraction from her own thoughts every Monday night; I was a happy, well-adjusted adult who could text her friends if she was having a bad day. Once the world opened back up and my social life resumed (along with the serotonin receptors in my brain), I couldn't see a reason to prolong the unpleasantness any longer. I would miss the online community, but not enough to stay in this bad relationship any longer than I already had.

Matt James was my last. Goodbye to all that.

Sophie Vershbow is a freelance journalist and marketer living in New York City. Her writing has appeared in *Esquire*, *New York Magazine*, *Vogue*, *Jezebel*, and beyond.

15

Pick Me (Or Don't)

Alana Hope Levinson

This story starts, not with *The Bachelor*, but with a different melodrama that similarly poisoned the minds of millennial women. It's 2005, I am in high school, and the medical soap opera *Grey's Anatomy* is on its second season—just hitting its stride. During episode five, the love story propelling our main character, medical resident Meredith Grey, played by actress Ellen Pompeo, hits a fever pitch. During surgery, Grey notices her married boyfriend, Dr. Derek Shepherd, looking up at his wife, Addison Montgomery, who is surveilling from the observatory room. Though earlier she had vowed to not be "*that* woman," Grey is sent over the edge by the observation, deciding to declare her love in a last-ditch effort to get him to sign divorce papers. Once they leave the operating room, Grey, on the verge of tears, doesn't bother to take off her deeply unflattering scrub cap to plead with "McDreamy." Her words have since become iconic:

"So pick me. Choose me. Love me."

In the almost twenty years since its debut, the quote has been repeated and remixed and GIFed and memed into oblivion. But it's the first bit—*pick me*—that's had the most lasting impact. A little over ten years later, in 2016, the #TweetLikeAPickMe hashtag went viral, with women assuming the identity of a pick-me girl—one who bends over backwards to court male attention, to show that they are "not like other girls," all in a pathetic bid to be chosen by a man. If you're struggling to grasp the concept, think of it as a more contemporary version of the "cool girl," as best defined by the monologue from Gillian Flynn's *Gone Girl.*

Seeing the term circulate on social media, it didn't take me long to not just understand the concept but flinch in recognition. After all, pick-me-ism is a founding principle of *The Bachelor*—which premiered three years before the aforementioned *Grey's*—a show I've devoured since I was barely sentient. *The Bachelor* is touted as many things, all of which it is: a monument to patriarchy, a death cult of monogamy, a reason straight people shouldn't have rights. But rarely do we discuss its groundbreaking role in the spread of the pick-me virus. The show is quite literally a bunch of women standing around in cheap prom dresses, desperate to be picked by a guy they barely know who doles out roses to the chosen.

Take season 24 of *The Bachelor*, which premiered in January of 2020, known to many superfans as one of the most chaotic (read: best) seasons, in part because of the easily produced and seduced Peter Pan-of-a-lead, Peter Weber, also known as Pilot Pete. Weber had just come off a season of *The Bachelorette* where he failed to win the heart of former Miss Alabama and America's sweetheart, Hannah Brown, but not before fucking her real good in a windmill four times. Though clearly a lover boy, Weber was branded a "nice guy" with a demeanor far softer than previous leads, and his job as a pilot—in 2016, Tinder's most swiped-right male profession—skyrocketed his desirability.

But there were some warning signs that perhaps our friend Pilot Pete was not ready for marriage: Brown found a condom in his car during her season's hometown date; at the start of his season, the twenty-seven-year-old lived with his parents; he had a deep and somewhat sick attachment to his mother, Barbara Weber, the most diabolical parent in Bachelor Nation history, whose later on-air histrionics were deemed "scary" by an ABC exec;[1] and at the time of filming, he definitely wasn't over his ex... Brown made an appearance on the first episode of Peter's season, and he asked her to participate in the competition for his heart, which she declined. (Later, in her memoir, *God Bless This Mess*, Brown revealed he told her off-camera he'd quit the show if she wanted to be with him.)

And yet—as is true for all leads—the women who trotted out to woo Weber believed he was the second coming of Jesus Christ. Well, that's not entirely accurate—it wasn't really about Pilot Pete as a human, but rather what he represented. As with all pick-mes, the goal was winning the prize, the man; whether or not he's worthy is sort of irrelevant. In the premiere, when the contestants hadn't even known this guy for more than a couple hours, they all harped on a similar theme in their confessionals. "He's just like that guy you dreamed about marrying as a little girl," one said. "He's the guy I've been dreaming about marrying my whole life," another opined. "I just hope that I'm the girl that he's been dreaming of. I feel so honestly that we could be the greatest love story of all time."[2]

In Homer's *Iliad*, one of the oldest surviving works of Greek literature, women are presented as prizes men compete over. They are objects given as gifts to the victor in both war and sport. This idea has persisted throughout history; the bible teaches that a "virtuous wife" has worth "far above rubies." The story told by *The Bachelor* and the pick-mes reveals how society now perpetuates the man as the ultimate trophy; the goal for a woman is to be chosen—not won. When you're indoctrinated to think that the position of "wife" is the most valuable one you can hold—and that men are the deciders of if and when you get that promotion—sobbing over some douche in a bad suit five minutes after meeting him makes more sense. They aren't crying over him; they are crying out of fear that they aren't worthy of ever being picked, of becoming someone's **Borat voice** wife.

Lest you think I'm turning my nose up at the contestants or other

1 Emily Longeretta, "'The Bachelor' Producer Admits Barbara Weber's Face-Off With Madison Prewett Was 'Truly a Little Bit Scary,' *US Weekly*, March 11, 2020, https://www.usmagazine.com/entertainment/news/bachelor-producer-barbara-weber-madisons-face-off-was-scary/.

2 *The Bachelor*, season 24, episode 1, "Week One," aired January 6, 2020, on ABC.

women I deem pick-mes, I should reveal that I consider myself a pick-me in recovery. Though the term "pick me" didn't exist when I was in high school, my symptoms were at their most severe when I began religiously watching *The Bachelor* in adolescence. (At a winter dance, my first boyfriend kissed a girl in front of me when he was drunk, and I quickly forgave him and blamed her.) Though I would have balked in dismay at the allegation—a classic pick-me move—I'd also claim I actually really liked the hardcore bands Steve told me about and was super okay with randomly being ignored in homeroom whenever he was too busy to acknowledge me. As a wise woman once said in a TikTok that is now lost to the sands of time: We are all on the pick-me spectrum. And I believe that at different points in a woman-who-dates-men's life—depending on our feminism and how much healing we do—we bounce around the scale like motherfucking Kinsey. Pick-me-itis is passed down through the generations, learned from our parents, and ignited with a blowtorch by trauma. This is what makes *The Bachelor* compelling to so many women. We are watching a melodrama that exaggerates the dynamics we see all around us.

But the waning popularity of *The Bachelor* is encouraging, suggesting that as the earth hurtles towards its demise, young girlies are seeking out a cure for that which ails their elders. *The Bachelor* has seen a decline in ratings since 2002, going from 18 million viewers at the end of the first season to just 6.3 million in 2024. The reason is obvious: People are less interested in an antiquated and conservative show that refuses to change along with culture; they didn't have a Black lead until 2017 and have yet to do a queer season, despite impassioned pleas from fans. But I think it's also that women are getting increasingly tired of consuming media that uncritically worships pick-me-ism when there are so many other options—shows like *Couple to Throuple*, for example. (Ratings are also plummeting for the "feminist" sister program *The Bachelorette*, whose latest season as of this writing saw the first Asian American lead picking between a guy who tweeted racial slurs and another with rape allegations).

The show's premise is increasingly ridiculous when you consider that with each passing season, it's basically just an audition to do tummy tea ads on social media. As with all reality shows, the rise of influencer culture has meant there's no illusion that some people are "there for the right reasons." We know they're all there to hopefully get free tickets to Coachella, and we try not to let it ruin the fantasy.

On the Bachelor Nation subreddit, I've seen it joked that Pilot Pete's season never really ended; a handful of the contestants were compelling (or chaotic) enough to still be relevant years later: At the time of writing, villain Victoria Fuller, who made it to the top three despite being accused of being a "home-wrecker" and later wreaked havoc on *Bachelor in Paradise*, has a resulting 700,000 followers on Instagram (more than some leads) and is dating a professional football player; model Hannah Ann Sluss, the winner who got engaged to Weber and was subsequently dumped by him, now has over a million followers and is married to NFL running back Jake Runk; and Madison Prewett, the Christian virgin runner-up who broke up with Weber after learning he slept with two other contestants before briefly dating him again post-Sluss, recently had a daughter with her pastor husband Grant Troutt, heir to a billion-dollar fortune. She now talks about the security of submission and how sin (premarital sex) keeps us from god to over 1.8 million Instagram followers.

Apparently, it pays to not get picked; these rejected pick-mes actually ended up winning in the long run. There's a lesson in there somewhere—that being picked by a shitty guy is actually worse for you. Meanwhile, Pilot Pete has been busy proving his haters right. After battling rumors he slept with a producer while the season aired, he went on to have a one-night stand with Hannah Brown and date contestant Kelley Flanagan (a woman he sent home before hometowns) three separate times. He is still a commercial pilot and, as of this writing, still single.

Even in fiction, it seems that reformed pick-mes end up vindicated in the end. In season 19 of *Grey's Anatomy*, seventeen years after her pick-me credo, Meredith Grey is in another off-on relationship with a doctor, but this time, in a monologue to boyfriend Nick Marsh, she picks herself. Still sporting an ungodly scrub cap, she says, clear-eyed, not through tears: "If I have to choose, I'm going to pick me. I pick my kids, and I pick what's best for us. And I am not going to beg you to love me."

For fans of the show, this development comes as no surprise. In 2017, Ellen Pompeo, now an executive producer on the show, revealed that she has always hated the "pick me" speech. "When I read that scene, I was horrified," Ellen confessed on her podcast *Tell Me with Ellen Pompeo.*[3] "And what's funny about that scene is that I'm bawling my eyes out, but I'm bawling not for the reasons in the scene. I'm bawling because I can't believe I'm on TV begging a man to love me." She then recalls how, recently, her twelve-year-old daughter Stella saw the scene on TikTok and asked her why she would ever do such a thing.

Stella not getting it is perhaps the greatest sign that we may see the end of the pick-me soon. Even if that means the end of my beloved *Bachelor*, I can't in good conscience say that's a bad thing.

Alana Hope Levinson is a magazine writer and editor interested in digital culture, trends, gender, and design.

3 Ellen Pompeo, host, *Tell Me with Ellen Pompeo*, "Rachel Lindsay," Cadence13, November 3, 2021, 12 min., 2 sec., https://podcasts.apple.com/us/podcast/rachel-lindsay/id1586148064?i=1000540594227.

16

How *Not* to Project Your Own Traumas Onto the First Vietnamese Bachelorette

Carolyn Huynh

A funny thing happened when Jenn Tran was announced as the first Asian Bachelorette… I felt an explosion of joy and dread all at once. I hadn't experienced that reaction since the first date I had with my now-husband. My group chats—of mostly Asian women—detonated. Some were long-time Bachelor Nationers. We all shared the same sentiments. *Will it be as bad as Matt James's season? Is she ready? Did her mom oppose it when she found out? Was she scared to tell her mom? Will it be filled with a bunch of mediocre white guys? Are they going to have any Asian men?*

But the real question we were all asking ourselves but didn't want to admit outright: *Is Jenn healed enough to be able to do this?*

With the announcement of the first Asian Bachelorette came the expected blanket statements all over my reality TV forums. People questioned her charm and personality, they tore apart her looks, and, of course, there was a big outcry that ABC didn't make Daisy Kent or Maria Georgas the next Bachelorette. Daisy and Maria were two of the more popular contestants from Joey Graziadei's *Bachelor* season—and conventionally (and arguably) considered prime Bachelorette material. I wasn't surprised by the discourse because even I had asked myself, *Why Jenn?* I'd been conditioned my entire life not to be chosen, so much so that it was normalized in my mind. Why on earth would America ever want to see a Vietnamese woman fall in love on national television? I was used to always being second place to a Maria-figure in my own life; why would it be any different for Jenn?

Did my traumas flare up? Absolutely. And so did my panic.

Like every other Bach Nationer, I'm used to the franchise appealing to their network audience's taste, which is typically white. Historically, the show hasn't done well with marginalized Bachelors and Bachelorettes. After Matt James's season, I took a break from the franchise because I was so disenchanted by everything that went down. The mistreatment and racism were glaringly obvious. But out of a mixture of bewilderment and the desire to support a fellow Vietnamese woman, I followed Jenn Tran on Instagram and braced myself for her season to start.

Leading up to it, my support was undeniable.

I liked all her posts and boosted them too. I was interviewed by *Yahoo News* in anticipation of her season. Hell, I began to see her season as my World Series. I even got a chance to meet her briefly at a Vietnamese event in Los Angeles where I eagerly begged for a selfie! I joked with her that night about whether the guy she was with had won her season. (He was simply her publicist.) I pored over each contestant's info like Pokémon trading cards. And I clocked the arrogant Vietnamese guy immediately—Thomas Nguyen—and I rooted for him before he even opened his mouth (big mistake). But my support for Jenn went deeper because she is a Southeast Asian woman, a Vietnamese woman whose parents are refugee immigrants. There was no explanation or extra encouragement needed from me.

At a base level, Jenn and I probably share similar traumas and have experienced similar moments of misogyny and racism. Not all experiences are the same of course, but we probably shared the same fears about dating—especially when it comes to abandonment and learning to love our beauty through a Western lens. Jenn is also the youngest daughter in her family, which comes with a whole host of its own troubles—the amount of translating she has had to do for her family; the emotional labor it took to be there for her mother and try to help her regulate her own traumas; and the fierce independence she had to force herself into to learn how to assimilate better and navigate the world without as strong of a support network as her friends probably had, especially those who already had generational roots and generational wealth in this country.

In essence, finding romantic love has always been pushed back for us. Survival was always first.

As the youngest daughter in a Vietnamese family, I worried about Jenn like a big sister. I am older than her by at least a decade (please don't do the math). Vietnamese culture is hierarchical, so in my eyes, not only was she younger than me, and not only was she my *chị em*, which is a blanket term which means sister, but Jenn was my *em*—my little sister.

Within my decade of dedicated (and oftentimes reluctant) growth, I had to go through my own witch trials—often held by a council of mediocre men—in order to find romantic love. Could I market myself as cute, but not sexy? Could I convince these men that I wasn't *that* codependent? (A blatant lie! I am happily a koala bear!) Could I actually see myself getting into rock climbing? (I lived in Seattle at the time.)

But I began to wonder *why* I had to mold myself so much just to get one middling date. These were the moments that radicalized me. I had to understand the politics that lived behind desire. *Did I even find these men to be actually attractive or did society tell me, as an Asian woman, to find them attractive? Did my generational trauma cloud my judgement?* I also had to lower my walls even more and finally allow myself to question my own sexuality. *Was I queer? And to what degree? Was I allowed to even have degrees of queerness?* I had to go through my own self-identity and self-determination journey. One of my first steps was to try to find joy in taking selfies because I'd been taught my whole life that my "type of beauty" wasn't for everyone. Once I really began unpacking everything, I realized that everything was political. Including those mediocre white men I used to chase.

But most of all, I had to learn self-love, which is the most difficult journey of all.

This is why I worried for Jenn in the way a big sister would. Because the journey toward loving yourself is damning. A certain type of raw vulnerability used to make me so uncomfortable that I would lie to myself, and convince myself that everything was just fine, all in order to avoid seeing the ugly truth—very *The Art of the Deal* core.

I settled into Jenn's season, popcorn in hand, with nothing but a feverish cheerleading attitude. At first, I was laughing and crying alongside her. I joyfully texted friends and pointed out how awful some of the men were, but also how *mediocre* they were. Why couldn't they find better men for Jenn? My old habits returned, and I was able to watch the season as a Bach Nation fan again.

Somewhere along the way, the season took a dark turn, and I watched as Jenn missed red flag after red flag. I'm a reality TV aficionado, so watching is always more entertaining when contestants are color-blind to any flags, but watching as Jenn's proverbial sister, I began to feel an emotional strain in our parasocial relationship. How could Jenn miss these flags? I, of course, rather than blaming the network, the franchise, or the men, blamed her immediately. I furiously texted friends: *Jenn needs therapy. Why is she chasing the mid white guy? OMG, I cannot support Jenn in public. I support women's rights and wrongs, but not this time. This is so cringe. Why? WHY? WHY!*

The parasocial relationship I had with Jenn was starting to really cloud my judgment. I couldn't stand her reactions, her choices in the men she picked. I was also shocked by how much she gave herself to these men, wholeheartedly and with such sincerity—I was shocked because I used to be so much like her. I used to throw myself at men, like throwing spaghetti against the wall, hoping something would stick one day. And now here I was watching Jenn let these mediocre men get away with murder. I was as harsh on her as a Vietnamese sister and mother who only know how to express their love through criticism. I wanted Jenn to do better, to pick better, to "stand ten toes down" for herself. I *needed* her to do better.

Did my traumas flare up again? Absolutely.

My panic only increased as the season went on.

Every Monday night, I would turn to my husband (who is also Vietnamese) and complain relentlessly. I watched TikToks and found discourse that validated my concerns that Jenn was simply too young and hadn't gone on her healing journey yet. I turned to Asian commentators who had a lot to say, and I nodded my head furiously. Jenn's actions and reactions validated all of us, all of us who stood on our moral high ground and pretended that we were past our healing journey and were now more self-aware than her.

I watched in agony as she picked the wrong men for her final three. I teared up when I saw her family on-screen—especially her mother. I watched as she struggled speaking to her mother in both Vietnamese and in English, and I witnessed her reaction in real time as she tried to figure out which language would be the best for national TV. My group chats slowed down. We had lost respect for Jenn as we watched her pick the worst guy of all of them. It only got worse when she proposed to Devin, and my group chats went completely quiet. My support for Jenn was silent.

Her journey went just as expected, and I wished her nothing but the best.

When the final episode and reunion happened, and it was revealed how Devin Strader had abandoned Jenn immediately after the season wrapped, the same dread from before began to crawl through my body. But this time, the dread shifted. I was no longer feeling dread about Jenn's actions, but rather about the mediocre men who continuously believe they can use and discard Asian women's bodies without consequences. Just like

I had been conditioned my whole life to be second to Maria-like figures, I had also been conditioned to accept that mediocre men's actions are normal and that we can't do anything but to accept them and move on.

Except I didn't want to move on. I didn't want Jenn to either. I wanted us to both choose pettiness this time. There was no such thing as the high road.

My triggers flared again! But now my anger was motivation, as it has always been during my radicalization. My group chats burst into action again as we all watched Jenn's mother cry on national TV for her only daughter. I watched a Vietnamese mother go through the same heartbreak as her daughter, and I grew furious. Something in my brain switched, and I realized that the so-called healing journey I had prided myself on would be all for nothing if I could not understand that the desire for self-determination and the road to self-love were so often blocked by systems outside of our control.

I began to watch Jenn through a different lens, one of radical empathy. Instead of seeing her as my *em*, my little Vietnamese sister, I began to see her as a marginalized woman who had been failed once again by the franchise and the network. Everyone had failed to protect her, and I saw the oppressive pattern work against Jenn's ability to find a real, healthy, romantic love. I began to cry for her again, but this time, my tears were rooted in anger at the injustices she faced. I worried for her mental health, and just like all my exes and all the mediocre men I'd crossed paths with throughout my life, I hoped that Devin would never find happiness again and would be blessed with a thousand STIs.

But after all my online discourse and social media pitchforks against Devin, I would crawl back into bed every night, completely exhausted, lay my head on my husband's chest, and lower my defenses. After all this time, I still can't comprehend what we have to deal with as Asian women. I was so tired. I would lay in the dark, listening to him softly snore, and recognize that my self-identity and self-love journey had barely begun. There was so much I had left to unpack and understand about myself, my own traumas, and my own queerness.

For now though, I rest. I rest, and I brace myself for the next marginalized Bachelor and Bachelorette to be picked. And hopefully, when that moment comes, I'll be able to contain my emotions more and not project. Though Jenn and I are not the same, we do probably share so much—just like how my husband and I don't need to explain our traumas to each other, Jenn and I wouldn't need to explain our traumas to one another—all three of us know what it's like to grow up Vietnamese in America, and because of that, I'm rooting for each of us to find our own, individual paths.

My support for Jenn picked up tenfold after her season ended, and I liked and boosted everything she did again. I watched her TikToks with joy and rooted for her on *Dancing with the Stars*. I cheered for everything Jenn did that brought her a step closer to happiness, and slowly, I saw her smile return. Jenn remains a *chị em* to me, a sister, but now I allow her to make mistakes without judgment—because mistaking criticism for love is something I am still unlearning today. Nobody is ever fully healed from all their traumas, all we can do is "keep the main thing the main thing" (as Jenn's second-worst contestant, Sam McKinney, kept saying during her season) and continue to hold the franchise accountable, and hope that progress comes one day. Until then, my group chats and I will be watching warily, as we always do, trying to find the small crumbs of joy where we can.

Carolyn Huynh is a novelist, screenwriter, and playwright. She loves writing about acerbic women who never learn from their mistakes, but yearn for joy. Her debut novel, *The Fortunes of Jaded Women*, was a Good Morning America book club pick and picked as one of the best books of 2022 by NPR. A homegrown Californian, she resides in Los Angeles with her partner and her demon girl dog. When she's not writing, Carolyn daydreams about having iced coffee on a rooftop in Ho Chi Minh City.

17

The Bachelor Has Entered the Chat

Renée Reizman

Every time I put on *The Bachelor*, I anxiously wait for my phone to blow up. The texts, which come from a group chat titled "The Real Rose Buddies," are not a distraction, but rather a vital component to my viewing experience. We are four devoted members of Bachelor Nation, all located in the same city but divided by gridlock, introversion, and malaise. The group chat, our personal live-reaction thread, unites us even when we don't have the willpower to leave the couch.

The Real Rose Buddies is a diverse bunch. Some of us have backgrounds that would never be featured on *The Bachelor*, and other parts of our identities would be the sob story fueling our narrative on the show. Between the four of us, two are disabled. One is Filipino, one is Persian, one is Jewish, and one hails from the American South. Three of us have graduate degrees, but we all grew up lower-middle class or poor. None of us are a size zero, but all of us are attractive. None of us have filler, but one of us got Botox to treat her migraines. All four of us are atheists. One of us is queer. One of us is an immigrant. All four of us are politically progressive and have attended protests in support of Black Lives Matter, defunding the police, and to end the genocide in Gaza. Three of us have absentee fathers, and one of us has a schizophrenic mother. One of us is married, one of us has sworn to a life of spinsterhood, and two of us are still in search of The One.

We are all too well-educated, too woke, and too cultured to indulge in *The Bachelor*, yet it is precisely for these reasons that we enjoy the franchise so much. Watching the show is a gateway into talking about serious topics. Contestant Chad Johnson's iconic "Fuck you, Chris Harrison!" outburst on *Bachelor in Paradise* opened up a discussion on toxic masculinity; Rachael Kirkconnell, who won the heart of Matt James, the first Black Bachelor, had a sorority formal on a plantation, which had us reckoning with the prevalent racist history of this country; and Marcus Shoberg, who vied for Jenn Tran's heart, told emotional war stories that got us ranting about the military industrial complex.

I joined the chat in 2016, during *The Bachelor's* twentieth season, in which Ben Higgins made history by telling two women he loved them. Entering this thread was very unusual for me. Back then, I was a reality television snob. I had never watched anything in the *Real Housewives* franchise, I couldn't name a single Kardashian that wasn't Kim, and I scoffed at the green card marriages holding toxic couples together on *90 Day Fiancé*.

But in 2015, *UnReal* hit our screens, and the critical darling had made it onto my watchlist. The barely-fictional portrayal of heartless producers, manipulation, and mess got me interested in watching the real series. I wanted to see if I could spot the machinations taking place just off camera. When a woman cried over another contestant stealing the Bachelor for a second, was it because a producer had told her a minute earlier that she was on the brink of elimination? Were all screaming matches spurred by a production assistant casually telling a contestant four rosés deep that they overhead another contestant shit-talking her dog? Did the devout Christian girls start showing a little more cleavage because a boom operator told them prudes would never make it to Fantasy Suites?

Luckily, I had a group of friends that were already *Bachelor* fanatics. We all lived in the same neighborhood, and they gathered every Monday to watch the show. They eagerly welcomed me into their viewing nights. These women were true believers in all the love stories and drama that unfolded on the television show. Yes, they had heard of *UnReal* and acknowledged that much of the show was produced, but for them, it didn't change the fact that Trista and Ryan Sutter, *The Bachelorette*'s first couple and the longest partnership in the franchise, had a genuine, enduring love that transcended the limits of reality television.

I started off as a cynical viewer, favoring the pettiness in early episodes and losing interest by Hometowns, when love stories began to outweigh the drama. On Ben's season, Olivia Caridi had been eliminated on her two-on-one and left stranded on an island, and a proposal couldn't top that. I kept watching, however, because I enjoyed spending time with my friends. *The Bachelor* watch parties were also a space for us to discuss our latest Tinder dates, vent about clients who didn't pay their invoices, and recap arguments we had with our mothers.

We stayed together through *The Bachelorette* and *Bachelor in Paradise*, but by the fall, we started getting too busy to keep watching every week in person. I started grad school, Samira moved to a new neighborhood, Stephanie had to start working weeknights, and Heather was taking scuba classes. Our viewing parties moved over to the group chat.

It was the perfect distraction for me, a fresh MFA candidate writing 10,000-word papers on Michael Asher's "Untitled," a public water fountain that was actually a conceptual art piece. I decompressed through the chat, switching my brain power to crafting a 10,000-word defense of Rachel Lindsay's decision to choose Bryan Abasolo over Peter Kraus. As I insisted that Bryan was the secure choice, I realized that I genuinely cared for Rachel's happiness. Putting myself into her shoes and dissecting her every action and emotion over the group chat had made me grow attached to our first Black Bachelorette. I did not want her to settle for Peter, who wasn't ready for commitment.

The chat had an important rebuttal: that hot tub scene with Peter tho…

A strange thing about reality television is that, even though a contestant appears as themself, we still treat them as fictional. Editors slice out context and nuance to present people as the most irrational versions of themselves. For a casual viewer, this turns contestants into caricatures, and because they are no longer behaving like real people, we stop seeing them as such.

The group chat, however, was adding that humanity back into the picture. Our gut reactions were often negative—Did Caelynn Miller-Keyes really ditch a hot guy in Mexico to live with Dean Unglert in a van?!—but then we would loop back to our own experiences. When I was twenty-four, I too dreamed of van life, and that would have been the perfect age to see the world with my crush and shower at rest stops. With no kids, no mortgage, and influencer cash paying for gas, I argued, why wouldn't Caelynn take up that opportunity?

Our conversations progressed past snap judgements, and we could locate the jealousy, insecurity, and hurt that was often the root cause for a thrown glass or a smashed cake. We also had watched enough of the show that we could tell when arguments were producer-driven and trained our ears to catch Frankenbites, which is when an editor cuts up audio from different takes and stitches them together to create a new, never-uttered sentence. It didn't excuse anyone's actions, but it gave us the capacity to forgive the contestants for their outbursts and to root for them.

By the time we got to Clayton Echard's season, I was fully hooked on *The Bachelor*. It became my mission to get us into a live taping, and months of lurking on Reddit finally paid off. I signed up for an email list, and in August 2022, we scored tickets to the "Men Tell All" taping for Gabby Windey and Rachel Recchia's dual *Bachelorette* season. The live show revealed many of the producer tricks I had long suspected. At one point, we were told to make faces, like gasping, pouting, or looking disgusted, which could be spliced between hot-seat interactions in the final edit to emphasize the audience's judgment regarding whether or not a man had come onto the show "for the right reasons." Two members of the Real Rose Buddies made the telecast's final cut.

Before the taping's calculated production could sour us on the franchise, Chris Harrison surprised the entire audience with a free Virgin Voyages cruise, one of the season's sponsors. All was forgiven. Only Heather and I could use the vouchers before they expired. We sent selfies to Samira and Stephanie from the same knockoff Yayoi Kusama Infinity Mirror Room that Rachel and Tyler Norris spun in during their one-on-one date, sailing somewhere between Puerto Rico and the Dominican Republic. An abundance of free champagne in hand, we toasted to Bachelor Nation and thanked them for enriching our lives.

My participation in the Real Rose Buddies chipped away my general smugness towards reality television, and I started to see the genre as a positive force. It was the catalyst for deepening the friendships I had formed with these women. Before the chat, we were mostly acquaintances, but now I consider them all close friends.

Through hours of texting, I've learned so much about the three of them. There are the more surface-level details, like that Heather is an aspiring writer, and she's written a memoir about her immigrant experience; that Stephanie is a massive fan of drum and bass music, and she travels to Europe every year to attend a notable festival; or that Samira is surprisingly fluent in Japanese because her family moved to Japan when she was a teenager.

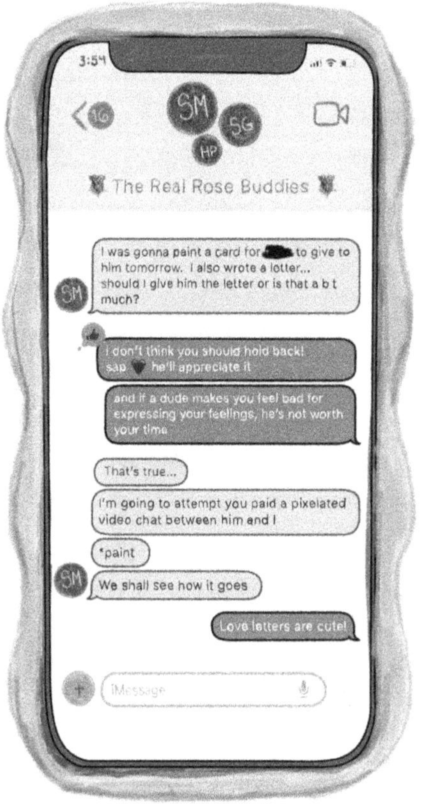

I've also learned that Heather is rock solid in a crisis. When she met her now-husband, a friend of his had committed suicide, and Heather skipped Arie Luyendyk Jr.'s "Hometown" episode so that she could guide her partner through grieving and healing. I realized that Stephanie is a hopeless romantic, and when Dotun Olubeko's mother said that she already thought of Charity Lawson as her own daughter, Stephanie sprinkled crying emojis throughout her messages, letting us know that she was getting emotional, and declared the contestants soulmates. And I admired Samira's vulnerability during a songwriting date on *The Bachelor*

Presents: Listen to Your Heart, which prompted her to share that she was writing a love letter and painting a birthday card for the person she was seeing at the time.

Because of the inherently romantic nature of the shows, the chat has given us play-by-plays of our dating lives, from good to bad. We were so skeptical of Heather's connection with her partner because they seemed to fall in love in a day, and the real world doesn't work like the Bachelor universe. We warned her about love bombing and braced for devastating red flags, like MAGA values, a secret child, or an arrest record. They never came. I happily ate crow a few years later, when he joined us on our cruise, and Heather showed off their new wedding rings: matching tattoos.

I have seen Stephanie go through numerous heartbreaks, just like me, and we have connected deeply on our shared perception that our careers and love lives have an inverse relationship. If our career is on the upswing, as Stephanie excitedly shared when she opened her own private practice, it seems that our romantic relationships will flame out. After Rachel Lindsay and Bryan Abasolo announced their divorce, I suspected that Rachel, whom I had vehemently defended, could not make it work long-term with Bryan because her career outshined him. Sometimes Stephanie and I fear we'll never find a man who isn't intimidated by our ambition.

The biggest romantic hardship came for Samira, who saw a fourteen-year relationship crumble during the sixth season of *Bachelor in Paradise*. As she tried to detail his indiscretions over the chat, we quickly rallied to become a support system in real life. Within an hour, the three of us had arrived at her tiny Koreatown apartment, armed with wine and weed, and squeezed into her bed like sardines in a tin. We hugged and spooned and then flipped on *Paradise*, sobbing upon seeing Demi Burnett and Kristian Haggerty become the first openly queer couple on the show. It was a historical moment for the franchise, but mainly it was a good excuse to cry.

When Chris Harrison lost his hosting gig in 2021, the chat reckoned with the idea that *The Bachelor* might not last forever. We had long overlooked the franchise's worst characteristics, like upholding rigid, heteronormative gender roles, casting a number of men with sexual violence allegations against them, or taking thirty-three seasons to cast a Black lead and still tokenizing its contestants of color. We also now had many other trashy dating shows, like *Love Is Blind*, *Married at First Sight*, and *Temptation Island*, that sparked conversations in the group chat. We knew we could exist without *The Bachelor*, and no one seemed as sad about the prospect of losing the franchise as I did.

The television show itself wouldn't be as enjoyable without people to discuss it with, and the Real Rose Buddies have become a core piece of my social life. If the franchise were to be canceled, I fear it would mean losing a connection to these women that I've been bonding with for the past eight years. There are so few television shows that have the lifespan of *The Bachelor*, and while we'll unite for the three-day binge of *The Ultimatum*, there is nothing like the continuous, ten-week fodder of *Bachelor* spin-offs to keep us tethered for nine months out of the year.

So many of my memories are tied to this chat, and the conversations paint pictures as vivid as real-life encounters. When the franchise is on hiatus, I notice how quickly my phone stops buzzing. Without our live-reaction thread, we also abandon the excuse to give each other updates on life events, dating stories, and work drama.

With every new season, I feel like we're students returning from summer break. We take turns giving updates:

Stephanie: I just got back from London

Heather: I'm learning how to surf skate

Samira: Guess who I'm talking to again?

Renée: Should we watch the premiere in person? Who knows how many seasons are left.

Renée Reizman is an interdisciplinary artist, writer, and educator based in Los Angeles. Her stories about arts, culture, and community have appeared in *The Guardian*, *The Los Angeles Times*, *New York Magazine*, *Hyperallergic*, *Observer*, and more. She is always looking for an excuse to take a road trip. Find her online at https://reneereizman.com or on Instagram @reneereizman.

18

What It's Like to Watch Black Bachelorettes as a Black Woman

Joy Alicia

When Rachel Lindsay was announced as the first Black Bachelorette, I gasped and clutched my imaginary pearls. The memory of my excitement then is still palpable, and the ripple effects of the franchise diversifying its cast continue to be felt. Black women across the country were filled with glee. A Black Bachelorette was a symbol of possibility, a glimmer of hope. Similar to when Barack Obama was elected president, Black Americans never thought we would see the day!

Naturally, it didn't take long for my celebratory serotonin boost to free-fall into panic. I predicted that Rachel would be targeted online and offline for securing a role once primarily available to white women. My fears weren't unfounded. Black actors cast in roles traditionally played by white stars are eviscerated by bigots in online comment sections. Challenging the status quo is often met with resistance, so I wondered if Rachel's potential suitors would genuinely embrace her and whether the loyal Bachelor Nation fan base would rally behind her.

I want Black Bachelorettes to be themselves, but I also don't want them to play into repetitive stereotypes about Black women. Over the years, some Black Bachelorettes understood the assignment, that being a Black Bachelorette was bigger than centering themselves, and the role should be used as an opportunity to showcase a Black woman's joy, humor, humanity, and sense of community. Other Bachelorettes never mentioned their race at all and struggled, or refused, to even mention that racism exists.

While each Black Bachelorette has had different approaches to their coveted role, one common thread among the Black Bachelorettes has been family. It was touching to see that all the Black Bachelorettes are close to their loving mothers and fathers, dispelling stereotypes about Black children being raised in single-parent households.

Black women continue to be in dire need of a rebrand—one that challenges deeply ingrained stereotypes in media and society. In his book *Dataclysm*, OkCupid cofounder Christian Rudder wrote that Black women were voted "less attractive than women of other races and ethnicities" by OkCupid's male users.[1] Statistically, Black women and Asian men receive the least amount of attention and engagements on dating apps, which only underscores the pervasive nature of these biases. In addition to that harsh truth, Black women on dating apps may be inundated with messages from Caucasian men with a Black-girl fetish or fantasy and certain Black men they may avoid them for a myriad of reasons. This complex landscape of racial bias and fetishization isn't new—Black women have been objectified and stereotyped since the days of slavery.

Minorities are often viewed through a stereotypical monolithic lens, and this tendency can shape how they are represented in media. One of the most effective ways to challenge internalized prejudice and implicit bias is through positive, authentic interactions or by seeing marginalized groups portrayed in empowering, multidimensional ways. Showcasing a

1 Ashley Brown, "'Least Desirable'? How Racial Discrimination Plays Out in Online Dating," NPR, January 9, 2018, https://www.npr.org/2018/01/09/575352051/least-desirable-how-racial-discrimination-plays-out-in-online-dating.

positive, multifaceted image of Black women can have a profound impact on shifting the opinions and perceptions of a diverse audience, so I'm critical of any Black Bachelorette who doesn't view her position as a potentially teachable moment for a widespread audience.

Before Nick Viall's 2016 season, Black contestants were often sent home fairly early each season on *The Bachelor* and *The Bachelorette*. Nick was an equal opportunity Bachelor, though. He dated Rachel for most of his season. While this may sound odd to white people, who see themselves predominantly represented on dating shows and in mainstream media and pop culture, Rachel's lengthy run on Nick's season was thrilling for me to watch because she was in an interracial relationship, a rarity for Black women onscreen and fairly uncommon for Black women in the dating world at large.

Given that *The Bachelorette* attracts viewers from across a broad spectrum of psychological, social, and economic backgrounds, the potential influence of Rachel's own season was significant. I believed the likelihood that more Black women would be cast as Bachelorettes hinged on the ratings Rachel's season garnered, so I watched all of her episodes as they aired.

Rachel becoming a lead was meaningful to me because, like many Black people, Rachel wouldn't pass the "brown paper bag test." This term refers to a discriminatory practice that was unfortunately common throughout the twentieth century and used to determine whether an African American would be granted access to certain social or professional spaces. In a variety of institutions—from sororities and fraternities to churches, nightclubs, schools, and even places of employment—if a person's skin tone was darker than the shade of a brown paper bag, they were often excluded. Those who were lighter than the bag "passed" and were given entry. Rachel, like me, would not have passed this test. But her very presence as the lead on *The Bachelorette* defied those outdated, harmful standards, marking a bold step forward in redefining beauty, access, and representation in mainstream media.

There is rampant erasure of dark-skinned Black women in entertainment and pop culture. Unlike stars like Beyoncé, Rihanna, Zendaya, Zoë

Kravitz, Doja Cat, and several other A-list Black women with mainstream success, Rachel doesn't look racially ambiguous or biracial. When I learned she was the new Bachelorette, I felt that Black women like me were officially allowed to exist in a space we had been shut out of.

A decade before Rachel's season, in 2006, *Flavor of Love* debuted on VH1, arguably the premiere Black reality TV dating show. Viral *Flavor of Love* memes still circulate today; the highly entertaining series remains a staple in pop culture. The *Flavor of Love* cast showcased many prevalent stereotypes about Black women. Like many viewers, I was hooked.

The women who competed for rapper Flava Flav's clock were loud, scantily clad, ready to fistfight, and spoke Ebonics. The series wasn't progressive enough to showcase classy Black women like Rachel Lindsay, Tayshia Adams, Michelle Young, or Charity Lawson—the Black Bachelorettes thus far—and there was no need to. Highlighting stereotypes proved to be a recipe for success. The show's season finale episodes garnered several million viewers, breaking records for VH1.

In contrast, *The Bachelor* and *The Bachelorette* don't center harmful stereotypes or resort to cheap tactics for views like *Flavor of Love* and many reality TV dating shows do. *The Bachelor* and *The Bachelorette* deliver substance, romance, international travel, hometown dates, fun excursions, and a proposal (most seasons **cough**). Seeing Black women being treated like queens by good-looking and successful men was affirming for single Black women seeking healthy, lifelong partnership and all who enjoy witnessing a love story bloom and grow.

Notably, Black women were overdue for gaining young role models whose accomplishments felt attainable. I don't see myself in entertainers or most public figures, but watching a Black Bachelorette seeking love is relatable. Seeing Black women—often labeled "strong," much to their detriment when seeking medical attention[2]—experiencing a range of human emotions in front of a national audience was revolutionary in its own right.

Black women are in every field imaginable—from STEM, where

2 "Denied," *Today*, accessed October 15, 2025, https://www.today.com/denied.

Kizzmekia Corbett was instrumental in developing the Covid-19 vaccine, to arts and entertainment to corporate boardrooms and local communities. But the reality is that the world doesn't always give us the same visibility or recognition it offers to those who are in the rarified air of fame and fortune.

Having a Black woman as the Bachelorette wasn't just a win in the world of reality TV; it was a victory for all the Black women quietly making waves in their own communities, professions, and families. Sometimes, the power of visibility is just as important as any other achievement.

During her season, Rachel cried, saying, "I get pressure from so many ways being in this position.... I already know what people are going to say about me, and judge me for the decisions I'm making. I'm going to have to be the one who has to deal with that and nobody else, and that's a lot."[3] I feel the subtext of Rachel's confession was a veiled fear she would be scrutinized for getting engaged to a contestant who wasn't African American. By following her heart and accepting a proposal from Colombian Bryan Abasolo, Rachel may have accelerated mainstream acceptance of a Black woman dating outside of her race.

I would be remiss if I didn't mention that one of Rachel's contestants, Lee Garrett, had posted racist tweets mere months before competing for her final rose. Rachel also had a contestant, DeMario Jackson, who allegedly had a girlfriend while dating Rachel. DeMario appeared to be a top contender for Rachel, and she was rattled to learn that he was, purportedly, a clout chaser. When learning about these men's actions, Rachel would walk away from cameras to compose herself so that she could deal with the challenges with poise and grace.

Other Black Bachelorettes had different hurdles. Tayshia Adams, a half-Black, half-Mexican Bachelorette, grew up in a white community where she always tried to assimilate. Tayshia admitted, when speaking about contestant Ivan Hall, that dating a man who was also half-Black would be a first for her. When Ivan brought up the protests in the aftermath of George Floyd's murder, Tayshia revealed that she was still

3 *The Bachelorette*, season 13, episode 4, aired June 19, 2017, on ABC.

processing the uprising: "It's overwhelming. Sometimes I feel like it affects me." Tayshia's stuttering and hesitation to share her thoughts troubled me as a Black viewer. She struggled to mention the Black Lives Matter movement or any Black issues. Tayshia confessed, "I haven't been able to talk to someone that really understands me." That's sad, and it made me wonder whether Tayshia has any Black friends.

Michelle Young, the third Black Bachelorette, did not disappoint me. When faced with a contestant who brought detailed notes about how to secure camera time, Michelle didn't morph into the stereotype of an "angry black woman." Instead, she asked him to leave without breaking a sweat or shedding any tears. What was most endearing to me about Michelle was her willingness to engage in conversations about race throughout her season. She didn't shy away from the complexities of her identity.

Growing up as a biracial Black girl in Minnesota, Michelle shared how she often felt like the "token" Black girl, who wasn't always seen or acknowledged for who she truly was. This experience of feeling invisible or like an afterthought was something she grappled with on her season. I found it powerful when she expressed her appreciation for a Black contestant who mentioned going to psychotherapy, noting that it's rare for Black men to talk openly about mental health. Black people tend to opt for church, prayer, and their support network of friends and family instead of psychotherapy or prescription drugs. From relying on churches for freedom (some churches provided a sanctuary to escaped slaves on the Underground Railroad) to the Civil Rights Movement and beyond, churches unify African American communities. Consequently, Black churches have been torched and bombed because they're a vital resource and refuge that provides relief and hope to residents in the communities they serve. Michelle's ability to have candid and nuanced conversations about the Black community proves that *The Bachelorette* can be a platform for meaningful conversations about identity, well-being, and the complexities of race.

Unlike Rachel, Tayshia, and Michelle, Charity gave an unfavorable representation of young Black women. Generally speaking, minorities aren't granted the same grace as their white peers. The most devastating and glaring example of this is the justice system, where white people receive lighter sentences than Black people for committing the same crimes. But it's true, too, of how viewers approach Black reality TV stars.

Although Charity is a dark-skinned Black woman with African American parents, she didn't mention her ethnicity and kept racial issues out of discussions throughout her season. She also kissed more men on night one than any other Bachelorette (to my recollection). Even if my guesstimate is inaccurate, I was appalled, because Black women have been hypersexualized since slavery, and Charity embodied the outdated trope that Black women are highly sexual, which couldn't be further from the truth, despite what rap lyrics and rap videos suggest.

It's important to strike a balance between individual agency and the responsibility that comes with representation. My hope is that, as more women of color take the spotlight in future seasons, there will be more room for them to just be themselves—without the weight of centuries-old stereotypes hanging over their every move.

Black women are a multifaceted tapestry of traits, characteristics, and personalities, but are still mostly seen and represented as an amalgamation of negative stereotypes. Our society hasn't embraced Black people's individuality yet. Rachel was aware of this and concerned about how she may be perceived by viewers, but Charity did not seem to be. Charity gave me the impression that she wanted to experiment with as many contestants as her hormones desired.

What was worse about Charity's season is that a Black contestant named Xavier Bonner, one of her final three, implied that he needed her to have sex with him on their overnight Fantasy Suite date. Xavier's ultimatum was unnecessary and ridiculous because sex is already expected during Fantasy Suite dates—he wasn't good-looking enough to try to coerce Charity into having sex with him, and Charity had options! Literally. Charity promptly sent Xavier home, but watching him represent the stereotype of a Black man wanting to be with a woman exclusively for sex was disappointing.

Despite some contestants being clowns, *The Bachelor* franchise helps viewers inch closer toward living in a color-blind society, like the mind-altering one featured in Netflix's *Bridgerton*. I wouldn't be surprised if the vast majority of contestants hadn't dated a Black woman before joining the show. Each Black Bachelorette did a great job of showing viewers that they're fun to date *and that anyone, of any race, would be lucky to be with them*. I feel slightly more seen, sought after, understood, and valued because there have been four Black Bachelorettes (and counting, hopefully)! I can't help but wonder whether, today, Rachel would still feel pressured to choose a Black fiancé. *The Bachelorette* should be credited for helping pave the way for all Black women on mainstream reality TV dating shows. Perhaps viewers looked at Rachel and Bryan and Tayshia and Zac as happy couples they rooted for despite being interracial couples. I commend the franchise for giving Black women, especially underrepresented Black women who wouldn't pass the paper bag test, a spotlight to bask in and a platform from which to shine bright.

Love is for everyone. These shows are more than just entertainment; they reflect how far we've come and, hopefully, offer a glimpse of how much further we can go in embracing love in all its forms.

Joy Alicia is the author of *So Drunk a Tooth's Gotta Go* and the founder of Online Dating Savior, a dating coaching service. She's also the host of *The Worstship* podcast.

Her work has been published in *Newsweek*, *Daily Mail*, *Blavity*, *Metro UK*, *The Bold Italic* and more. Joy has performed stand-up comedy in California, Texas, and Oregon, captivating audiences with her observational humor. She currently calls Southern California home, where she lives with her dog, who she's convinced pretends to have an avoidant attachment style to score extra treats.

19

Will You Accept This Spoiler?

Iftin Abshir

In my first semester at the University of Southern California School of Cinematic Arts, my friends and I attended the graduate student conference, First Forum. After a morning filled with fascinating discussions and thought-provoking talks, a peer presented a paper about the niche *Survivor* fan community that utilizes edgic, a combination of the words *editing* and *logic*. It's a technique that uses media theory, reason, and statistical analysis to determine the winner of a season before they're made public. This practice grew out of the spoiling *Survivor* fandom, which through various forums—most famously the *Survivor Sucks* blog—worked together to "spoil" the show by discovering and sharing details such as filming location, contestant names, and elimination order before a season aired.

As longtime reality TV junkies, my friends and I were immediately intrigued by the topic of spoiling and edgic, and during our lunch break, we debated whether it could be applied to other reality shows. *The Great British Bake-Off*? Definitely not; the contestants are too nice, and the editing so positive. *The Amazing Race*? Again, no, because the producers are on record saying they take the "race" aspect of the show seriously and try not to interfere with the results during filming or editing. *Big Brother*? Nope, because it takes place in close to real time, and edgic involves analyzing editing patterns and character arcs that can only be recognized in a show that is filmed first and edited later. Finally, someone suggested *The Bachelor*, and it was a perfect fit; it helped that we were already fans and therefore had years of viewing history.

My friends began making regular Monday night pilgrimages to my apartment for *The Bachelor* over the next two years. We talked; we tweeted; we even started a blog digging into every clue, breaking down the smallest spoiler, and tried our hands at applying edgic to our favorite guilty-pleasure show. Like so many others, we found a community in watching and, as media scholars, dissecting and analyzing every little detail of the show.

But I wonder: Why were we so drawn to spoilers? Fan engagement within *The Bachelor* franchise is not only acknowledged but, in many cases, also promoted by *Bachelor* producers. Activities such as *Bachelor* viewing parties, brackets and pools, and the *Bachelor* Fantasy League can all be considered "approved" fan-engagement practices. One that isn't well-received, though, and would be considered "unapproved," is spoiling—attempting to determine certain elements of the show before they air during the season. While I try my best to stay away from potential spoilers these days, the desire is still there; I want to know what happens at the end. It's like being in on a tightly-held secret, and once you know, it becomes even more fun to look for clues that hint to the eventual ending.

So, the question remains: Why do we enjoy spoilers?

Embedded in the name "reality television" is the assumption that the people, locations, and situations portrayed on the show are inherently real and accurate representations. However, the need for television to also be entertaining means that reality TV producers have increasingly taken on a role of creating a narrative for audience consumption through the careful manipulation of situations and selective editing practices. While these elements combine to create an engaging narrative for audiences, they also contribute to the constructed-ness of reality programming.

Critical to understanding the pleasure of spoiling is what Dana Cloud calls the *irony bribe*. According to Cloud, this notion is related to the "constructed reality" of reality TV. The irony bribe corresponds to the paradoxical nature of reality television in which viewers can regard the program as "real" and "not-real"—and, therefore, both worth viewing and worthless at the same time.[1] In other words, even though the reality portrayed on *The Bachelor* franchise is heavily manipulated and crafted by the shows' producers for the specific purpose of entertainment, the world of the shows takes itself completely seriously in relation to the romance and drama presented on-screen. (Interestingly, this is also why the campy and tongue-in-cheek opening credits for *Bachelor in Paradise* feel like a breath of fresh air: This iteration of the show recognizes and embraces its own ridiculousness.) The irony stems from the fact that, in spite of how a reality show such as *The Bachelor* is presented, it will never be entirely "real."

Mary Beth Haralovich and Michael Trosset write that "narrative pleasure stems from the desire to know what will happen next, to have that gap opened and closed, again and again, until the resolution of the story."[2] These feelings of anticipation associated with the narrative pleasure an audience experiences essentially come down to two elements: uncertainty due to chance and uncertainty due to ignorance. The uncertainty due to chance stems from the comprehension that any particular outcome results from some degree of statistical unpredictability, while alternately, uncertainty due to ignorance describes a person's lack of knowledge.[3] For example, in a scripted narrative, all the story's elements—such as characters, conflicts, and conclusions—are crafted by writers long before the audience encounters them. There is only one predetermined direction the narrative can take; the uncertainty the audience experiences is due to ignorance of how it will unfold.

1 Dana Cloud, "The Irony Bribe and Reality Television: Investment and Detachment in *The Bachelor*," *Critical Studies in Media Communications* 27, no. 5 (2010): 415, https://doi.org/10.1080/15295030903583572.

2 Mary Beth Haralovich and Michael W. Trosset, "'Expect the Unexpected': Narrative Pleasure and Uncertainty Due to Chance in *Survivor*," in *Reality TV: Remaking Television Culture*, ed. Susan Murray and Laurie Ouellette (New York University Press, 2004), 83.

3 Haralovich and Trosset, "'Expect the Unexpected.'"

In reality TV, we already have an inherent understanding of the artificiality of the narrative—so how do we find other ways of receiving pleasure? The highly produced nature of *The Bachelor* means that it becomes more obvious with each episode that the audience is experiencing uncertainty due to ignorance because the production team already knows how it all ended—in large part because there is a significant gap between when the show is filmed and when it is aired.

In order to fully engage with the narrative pleasure of uncertainty due to chance, viewers must be able to engage with each episode as if it is happening in the present; once they've broken down this critical barrier between past and present, they shift to uncertainty due to ignorance.[4] With this shift, audiences may feel that they are losing some of their agency in that they are not experiencing the developing romance along with the contestants, but are instead being presented the story the show's producers have crafted. In order to reclaim some of their lost narrative pleasure, fans begin using spoiling as a means to circumvent the traditional consumption pathways laid out for them by *The Bachelor*'s producers. Fans essentially short-circuit the cycle of chance and take the narrative back into their own hands.

In the practice of spoiling, there are many ways fans can gather information and different levels of involvement. The main layers are prediction, speculation or sleuthing, and spoiling. While all three methods involve analyzing the program to determine potential outcomes, the methods employed are quite distinct and differ in the extent to which a viewer invests in the manufactured reality of *The Bachelor*. The least invasive mode is prediction, in which the viewer limits their investigation to information garnered only from the episode itself. For example, forecasting which contestants will be eliminated at the rose ceremony based on the types of conversations they had with the Bachelor.

The next level of engagement—which I primarily used to win my *Bachelor* Fantasy League!—is speculation or sleuthing, which involves the use of additional information such as analyzing promos or social media

4 Haralovich and Trosset, "'Expect the Unexpected.'"

posts for the upcoming episode to look for clues as to who might still be in the competition, who gets one-on-one dates, and where the show might be filming. In 2017, *The Bachelor* franchise, in collaboration with ESPN, launched the *Bachelor* Fantasy League. Fans created groups with their friends and competed for points based on a series of questions that involved predictions about the next week's episode. Of course, my friends and I made our own team and played along. However, unlike a fantasy football league, in which individuals can use data and player statistics in order to make educated guesses about upcoming games, the questions asked in the *Bachelor* Fantasy League—such as "Will there be a hot tub on the date?"—made it very difficult to answer with any kind of certainty. I spent a long time combing through previews looking for any kind of clues that would give me an advantage in answering those weekly questions.

Finally, the most in-depth type of spoiling involves collecting information not provided in any of the network's official channels—such as looking for which contestants have reactivated their social media accounts and how they've interacted with and followed other former franchise contestants—so as to predetermine the order of elimination while the program is still in production.

The focus of all spoiling is the determination of crucial information for the season. Within spoiling communities, emphasis is placed on determining the order of elimination of the contestants, hometown date recipients, and the eventual winner of the season. In addition to wanting to determine particular events from the program *before* they are shown on television, other types of spoiling are concerned with the discovery of events that are *not* shown during the episode at all.

An example is from a group date in St. Thomas during season 21 with Nick Viall. Six women were split into two volleyball teams where the winners were promised extra time with Nick that evening. This last detail was alluded to in clips of contestants crying on the beach talking about how time with Nick is so important, and how it hurts not to get it. However, when the program returned after the commercial break, all six women were at the cocktail party with Nick, which made the previous clips of crying women seem totally out of place.[5] As longtime *Bachelor* spoiler Steve Carbone, known online as Reality Steve, reported, the original plan had indeed been to only take the winning team to the cocktail party, but because season front-runner (and Nick's favorite), Vanessa Grimaldi, was on the losing team, producers had to allow everyone to attend.[6] The messy editing led to fans wanting to know what went on behind the scenes.

Often the only people who *truly* know that are the contestants themselves, and occasionally they are the source of certain spoilers. In what I call *unintentional spoiling*, contestants accidentally reveal unreleased details. This could be as simple and discreet as an eliminated contestant immediately following other former *Bachelor* contestants on social media after being sent home, or as dramatic as Kaitlyn and Shawn's Snapchat snafu. In this well-known and widely covered incident, season 11 Bachelorette Kaitlyn Bristowe and her final rose recipient, Shawn Booth, accidentally sent out a public Snapchat photo of themselves cuddling in bed long before the season finale aired. In a less obvious social media slip-up, season 28 Bachelor Joey Graziadei was caught posting TikTok videos and Instagram stories in the same location as the season's eventual winner, Kelsey Anderson; a group of eagle-eyed fans soon spotted the similarities and concluded the two were together and engaged after filming ended.

In contrast to other reality shows such as *Survivor*, which films on closed sets, the public locations used for many dates in *The Bachelor* and *Bachelorette* have led to a phenomenon I refer to as *real-time spoiling*. The dates' public locations make it much easier for fans to see filming as it occurs, take pictures or videos of the filming process, and post the pics online. The type of information gained with this particular type of spoiling is especially valuable in fan communities when it comes to determining hometown date recipients.

5 *The Bachelor*, season 21, episode 6, "St. Thomas," aired January 30, 2017, on ABC.

6 Steve Carbone, "The 'Bachelor' Nick Episode 6 Recap Incl What the Hell Was All That Last Night?" *Reality Steve*, February 7, 2017, http://realitysteve.com/2017/02/07/the-bachelor-nick-spoilers-episode-6-recap/.

As a media scholar and viewer, I recognize spoiling as a valid resistant reading strategy[7] with which fans are able to engage with *The Bachelor*, but the practice and those who engage in it are frowned upon by *Bachelor* producers. Prior to the season 24 finale, creators of the show and that season's lead, Peter Weber, touted it as the first unspoiled season *ever*. While promoting the finale during the "Women Tell All," host Chris Harrison went so far as to claim that even Peter himself didn't know how the show would end.[8] Why is there such an emphasis on claiming the show to be unspoiled? *Bachelor* producers have always tried to keep each season's ending as secret as possible. In an interview on *The Ben & Ashley I Almost Famous Podcast*, Harrison spoke about this, saying, "People live their life to try and spoil other people's work… It just never ceases to amaze me that there's people in this world who are like that, but there are."[9]

While the fan-producer relationship inhabits a kind of symbiotic space, there is also tension baked into this connection from its very inception. Media producers need fans to support their work (through views, social media engagement, merchandise purchases, and so on), but at the same time, they try to keep fans at arm's length for fear of having their hard work ruined. Conversely, fans can be dependent on the media producers to continue making their favorite TV shows while also being critical and attempting to hold the franchise accountable for what audiences consider inappropriate behavior or representations. Fans are not intentionally trying to invalidate the production; rather, spoiling is a means through which viewers are able to reclaim their own experience of reality through the show.

The line between reality and unreality is constantly negotiated by both the producers and the audience, and it is within this realm that spoiling

7 Derived from the work of British cultural scholar, Stuart Hall, a resistant reading of *The Bachelor* involves deliberately interpreting the program in a way that is in opposition to the narrative presented by the show's producers.

8 *The Bachelor*, season 24, episode 10, "Women Tell All," aired March 2, 2020, on ABC.

9 Ben Higgins and Ashley Ioconetti, hosts, *Ben & Ashley I Almost Famous Podcast,* podcast, "Saving Yourself with Chris Harrison," February 25, 2020, https://omny.fm/shows/the-ben-and-ashley-i-almost-famous-podcast/saving-yourself-with-chris-harrison#description.

flourishes. By taking part in spoiling practices, fans are pursuing a viewing experience that is distinct from the goals of the producers but no less valid. Through spoiling, viewers circumvent the traditional consumption pathways laid out for them and can transcend the artificiality of the highly produced romance in order to find the "real life" love story developing off-screen. So whether a viewer is a dedicated fan, a casual watercooler conversationalist, or an avid hate-watcher, the need to believe in the authenticity of some aspect of the story being presented drives many to look for new ways to connect to #BachelorNation.

Iftin Abshir is currently working on her doctorate degree in cinema and media studies through the University of California, Los Angeles. Her dissertation research is a pop culture interrogation of dating on reality TV, focusing on the intersection of culture, gender, sexuality, race, and class. Other research interests include fan studies, transmedia studies, social media and influencers, and Disney studies. Her work has been presented at conferences such as the Society of Cinema and Media Studies, Popular Culture Association, and Pacific Ancient and Modern Language Association.

20

Chiaroscuro

Shir Kehila

In my mid-twenties, having chased boys across the Atlantic for years, I fell in love with a man who could hardly leave his room. When he did, it was with an eye mask and noise canceling headphones—cut off from the world even while moving through it. "Here comes the Martian," he'd say, making his way to the stairs with a palm on the wall. He never called himself an "alien." That was me.

With my student visa renewed, I moved to New York City for grad school. Every three weeks, I took a 3:00 a.m. bus to Boston, an 8:00 a.m. to Bangor, and a 2:00 p.m. to Bar Harbor to spend three nights with Nathaniel. I was used to this kind of trip—the sleepless, sugary buzz of expectation—making my way to someone while looping the same few songs for an hour each. If I'd had a "type" before, it had been the guy who couldn't stay put but wouldn't come to me. With Nathaniel, the opposite was true. He wanted to come to New York—he'd never been—but could only stay in the room, curtains drawn, earplugs in, white-noise machines whirring while, downstairs, his parents made "kitchen noises," which was what we called "cooking."

"Just make sure," a family friend told me in the city, "that you aren't skipping your life here." But my life wasn't in the city. It had been in the dark room in Maine, on Nathaniel's futon, while Wilco's "Far, Far Away" played in the background.

A few months later, life in the city moved indoors. My classes moved online, and I moved into the dark room with Nathaniel. I felt more seen there, often, than out in the light—my mood shifts somehow detected by Nathaniel before I could even sense them. We'd talk while brushing our teeth, while one of us was in the shower—needing, we felt, all the time we could get. And yet our relationship became daily too: detailed, de-idealized. It became the lingering smell of steamed veggies, and scented candles, and sheets I should have washed but didn't. I'd become, along with Nathaniel's parents, a caregiver. I was still in school, jealous now of the far, far away New York outside my classmates' windows—staring at the Zoom square in which, after the vaccine rollout, three of them squeezed in, notebooks and shoulders touching. Nights, too wiped out for work but too worked up to sleep, I stayed up watching *Narcos*. I watched *Derry Girls* and *Gilmore Girls*, *Sex in the City* and *Sex Education*. I wasn't very discerning. But I didn't mean to watch *The Bachelorette*.

The day my vaccine became effective, I got the bus down to Boston to visit a friend. The plan was to gab each other's ears off, which we both needed, and stay out of the kitchen, which I did. "I don't know if it'd be your thing," my friend said, "but there's a new *Bachelorette* starting Monday." I shrugged, trying to keep my face from showing just how flattered I was that my dear, college friend—who'd seen the worst of my boy-chasing—would doubt it was "my thing." Just how relieved, too, for another excuse, when I hadn't made it myself, to watch something more.

"You both know Katie?" I asked my friend and her roommate just a few minutes into the premiere. I was already, somehow, lost.

"Yup," they said, and gave me the brief on the new Bachelorette, Katie Thurston. "She was on James's season," the roommate said.

"Very sex-positive," my friend added. Soon, the ads were over, and I jumped into the story because I wanted to hear the man on-screen say what everyone else already had. He was *so* excited. Katie was *so* beautiful. *So*—yes!—sex-positive. This wasn't repetition—Gertrude Stein would have claimed—it was insistence! The show was an echo chamber, and I was drawn inside by voices drowning one another, each conviction containing its own contradiction.

In episode two, still at my friend's, I learned everyone played not only the sanctioned game of the show but also that of outing the "real" players, which was to say, those who weren't really playing. *OK*, I thought, *I could follow this.* The next week, I watched on my own. The next summer, I watched another season. I did so because, while my "dates" with Nathaniel happened in the dark room of his childhood, it was easier to watch romantic helicopter rides than to see my friends move in with their partners. It was easier to watch Gabby Windey and Rachel Recchia slide into hot tubs and board a cruise ship than to watch my friend turn the key to her apartment, where her boyfriend sat on the couch—light filling the half-painted living room that was all their own.

The more exorbitant the luxury, in other words, the less I envied it. *The Bachelorette* was accessible to me precisely because its world never would have been. There was comfort in watching adventures so lavish, so glamorous, they were unattainable not only for us, but for most people—not because Nathaniel was ill, but because we weren't rich. There was comfort in being the rule, in this sense, rather than the exception—in sharing an economic reality with our friends, if we couldn't share any other. Our friends, too, weren't likely to set foot on a yacht, but they *could* walk on the beach at sunset, run to the store for bread and hummus, take turns washing dishes. This I envied: the things we could have done had Nathaniel been healthy, not in some other world, but right here.

Early on in our relationship, we fantasized about getting dinner in town. "I'd probably get a heart attack," I said. What I meant was, I'd be so happy, it might kill me. But I also admitted, without meaning to, that I didn't know how to picture us out together. It was easier to flip the familiar image, where one of us was ill, than to inhabit an entirely different one. It was easier to imagine a medical emergency than ordinary pleasure—easier to interfere with the dream than to dream it. If I kept the fantasy vague, my subconscious assumed, I could also keep it boundless. The catch was, I had to dream myself out of it too.

Around the same time, Nathaniel told me he was afraid to get better. Five years into illness—into life "under a rock"—he didn't remember how to be in the world. He couldn't imagine what it might take to re-enter and navigate. Even in his mind, Nathaniel was hesitant, like me, to leave the dark room. We were both comfortable there, if also constrained; Nathaniel's parents got the groceries and paid the bills and never asked when I might leave. So I stayed, watching, from within our cocoon, the bright unreality of *The Bachelorette*—both a negative image of ours and its eerie reflection. We, too, had to make up our minds about marriage. We, too, had our deadline set by a corporation—not the American Broadcasting Company, but its evil twin: Citizenship and Immigration Services.

While I didn't wonder whether I'd find "the one," I wondered whether I could keep him. What Nathaniel and I had—both in spite and as a result of his illness—was the healthiest relationship I'd ever been in. He couldn't afford to ignore his needs or pretend to manage on his own; he needed to ask for help and communicate his boundaries. There was enough room between us, I felt—despite a lack of physical space—to come together rather than merge into one. And yet, could I marry him not knowing if he'd ever get better? If he'd ever drive himself to doctor's appointments, or make his own dinner, or a meal we could both eat? Was I ready to remain, perhaps indefinitely, my partner's caretaker?

A year after finishing grad school, my student visa was running out. The deadline was hard and nonnegotiable; it was the "real" world grinding up against the dark room. Of course, the distinction itself was unreal, and the world had been inside with us all along, in Nathaniel's medical struggle, in the disquieting sense that we were somehow behind on our lives. *The Bachelorette*'s overflowing, seductive reality was, I felt, a way to make up for our lacking present—for our latent futures. It was a way to access, if indirectly, the freedom and possibilities we didn't share. The show was a reminder that I still had them. It was also a reminder that I had, with Nathaniel, what the Bachelorettes were after.

A viewing experience marked by contradiction wasn't only common, I learned, but academically researched. *The Bachelor* tempts us, scholar Dana Cloud claims, "not only with the fantasy of mythic romance" but also with the pleasures of "recognizing the fantasy's folly."[1] The pleasures, that is, of rejecting what we may still want, despite ourselves. She calls this *the irony bribe*: a simultaneous reward for both our earnestness and cynicism, our investment in and detachment from the show, our oscillating belief in and disillusionment with love. We're tempted just as much by the fantasy's success, it seems, as by its failure—which is, perhaps, its own kind of success. Because a breaking fantasy is also a fulfilled one: restored, by being shattered, to a thing beyond our reach.

"Viewers can regard the program as 'real' and 'not real,'" Cloud writes, "and therefore worth viewing and worthless at the same time."[2] *The Bachelorette*, to me, was worth viewing not only for the "real" or "not real" but also for the challenge to tell them apart, for finding how often I couldn't. What portion of our lives, one of my teachers once asked, do we spend daydreaming? What reality wasn't, in some ways, imagined?

"In the fantasy...," Leslie Jamison writes in an essay on daydreams, "I found the consoling purity of unequivocal feeling states: fear and love. It was a fantasy of emotional simplicity: melodrama as antidote to the muddled emotional contradictions of reality."[3] What I got from *The Bachelorette*, I think, was the opposite kind of antidote. The constant drama on the show helped me appreciate the "muddled emotional contradictions" of my life with Nathaniel. It helped me appreciate what I otherwise found frustrating: Nathaniel's methodical approach to conflicts ("Can we talk about

1 Dana Cloud, "The Irony Bribe and Reality Television: Investment and Detachment in *The Bachelor*," *Critical Studies in Media Communications* 27, no. 5 (2010): 415, https://doi.org/10.1080/15295030903583572.
2 Cloud, "The Irony Bribe and Reality Television," 415.
3 Leslie Jamison, "Dreamers in Broad Daylight: Ten Conversations," *Astra* (2022), October 11, 2022, https://astra-mag.com/articles/dreamers-in-broad-daylight-ten-conversations/.

talking?"), his scribe-like attention to detail ("Let me make a note."), and his reluctance to assume my intentions (*Didn't he know?!*). In centering the "fantasy of emotional simplicity," the show wasn't only a way to live vicariously—to witness a reality I'd never inhabit—but to reframe the one I did.

Part of *The Bachelorette*'s appeal, for me, was in these dualities. Watching, I became something of a seeing, unseen specter—a ghost of myself and others—hovering over the stirred-up snow globe of the show, both hiding from my reflection and manipulating it. *Couldn't I have done better?* I kept asking myself, shaking my head at this or that reactionary scene. *Wasn't I, already?* This was another bribe: the temptation to watch contestants under the bright, merciless lights of the set, while watching myself under brighter, but more merciful ones. To haunt them was to haunt what they were haunted by—what so many of us have been—what I still was. To be a spectator was to haunt the fantasy back. It was both a distraction from and a salve to the fact that, whenever I judged a contestant, it wasn't because I could've done better, but because I'd already done the same.

"Are you really going to marry Nathaniel?" a friend asked.

"I think so?" I said. The doubt wasn't about him, I tried to explain, but about a shared life of unshared domestic labor. My friend asked about our finances, the reality of long-term care, and my own dreams. And because I had no answers, I cried. I couldn't imagine leaving either. I didn't want to.

So I married Nathaniel. And then he got better.

I wish I could tell you it was me—that marriage really had, as the fantasy would go, healing properties. But the timing was coincidental. Nathaniel just happened to be prescribed, after much trial and error, something that worked like magic. It kind of *was* too: daydreams.

The brain rehabilitation program Nathaniel started called for three visualizations each day. A mix of memories and desires, they had to be as sense-based, vivid, and as specific as possible. Imagining, say, the texture of sand, the smell of sunscreen, the old-lady laughter of seagulls, Nathaniel's brain transported itself to the beach. Neurologically speaking, it was no longer in the dark room. The brain, it turned out, can't tell the difference between direct and dreamed sensations. Our dreams, then, are experienced as real. By which I mean, lived.

"We went on a bike ride," Nathaniel would sometimes tell me, or, "We went dancing in Buenos Aires!" The visualizations became memories. That I wasn't party to the conjuring meant I couldn't be the party pooper. I couldn't dream the dream's end at its very beginning. Instead, I got to hear it as a story—a sweet but distant scene I somehow happened to forget. But I was so happy to live it, again, for the first time.

Nathaniel isn't yet well enough to work, or go back to school, or drive. But he's well enough to cut carrots and do laundry and wash dishes. This summer, I watched him play his piano and pick blueberries and hike mountains. I watched him jump into a misty lake, then found myself in my white, cotton underwear—a pair I'd worn on purpose as an excuse, a way to prevent stripping, to write myself off this scene too. But Nathaniel took my hand, and I counted down, and then, we were in.

Without noticing, I stopped watching *The Bachelorette*. I stopped watching most everything else. One night, though, while scrolling through Netflix with Nathaniel, we came across the trailer for the UK edition of *Love is Blind*. "Would you watch this?" he asked.

"I will if you do," I said.

Nathaniel hardly ever says "no" outright and didn't this time, either. But he did say there was so much else, out there, that he wanted to see first.

Shir Kehila is a freelance writer, editor, and translator. Her writing has appeared or is forthcoming in *The Boiler*, *Kairos Rivista*, *The Albion Review*, and others. She holds an MFA from Columbia and received scholarships from the Bread Loaf Writers' Conference, Tin House Summer Workshop, and Monson Arts' residency program.

21

Trauma as Currency

Jessica Masterson

It is a tale as old as *The Bachelor* universe itself: the lead and a lucky one-on-one contestant share a candlelit meal (or, more accurately, *don't*) and take turns baring their ultra-white incisors at one another until the piped-in music takes a turn for the serious.

"I really like you," intones the lead, "but it just feels like you have some walls up." This is the cue. The contestant inhales deeply, turns to the lead, and spills: a past marred by abuse, perhaps; maybe the death of a parent; or, in the puritanical early seasons of the show, having come from a "broken home" (in other words, having divorced parents).

I don't mean to brag, but I have experienced all of these things. And as both a *Bachelor* viewer from way back (a friend and I still quote lead Matt Grant's enthused In-the-Moment[1] during a one-on-one in *The Bachelor: London Calling*: "I'm with a *hot* girl, in a *hot* car, on a *hot* date!") and a nerdy academic who often looks to the theories of long-dead white guys to explain present events, I see this recurring practice of sharing trauma as

1 Editor's note: Per *Refinery 29*'s glossary of *Bachelor* terms: "In the Moment (ITM): On-camera confessionals during which contestants tell viewers (read: producers) how they're feeling about a given situation, fellow contestant, or even the bachelor/bachelorette him/herself." https://www.refinery29.com/en-us/2018/12/219943/bachelor-terms-dictionary-guide

fundamentally ritualistic: It almost always occurs on a one-on-one and is usually preceded by the requisite, successive ITMs in which the lead signals their reservations about the contestant who just seems a little "closed off" and the contestant gears up for the big revelation. Once the trauma is unloaded, the lead responds, more often than not, with a note of thanks and, most importantly, with a coveted long-stem red rose. In trading tragedy for a tea rose, the contestant secures a spot for at least the next week.

As an impressionable young adult when I began watching *The Bachelor*, this ritual led me to internalize that a) these experiences carried with them the whiff of shame, vulnerability, or embarrassment; b) the "right person" would reassure you that you weren't some disgusting, reprehensible creature because your parents were divorced; and c) there was some reward to be gleaned from divulging these deep, dark secrets if done correctly (read: *with tears*).

As a more seasoned (if still impressionable) adult, I see this pattern as a naked exchange of what French sociologist Pierre Bourdieu termed "social capital." I won't bore you with all the details (though trust me when I say that I really, really want to), but one of this guy's major contributions to social thought was the idea that the concept of "capital" could apply to other contexts besides economics. Capital could also apply to, say, the particular, class- and race-based trappings of culture such that in certain interpersonal "markets," knowledge of neo-Expressionist visual artist Jean-Michel Basquiat is worth far more than knowledge of comedian Gabriel "Fluffy" Iglesias. Bourdieu also noted that we could tie capital to humans' linguistic and paralinguistic exchanges.[2] Once you start to view human speech in the way sociolinguists do, as a series of "bids" to be recognized as a certain kind of person doing a certain kind of thing, you might notice that conversations are essentially just a turn-taking exercise of "Look at me asking you a question! Aren't I so inquisitive/interested/curious?!" and "Look at me answering your question! Aren't I so thoughtful/interesting/knowledgeable?!"

2 Pierre Bourdieu, *Language and Symbolic Power*, ed. John Thompson, trans. Gino Raymond and Matthew Adamson (Harvard University Press, 1991).

Viewed in this light, the trauma-sharing ritual of *The Bachelor* and *The Bachelorette* becomes more than a predictable, eye roll-inducing quirk of the show; rather, it is a viable means for a contestant to exchange one form of currency (the trauma) for another (the rose). Each of these is, of course, symbolic: Revealing painful experiences—particularly those tinged with the stigma of shame—is taken to be a sign of growing trust, while the rose serves as a physical embodiment of the lead's continued interest in the contestant. In the market of any given season, this exchange is the engine that actually propels the show to its inevitable (and, to my mind, frequently anticlimactic) conclusion.

In a post-#MeToo climate, both flagship shows have seen more frequent and more serious admissions of trauma, including domestic violence and sexual assault. In some windowless corners of the internet, this trend has led to increased accusations of "trauma dumping" being lobbed at the contestants, as in Joey Graziadei's season. In this mode of thinking, trauma dumping is a form of emotional abuse characterized by the nonconsensual disclosure of traumatic experiences without regard for their impact on the listener. It's easy to see how this label might be affixed to various instances in the franchise's history.

But when I consider specific conversations the online commentators point to—including Brooklyn Willie's tearful discussion of her past experience in a physically abusive relationship during Zach Shallcross's season, or Kelsey Toussant's divulging of her religious trauma to Joey Graziadei—it seems that writing off these vulnerable admissions as mere *dumping* occludes a central feature of the show's machinery. I think it's less accurate to say that it's *dumping*—which implies a lack of consent from the lead—when the show's structure, honed over decades, is one that positions trauma-sharing as a reliable form of getting ahead in the competition. As Peter Weber assured contestant Kelsey Weier after she confided about her parents' divorce and her subsequent estrangement from her father, "You being so real and opening up, that's all that I'm asking for." To pervert a line heard from presidential campaign cycles of yore, *It's the social capital, stupid!*

You might be asking yourself at this point, "So what, Jessica?" And honestly, IDK! To be slightly confessional, I come to this franchise as someone with parents whose messy divorce continued to send shockwaves through my family right up until my mother's passing from cancer a few years ago. For me, the apparent uptick in this so-called trauma dumping in more recent seasons of *The Bachelor* has been cathartic, particularly as contestants have shed the shame that can accompany so many painful experiences and as leads have gotten better at receiving these confessions with genuine care in addition to the requisite rose-giving. I've noticed, too, that psychotherapy has made several high-profile appearances in recent seasons, from Aaron Bryant openly talking about the benefits of therapy in his life on Charity Lawson's season to Gabby Windey's multiple forthright declarations of how much therapy helped her in healing her own familial and relational trauma. The normalization of trauma as a part of life—and the admittedly small steps by leads to listen and affirm—signifies important progress.

On the other hand, there still seems to be a barrier to talking about certain forms of trauma, namely racial trauma. The sad stories privileged by the franchise's format are those with a clear narrative structure and, ideally, a redemptive, empowering arc. For many people of color in the US, the intergenerational nature of racial trauma within a racist society means that there *is* no fully overcoming it. I think about Jubilee Sharpe from Ben Higgins's season, who was predictably positioned as the villain and called "complicated" by erstwhile host Chris Harrison. As a transnational and transracial adoptee, and the only monoracial Black woman on her season, Jubilee drew ire from fans and her fellow contestants for provocatively proclaiming herself the only "real Black girl" in the cast. The attempts by Harrison to litigate these comments on the "Women Tell All" episode were comically inept and hopelessly shallow. Indeed, this is because until very, very recently, the concept of race has been treated by the show as simply another way to stir the pot for the sake of drama (like casting Lee Garrett—a man with a social media history full of racist remarks—on Rachel

Lindsay's season) or to provide pseudo-catharsis (as in Matt James's much-hyped reunion with his estranged father).

Racial trauma ontologically resists the hopeful arc that the show is intent on displaying whenever trauma is introduced, and similarly, while a few contestants have bravely shared their histories with eating disorders, the stunning lack of fat folks—particularly women—on the show means we don't hear stories of folks who are okay with existing in bodies that refuse to conform to oppressive societal standards. As a fat person myself, I was disappointed (though not surprised) to hear Zach Shallcross explain his former fatness as owing to his lack of self-love. In his retelling, once he started to love himself, major changes in diet and exercise naturally followed (post-season, he admitted that many of the tactics he employed to lose weight were characteristic of disordered eating). Fatness, in the *Bachelor* universe, is a kind of solvable trauma, not unlike leaving an abusive relationship or overcoming the grief of losing a parent. In all cases, of course, the reality is far more complex and nuanced than the show is interested in (or perhaps capable of) portraying.

All of this brings me back to the accusations of trauma dumping. While some of the tragedies confessed on the show are sudden and unexplainable, I think it's interesting that certain viewers are more inclined to criticize contestants for sharing their traumatic experiences than to ask why it is that so many of us have suffered some form of abuse in our lives. According to the National Sexual Violence Resource Center, nearly one in four women in the US have experienced rape or attempted rape in their lifetimes, and 81 percent of women report experiencing some form of sexual harassment, abuse, or violence.[3] Folks, this is *not okay*. Though I understand that we are unaccustomed to demanding much from our entertainment media, one might imagine that a show like *The Bachelor* and its offshoots—as programs consumed mostly by women—could take a more

3 "Understanding Sexual Abuse, Assault, and Harassment," National Sexual Violence Resource Center, updated 2025, accessed April 28, 2025, https://www.nsvrc.org/resource/2500/understanding-sexual-abuse-assault-and-harassment.

activist stance towards sexual violence than simply flashing a generic title card with crisis hotline info at the end of an episode. I've learned by now that I can't count on *The Bachelor* to do right by people of color, or fat folks, or, more broadly, *women*—but dang it, I think we can and should still demand better.

So, for the time being, I invite you to watch the next season of *The Bachelor* or *The Bachelorette* with a critical eye toward how trauma is presented—whose trauma is given airtime, how it is received, and whether it conforms to or (hopefully!) subverts the happy-ending imperative. Do the folks sharing seem like they *want* to talk about these aspects of their lives? Is there genuine catharsis to be gained? Does the vulnerability feel reciprocal? At the end of the day, I want you to remember ol' Pierre: It's not really so much about the trauma itself; instead, each of these folks has a form of social capital to trade with the other, and if they follow the tacit, agreed-upon rules, it will be a successful exchange. Each of them just has to, as they say, "trust in the process."

Jessica Masterson is a professor and researcher in the Pacific Northwest. When not professing, she obsessively consumes pop culture and occasionally writes about it.

22

An Enduring Love

Stevie K. Seibert Desjarlais

I've been in Bachelor Nation since the very beginning. I was in high school in 2002, so even though she has no recollection of it, I must've watched the first season with my mom. I remember how scandalized we were by the "dessert in the sheets" room service that the final couple—Alex Michel and Amanda Marsh—ordered to their suite. It came complete with a rubber sheet and various syrups. That was spicy TV for the early aughts and for teenaged me! (Isn't memory a funny thing? Why would I retain this information rent-free instead of something more meaningful or practical?) Since that first season, I've realized something about myself: A big part of my viewing pleasure comes from watching with others, preferably with those who play the believing game with me as I look for authentic human connection on-screen. Aside from watching early episodes with my mom, I've coaxed other family members to tune in with me, and have even proselytized a bit to convince friends, like Ilana Masad and Katie McWain, to invest energy into the shows.

Once, when I was home visiting, I (as an adult) pleaded with my dad to watch *The Bachelorette* with me. Not because I wanted to convert him into a viewer, but because he has unyielding control of the TV remote. Oh man, did I live to regret my choice. He provided a relentless stream of commentary—something akin to *Mystery Science Theater 3000*—and none of it was positive. Most memorably, he made fun of the men crying on-screen. To date, that was the only episode of the franchise I've ever asked and gotten him to watch. Days later, we were watching *First Blood* (remember—unyielding control of the TV remote) and, when Rambo started to cry, I asked my dad why he wasn't mocking him. Crying over comrades lost in war was a legitimate reason for a man to emote, he told me, but feeling left out on a competitive dating show was *not*. My dad put it in different words, but I understood the line he was attempting to draw even if I didn't agree.[1]

While I haven't watched every season, I've committed to consistent viewership since 2015. Then and now, my memories of what I see on-screen are more often than not tethered to the relationships that I have with the people I watch with—my mom, my dad, my spouse, my friends… I've willingly and unwillingly pulled them into my fascination with this show at one time or another. As someone who professionally studies gender and pop culture, I've got a built-in defense for why I continue to engage with *The Bachelor* franchise; even so, defending the shows is not a hill I will ever die on. But I cannot let it go just yet, either, because it links me to some of my best memories of Katie.

You don't need me to tell you how hard it is to make friends as an adult, right? When I found myself back in grad school in 2014, I had already moved across the country a time or two with my husband. Getting a PhD in English was an opportunity to pursue a dream. But it was a tough adjustment after having been away from academia and being a little battle-worn from real life stuff. I met Katie during orientation week, when she led a session on teaching college composition. With Katie—now it's all going to sound as cliché as the catchphrases on the show—it felt like an instant attraction. She was so smart, so adept at the work she did with

1 Update: During Mel Owen's *Golden Bachelor* season, I suggested that my dad watch some episodes and to my surprise, he did! He identified the women that he found most interesting, but said, "I am definitely not the target demographic."

her teaching and research, so thoughtful and kind too. These descriptors fall short of conveying the extent of my appreciation for who Katie became as my friend at that point in both of our lives. Do you know the feeling of having someone who you can let it all hang out with? Katie was a mentor to me professionally (despite being two years younger)—and she was someone who I could really be human with.

Once Katie started watching *The Bach* with me, she was a quick convert. She mirrored my own enthusiasm back to me as I analyzed the mannerisms of the people we watched on-screen. She would often let me know what her dad (whom she convinced to watch too) would say about the show's dating dynamics. Most memorably, when watching *Bachelor in Paradise* for the first time, he said something to the effect of, "This is not a high-quality show." It made Katie and me laugh because, *duh*.

Peter "Pilot Pete" Weber's season was the first I had to watch without Katie, following her death in September 2019. I like to know what's coming, which is why I read spoilers, so I knew Pete had been picked when Katie texted me just a few days before she died, saying, "I want to know who the new bachelor will be! (But don't tell me if you've read spoilers!)" She never did find out, and I wish I could've told her how disappointed I was that it wasn't Tyler Cameron. Both Pete and Tyler were contestants on Hannah Brown's season of *The Bachelorette*, which Katie and I watched closely at my weekly viewing parties. Notoriously, Hannah B. said on-screen that season, "I've had sex…and Jesus still loves me." The screaming in my living room that night was louder than ever—had anyone on the show ever been so clear about their sexual independence while also affirming their faith? It was fascinating! What an unexpected combination! It isn't so much that Katie or I thought that Hannah B., or any of the other people on-screen, were heroes or role models. They were and are human, and that's what makes them interesting.

What I felt about Pilot Pete has long been par for the course in *The Bachelor* franchise. Many of the men are so damn disappointing: They lack emotional maturity and/or fail to break away from heterosexist norms. When there was truly a standout—a man with the capacity to show respect for a woman in the given parameters of the show—I would discuss with Katie what made him distinctive. We would ask ourselves: Is he a feminist? Does he represent a different sort of masculinity? If the Bachelorette doesn't pick him, shouldn't he be the next Bachelor? Trust me when I say that even though we drank wine while watching, the depth of our analyses into masculine performances went further into the weeds than most *Bachelor* viewing parties across America.

Oddly (sometimes it feels downright ridiculous), my grief for Katie, such an important person in my life, is tangled up in these silly shows. Along with lamenting Pilot Pete as that season's Bachelor (a disappointment that just keeps on giving), I also wish I could've told Katie how much she meant to me, how much I appreciated that I could share my thoughts with a friend candidly and have my thoughts be received with mutual honesty. I know that I did say such things often because it was no secret that she had a profound impact on me. But I would love the opportunity to say it again, and again. I would love the chance to talk about this franchise with her again, to share with her the shifts that I've seen on-screen in terms of the ways men, women, and the mess of dating experiences have evolved or devolved in the last few years. Our friendship was so much more than her attending my weekly watch parties—she championed me through grad school and showed up for me in ways that nobody had before and nobody has since. But the mindless fodder of dating on television and the surprisingly mindful conversations that were borne out of watching together are entirely woven through my memories of Katie. It's the companionship that I miss the most.

I especially wish Katie could've shared Gabby Windey and Rachel Recchia's season with me. Many folks assumed that the two women who had been simultaneously and unceremoniously dumped by Clayton Echard (another disappointing Bachelor) would be pitted against one another (which had happened to Kaitlyn Bristowe and Britt Nilsson). As women with similar aspirations, Katie and I could've felt pitted against one another too. This happens to women more broadly. But there was something about Gabby and Rachel—the way they consistently showed up for one another—that reminded me of my friendship with Katie. The way they looked at one another, leaned on one another both physically and emotionally throughout the season, and then later, when sitting on the couch side-by-side during an epic After the Final Rose clusterfuck.

There were times when Katie and I leaned on one another too. If you watched Gabby and Rachel's season, you might recall a certain dude that called Gabby "rough around the edges." *That guy* couldn't be bothered to show basic respect to women *even while being filmed for a nationally watched television program.* Don't we all know *that guy*? In fact, one such guy told Katie, "I respect women, I just don't respect you." When she told me, I was floored. I was taken back to that memory when I saw Rachel fired up, asking Gabby if she wanted to confront the men who put her down. Friends show up when *that guy* tries to make us feel small and unworthy. Seeing friends on-screen hold space for each other and challenging the men that they were dating to be better—well, I guess that's a big part of why I keep watching. I'm looking for glimpses of that type of companionship that was so dear to me.

Now that I am without a local viewing party, I still get texts from friends and family when they see a headline or promo that is especially salacious to get my hot take. (I would also like to note that I don't watch alone: Ilana and I tune in on Hulu the day after airing so that we can, first, avoid commercials; second, watch at the same time even though we live in different time zones, and, third, react in a constant stream of texts.) I appreciate that I hold expert status in their eyes. But there isn't anything quite like being able to pick up an ongoing back-and-forth rant that spans years without having to establish context. Even my references to Pilot Pete, Tyler Cameron, Clayton, Hannah B., Rachel, and Gabby are a testament to the specificity of this franchise.

Making friends as an adult is daunting because when you are cast out into the big ocean of human experience, it can feel impossible to find common ground in which to plant seeds capable of growing strong bonds. Had my friendship with Katie been entirely professionally based, I know that I'd still be better for knowing her. But the fact that we had more—like this pop culture springboard for conversations (that covered many topics that don't just come up naturally)—meant that we had a vehicle for dialogue outside of our particular teaching and research interests. On the shows, the friendships that the women make among themselves, independent from and frequently more intimate and longer lasting than the relationships they have with the Bachelor, are the real love stories.

Recent *Golden* additions to the franchise underscore this longing for connection—the human need for companionship, to be seen for all that we contain as complex beings. If you're looking for a good ugly cry, watch Jonathan Rone on the first season's "Men Tell All" episode of *The Golden Bachelorette* as he shares the sticky notes that Mark Anderson wrote to him while they were both staying in the Bachelor Mansion.

> Jonathan,
>
> Just in case I don't get to stay…
> I am humbled to have met you. I have enjoyed this time shared. Place this sticky note on your mirror and remind yourself that you are a fantastic human being!
>
> Mark

The second sticky note says:

> I am STRONG
> I am INTERESTING
> I am HANDSOME
> I am DESERVING
> I am ENOUGH

On-screen, both men—and many of the others on stage—cried. For me, it's a moment that bundles up everything: men demonstrating beautiful emotional maturity and connection—a type of masculinity that is worthy of recognition; friends showing up for each other; reality TV capturing humans taking the time to be fully human.

Sometimes, it feels like there is so little energy left over from our busy lives to honor friendships. Other times, the smallest gestures, like a sticky note or coming over to watch a trashy reality TV show on a weeknight, can demonstrate the beating heart of companionship. When I landed my first academic job—a teaching post-doc—Katie sent me a note of encouragement. I reread it all the time and carry it in my work bag. Even though Katie is no longer with me physically, her voice still echoes in my mind as I advance, overcome hurdles, and watch new episodes; it's an enduring love story.

Stevie K. Seibert Desjarlais is an assistant professor at the University of Nebraska-Omaha. Her teaching and research interests include representations of gender, race, and class in US literature, film, and pop culture. Her writing appears in the *Quarterly Review of Film and Video*, *Journal of Popular Film and Television*, and *Pedagogy*. Even though she now lives in Nebraska—with her husband and animals—Stevie is a Southern Californian at heart.

23

The Real Final Rose is the Friends We Made Along the Way

Erin Kayata

Perched on the couch in my living room, my friend Linsey and I are deep in discussion over glasses of wine and a board piled with all of Trader Joe's finest dried fruit and cheese options.

The topic of conversation is antebellum balls. They are a foreign concept to me as a lifelong northerner, but Linsey, a Texan by birth, has a little more insight. She fills me in on what they are, and together, we discuss their racist roots in the Civil War era. I never realized what a huge part they were of Southern culture or how much Linsey knew about this world, despite having known her for years.

What prompted this conversation? The final episodes of Matt James's season of *The Bachelor*. While the season was airing, it had come out that on top of attending a plantation-themed party in college, frontrunner Rachael Kirkconnell had liked racist posts and allegedly bullied girls in high school for being attracted to Black men. The fallout over this would eventually lead to longtime host, Chris Harrison, being released from the franchise.

But at that moment, Linsey and I were just weighing in on how, if at all, Matt and Rachael could move forward, given her past actions. (Consensus: It's not up to us white women, obviously, but up to Matt, who did ultimately decide to ride off into the metaphorical sunset with Rachael, albeit without the signature *Bachelor* engagement.)

"Oh my God, this is like watching baseball with two physicists," Linsey's husband interrupts us from the corner of my living room where he's perched on a rocking chair, evidently shocked by how much analysis we can do from one episode of *The Bachelor*.

He's not the only one. If you'd told me a few years earlier that I'd be watching *The Bachelor* religiously, never mind having a conversation about race prompted by an episode, I would've found that as unbelievable as the concept of the show itself.

The first season of *The Bachelor* aired when I was in second grade, so for most of my life, the franchise has been cafeteria and water cooler fodder. But I was single when I aged into the show's main demographic. I knew firsthand how hard it was to find love on a dating app. I didn't believe anyone could find it in a pool of only thirty or so people and had no interest in watching a series that seemed to set its participants up to fail.

I got into *The Bachelor* for the same reason people (supposedly) apply to be on the show: I was searching for connection. Before Linsey was my friend, she was my roommate. Life circumstances threw us, along with our friend Macaela, together into a two-bedroom apartment in Stamford, Connecticut, which we turned into a three-bedroom using a temporary wall.

But to make the space actually feel like our home, we established rituals. Every Monday, Macaela would make popcorn in a pot on the stove with the perfect ratio of salt and butter and we would sit on the brown couch with the squishy cushions and watch Colton Underwood on *The Bachelor*. I didn't plan to watch at first, but I would sit with my roommates for the company. And like contestants on the show itself, I gradually fell in love...not with the Bachelor himself, but with the series and making fun of it with my new roommates and now friends.

Over time, we began adding more people to our watch crew. My coworker, Jo, began joining us during Hannah Brown's season, often bringing ingredients to make a complex cocktail in our tiny kitchen before the episode started. Then we'd sip while watching Hannah make the mistake of choosing dog food jingle Jed Wyatt over the dancing contractor, Tyler Cameron.

This was the same season that one of the contestants, Luke Parker, had an explosive argument with Hannah over her sexual history, criticizing her for having sex outside of marriage. After telling Luke he can't tell her what to do or not do when it comes to the upcoming Fantasy Suites, Hannah finally ends the fight by declaring she has had sex and Jesus still loves her.

Many around the United States applauded Hannah for her response, myself included. To me, Hannah's ownership of her sex life reflected my own feelings. Not everyone in our watch group agreed.

I was raised Catholic with abstinence-only sex education, yet for me, Catholicism was more a family tradition than something I took seriously. But for some in my watch group, religion was more than just being forced to go to church on Sunday and holidays. It defined the way they lived their lives and included their stances on premarital sex. I found out that some *did* believe in the abstinence I came to shun in my late teens.

None of my friends were fans of the way Luke had spoken to Hannah, but some did understand his point: As a fellow Christian, he was trying to call out what he considered to be a sin. He just did it wrong. "That episode was really frustrating," one of my friends said at the time, criticizing Luke P. for the sense of superiority with which he approached Hannah. He should've been coming instead, she told me, from a place of love.

Luke P. and Hannah's argument nuked their relationship on the show. He quickly went from a top contender to getting sent home—twice. (Who can forget how, when he returned during a rose ceremony after their fight, Hannah simply moved the podium past him in an attempt to ignore his persistence?)

Their argument had the opposite effect on my friends and me, though. I didn't agree with their views on premarital sex being a bad thing. But our conversation gave me a better understanding and respect for Christianity than years of CCD (Sunday school, for those who aren't Catholic), which primarily consisted of going through workbooks on the Bible in my church basement. And while we disagreed on the "right" and "wrong" of premarital sex, we agreed where it was important: approaching someone from a place of judgment is bad.

This disagreement turned out to be an excellent test of our friendships' strength. After that, some of my friends came to me about having sex for the first time after years of abstinence, asking me about my experiences finding and going to a gynecologist. Soon, we were swapping stories about getting IUDs. "Talking about sex on the show helped me feel comfortable broaching the topic with you guys," my friend told me later.

Over the next year, our watch parties became a standing appointment of sorts, and people could pop in and out each week as they pleased. By the following year, we had at least half a dozen people gathered in our living room on Tuesday evening to watch the season finale for Pilot Pete (Peter Weber).

We didn't know it'd be the last time we'd gather. The next time we tuned in to watch was through Zoom. Our Connecticut crew was now scattered around the country, quarantining from spots in California, Texas, and Massachusetts.

While we found that *Listen to Your Heart*, a musical *Bachelor* spin-off that lasted for one forgettable season, didn't do much for us, it was a routine in a time that had both too much consistency and none at all. Our apartment gatherings had been our constant. Now, instead of meeting in our living room, we were propping our laptops on coffee tables and kitchen counters as we made dinner, tuning in while doing the dishes, eating, or sipping more homemade cocktails.

We watched as *The Bachelor* ventured a Covid season with Clare Crawley and then Tayshia Adams (the latter remains a group favorite). By the time Matt James's season rolled around, Linsey was back in Connecticut, and we would sometimes venture an in-person viewing.

As a group, we saw one on-air relationship after another crumble when it came to disagreements. Meanwhile, our relationships grew as we discussed the same issues that plagued the franchise's fleeting romances.

The show became a jumping-off point for conversations about religion, having children, and trauma. On paper, it would seem as though these topics would tear us apart. My watch group and I probably seem to have less in common than some of the contestants do with each season's lead. Among our mix is a married mom of two, a couple of married women who haven't committed to parenthood yet, a few single women, and some in new relationships. Most of us are straight, but some of us are queer (one of my friends used Gabby Windey's coming out to broach her own sexuality with us). We all grew up in different parts of the country, from Fresno to Boston.

Through *The Bachelor*, I found that I shared a lot in common with people who seemed so different from me. We loved Tayshia and how she sent home one of her finalists for not being on the same page as her religion-wise (a smart decision, we all agreed) but got frustrated with the male contestants who seemingly weaponized therapy talk. We also agreed the "trauma dump" dates (usually the first one-on-ones) were just a cheap way to feign intimacy. Overall, we all agreed with my original analysis: The show was not a good way to find love.

In 2021, Covid restrictions eased, and we were able to reunite in person for the first time at the New York City Marathon (where we cheered on our friends from the sidelines, as well as our beloved Tayshia, who flashed Macaela, Jo, and me a dazzling smile as she sprinted by). But we were all still living in different parts of the country. At a time when many were shying away from virtual get-togethers, burnt out on a year of connecting online, we continued to log on each week to watch.

I recently asked my friends why they think we kept coming together.

"Sometimes I feel like you want something more than just, 'let's get together,'" Jo said. "I don't know why it's so hard sometimes to be like, 'we're just gonna have a monthly get together,' but it was nice to have a set time every week or two weeks where we were all talking."

"We have so many things to talk about," Abby added. "But this was a backdrop."

Over the years, our weekly sessions became about far more than just the show. I tuned in for *The Bachelor* drama as much as I did to see what vintage market find Abby added to her new studio apartment on the Upper West Side or how Liz's classes for her master's were going.

The morning of one of our watch sessions, I woke up to a text from my mom telling me my grandfather was diagnosed with Alzheimer's. I went through the day in such a daze that I didn't even realize I'd cut myself on the glass of a photo frame I was moving until I was bleeding. I knew I needed a night to decompress alone.

If this had happened a few years prior, I wouldn't have known how to share the news with my friends without seeming depressing. Having our weekly watch session gave me an easy way to bring it up without feeling awkward. When my grandfather died two years later, I found flowers and a care package on my doorstep after the funeral, sent by my friends who'd seen me through the whole journey of his illness.

Today, our *Bachelor* crew is down to six. We haven't watched the show in a while and, to be frank, I don't know if we ever will again. (I have qualms after seeing the show's lack of diligence in vetting its contestants, particularly for Jenn Tran's season.) Much like many established couples from the show, we have distanced ourselves from the franchise.

Macaela, Linsey, and I moved out of our shared apartment in 2020 and now all live in different states, and most of our other watch group friends are back in New York. Part of my daily routine now is popping into the group chat the six of us share, usually when I'm bored at work and want some different thoughts about the latest political news or where to buy new dress pants. I didn't expect to find love on this journey, but like every other *Bachelor* contestant, I was surprised when I did…only this time, in my friends.

Erin Kayata is a writer, journalist, and pop culture enthusiast. Her work has appeared in *Tangled Locks Journal*, *The Manifest Station*, *Reader's Digest*, and *USA Today*. She has also worked as a staff writer for *Boston* magazine and Hearst newspapers. She lives in the Boston area with her husband and their cat.

24

Late-Stage Heterosexuality and Me

Milo R. Muise

When my friends ask why I watch *The Bachelor*, I say that I'm tuning in for the end of heterosexuality. Just as late-stage capitalism describes an unsustainable and exploitative final stop on the Capitalism Express, *The Bachelor* depicts decidedly men and decidedly women clinging to the last shreds of their "straight lifestyle" as the whole enterprise collapses. *They can't* still *be doing this*, I think as the Bachelor asks four fathers he's just met for their daughters' hands in hypothetical marriage. *We must be close now.*

My viewership began as part anthropological, part vengeful, part schadenfreude. "Straight culture" has always been a mystery to me, an oddity made all the odder for its naturalization. Throughout my life, I have been placed outside of its normative bounds over and over, first as a bisexual, then a lesbian, then a queer person, then a queer transmasculine person, and finally a queer transmasc polyamorous person. Though I never particularly mourned my rejection from this particular scene, it can be painful to be in a marginal position vis-à-vis your peers, at least before you discover the power in being outside the system. Watching *The Bachelor*, I got to peek into a party I wasn't invited to and confirmed that the party sucked.

As with any bad party, there are tears. A recent trope plays the sounds of one of the contestants (usually a woman) sobbing over images of empty hotel hallways, Airbnb rooms, and/or airplane hangars. (The men's tears are a purely visual medium, meant to inspire a sense of humanity that their manicured appearance and often stilted speaking patterns might otherwise lack.) Disembodied crying has never been deployed more powerfully than at the end of Arie Luyendyk Jr.'s infamous *Bachelor* season. Amid one of their post-finale Happy Couple Weekends, Arie informed his fiancée, Becca Kufrin, that he had decided to end their engagement and propose instead to his runner-up Lauren Burnham. After a visceral confrontation, Becca ran into a room and closed the door, unavailable to the cameras but still miked. What followed was a series of matter-of-fact static shots of the sterile Airbnb, each animated by the haunting sound of Becca's sobs. Her cries echoed through each empty all-white room, its cream furniture and mass-produced wall art looking on indifferently. It was a place so new, with its grey laminate flooring and freshly sodded backyard, that one could reasonably expect that this event was its first trauma.

But on *The Bachelor*, nothing is a new build: not its values, not its language, and especially not its trauma. It is as if I am watching a historical reenactment from the not-so-distant past, just dressed in current fashions and set design. Marriage is still a sacred institution, an indicator of one's moral fortitude, and also financially motivated, though the way *The Bachelor* monetizes its influencer couples is a novel development beyond dowries and tax incentives. Contestants who come from divorced families fret about how to convince the lead that they have not been tainted by their checkered past and are, in fact, capable of commitment. As recently as 2021, lead Matt James earnestly proclaimed to come from a "broken home," a phrase that was outmoded even during my parents' divorce in 1995.

My entry point to the franchise was through *The Bachelor*'s claim-to-feminism *The Bachelorette*. It was the spring of 2016, and every week, my partner and I would huddle on the miniature couch in our Portland, Oregon, apartment to watch the next climactic installment. Politically, White Middle America (a core *Bachelor* audience demographic) was liberal obsession, portrayed as a "forgotten" people who were now exacting revenge via Donald Trump. Personally, I was three years on testosterone, and my long-term partner Katie and I had just opened our relationship after a year of rigorous intention-setting. We were compelled by the show's contradictions—its concomitant performance and refusal of polyamory, for one—and how watching a show that overlooked our existence on nearly every level made *us* into a contradiction.

Mostly, though, we were compelled by JoJo Fletcher. A charismatic Texas beauty queen with a captivating heartbreak narrative from her season as a contestant, she was undoubtedly the star of the show. JoJo was unapologetic, willing to put her men in their place, while also wielding a quick, intelligent sense of humor. This was *her* journey, and she was going to get what she needed out of it. Remarkably, she did; her marriage to (spoiler) Jordan Rodgers is one of the relatively rare show relationships that has survived to the present day. She was the kind of woman I never could have been, dating men I had no interest in being, and yet. *I want to drink wine on a couch with her*, I'd say, *and I don't even like wine!*

In hindsight, JoJo was a perfect introduction to *The Bachelorette*, effortlessly embodying an impossible role. A modern Bachelorette, like a certain kind of modern heterosexual woman, must be independent, but not so independent that her man is unnecessary, or worse, emasculated. She thinks for herself, but that thinking never leads her too far from the traditions that raised her. She is liberal-adjacent (on some social issues, anyway) and Christian, but not to the point of alienating conservatives or secular society. Caught in so many double binds, it is a miracle she even makes it up the Mansion's front steps.

I was facing my own set of gendered obstacles, having reached a stage of my transition where the world was beginning to reliably cast me as a Man™, regardless of my non-binary identity. There are, of course, far worse things than being erroneously perceived as a white guy, but I felt as miscast as the one vaguely alternative woman exiting the limo on the first night of every *Bachelor* season. *Me?* I'd think whenever a stranger referred to me using "he," or a man clapped me on the back in a menacing show of fraternity. Every office party and extended family gathering felt like an adolescent initiation, a test of whether I had learned my lines or still needed the script. Acquaintances started asking Katie and me when we were going to have kids, something that had never been a topic of conversation before. I found myself in a dilemma faced by many a transsexual of yore: I had accidentally transitioned us into heterosexuals!

I started campily committing to the bit, trying to see how long I could last in a conversation before my cis dude persona began to strain credulity. I felt like an interloper, an ineffectual spy that was, nevertheless, going undetected. *Is this how they feel?* I wondered as I watched the cast commit to their own bits: Villain, Bullying Victim, Diva, Girl/Boy Next Door, Constant Crier, Scammer, Single Mom/Dad, Diplomat, Weirdo. No one commits more than the Alpha Male who enacts a performance of masculinity so exaggerated it slips into parody: a man reduced to his protein intake, chivalry, and near homosocial rivalry with other men. *Is he just waiting for someone to call his bluff?*

Love always involves fantasy, and heterosexuality tends to necessitate a bit of role play: No one is the Man™ or Woman™ heterosexuality requires them to be. What makes *The Bachelor* interesting is how it manifests this blend of artifice and reality. We watch people who are very likely in love *pretending* to be in love, an uncanny mimicry that rings both true and hollow. *The Bachelor* is a show of edits and omissions, as highly produced as Heterosexuality™ itself. The cast goes through the motions of a fairy-tale romance, but they never get to eat their candlelit dinner, acknowledge their jet lag, or have an important conversation during the day, no matter how awkward it makes their one-on-one.

When they do talk, there isn't much to say. The show employs a repetitive lexicon that is impressive for its paucity. The contestants repeat the cliché scripts that preceded them: They can *see themselves falling*, they *have walls up*, they've *been hurt before*, they need to *follow their heart*, they *just can't get there*, they were *blindsided*, and incredibly, this limited vocabulary (freighted with the historical weight of their ritual usage?) results in feeling *seen*, *known*, and even *loved*. Conversations often skim or altogether avoid important topics like one's parenting philosophies, how one handles conflict, or what one is looking for in a marriage. Instead, the contestants recount tedious interactions we've already seen as a show of intimacy (*Remember when you came up to me during the volleyball game group date? That meant a lot*), or divulge their One Big Trauma, which the lead receives with compassionate eye contact and some variation of *I'm so sorry that happened, but I know that it shaped you into the strong woman/compassionate man you are today*.

There might be moments on the show that feel dramatic or sweet or vulnerable, but they're also at least a little calculated. It is only in the final scene of each episode, hidden after the end credits and the next week's promo, where we occasionally get a flash of genuine relating. Here, the producers give us a blooper, or a sweet, silly moment between the lead and one of their dates. I get more insight into the relationship in these thirty-second increments than I do in two-hour episodes. A contestant that had previously seemed dull suddenly comes to life; a chemistry that had seemed forced turns electric. *Oh, I get why she likes him now. He's funny!*

These examples are sparse; *The Bachelor* is too invested in heterosexuality's rules and regulations to allow for much spontaneity. Rules are, understandably, comforting. They tell us who and how to be, they give us a clear set of "right" and "wrong." Yet, they are never quite as straightforward as they lead us to believe. When is the appropriate time to sleep with someone, to tell them you love them, or to move in together? Can you be in a healthy monogamous partnership and still have cross-gender friendships, get crushes on other people, or go to strip clubs? Many people might think that these questions have obvious answers, and yet those "obvious" answers differ from person to person. An entire industry of sitcoms revolves around the miscommunications that abound in heterosexual dating, but *The Bachelor* takes a more tragic approach. In these moments, the producers' manipulated illusion falters and, briefly, if we catch it, a sliver of the world beyond this fantasy comes into frame.

On Clayton Echard's season, his post-fantasy suites Rose Ceremony was devastated by a shocking admission: He had "been intimate" with two of the three finalists, and he was in love with all three. Susie Evans, edited to appear as Clayton's first choice, self-eliminated prior to the ceremony, leaving Rachel Recchia and Gabby Windey with a heartbroken lead. He stumbled his way through a series of confessions that didn't leave anyone feeling *chosen*. The women's upset was understandable but also illustrated their desire for a monogamy the show won't give them until after the final rose has been handed out.

Rachel and Gabby fled to different corners of the large glassy building, the sounds of their crying reverberating off the cold concrete floors. While Clayton talked with host Jesse, their sobs played as a ghostly chorus in the background. Their suffering became intermixed; despite their distance from one another, they cried together. From this shared pain, they would go on to form a friendship more compelling than many of the straight romances *The Bachelor* produces.

For ninety-seven percent of the cast (sometimes even one hundred percent!), *The Bachelor* is about a failed relationship, not a successful one. Many tearful limo riders hold themselves responsible for this statistic. *If only I had been enough. Why wasn't I enough? I'll never be enough!* That last piece is true—but it is a structural failing, not a personal one. To imagine that a single person could unfailingly meet all of one's emotional, sexual, romantic, spiritual, intellectual, and social needs is one of the show's most pernicious fantasies.

As the seasons continue, the casualties of heterosexuality only grow in numbers. Cry in your limos, your hotel rooms, overlooking your beautiful vistas on your verandas. Once you've dried your tears (or, better yet, worn your memeified crying face on a t-shirt as Gabby did), you're invited to join those of us who have crossed over to the other side. The heterosexual apocalypse is upon us, and it's time to celebrate.

Milo R. Muise is a trans writer from New England. An alum of the University of Idaho's MFA program and the Tin House Summer Workshop, they also received a 2018 Oregon Literary Fellowship in poetry. Their debut chapbook, *TL;DR*, is out now with Newfound Press. Milo lives in Portland, Oregon, with their loves and their dog, Rigatoni Collette. You can reach them at www.milo-muise.com.

25

Watching *The Bachelorette* as a Certified Forensic Interviewer

Sarah Gerard

I'm taking an online course to become a certified forensic interviewer. My classmates are from the loss prevention, government, human resources, law enforcement, and private investigation sectors. I'm in the last category. Our instructor calls us *elite interviewers*. He's been an interrogation trainer for thirty-three years and is an expert in human behavior. This class will bring us to the cutting edge of gathering intel from victims, witnesses, and suspects.

Tonight, my husband and I are catching up on the latest episode of Jenn Tran's season of *The Bachelorette*. We first noticed Jenn on Joey Graziadei's season, when they surfed and made out on the sand, but she didn't make it into the top three. On last week's episode, we watched her making out with Sam McKinney. Again. Because they have nothing to talk about, which is glaring to us, but Jenn has yet to notice. Sam has noticed, though, and he's trying to hide that his lack of a personality is the problem.

We don't trust Sam M., twenty-seven, the contractor from Myrtle Beach, South Carolina. Jenn called him a "sexy cowboy" in the first episode while the music suggested he would go far in the season. "I will always keep the main thing the main thing, and my main thing is finding my person," he'd said for the first time—of many. He told Jenn he'd been single for a year, which would turn out to be a lie. He also said he'd previously been engaged to a girl he'd met in middle school. Their life was planned out, but she "ended up cheating."

This passive verbiage bothered me. I'd characterize it as an explanatory denial, the subject explaining why they wouldn't have been involved in something, like the end of a relationship, rather than making a direct, emphatic denial of involvement. It's a way of trying to take control of the narrative and a lie of minimization. Sam M. can't admit that he was at least partially responsible for the end of his relationship. That her cheating was but the last straw.

Underscoring this, I find Sam M. to be closed off. Garbled. His mumbling makes it difficult to understand what he's saying. It's as though his voice wants to hide behind his lips, doesn't want to be clearly heard, because then it might be studied for signs of lying. Sam's hand frequently travels to his mouth as though to stop what's trying to escape. His face is emotionless, revealing nothing.

Let's assume that, in any given season, someone is always on *The Bachelorette* for the wrong reasons. That's the crime under investigation and our objective as elite interviewers is to apprehend them as quickly as possible. So, we start with behavioral interviews. Their purpose is to identify the truthful contestants and remove them from suspicion. A byproduct of this process is that we identify the untruthful ones.

Behavioral interviews begin with the gathering of biographical information. Jenn asks questions that the guys are likely to answer truthfully:

What's your name? Where do you live? What do you do for work? This gives her a sense of their behavioral norms—how they talk when they're not trying to hide something. It also helps her build rapport. During which, she can try to find common interests with these guys, things they share.

Then, she focuses on the issue under investigation: Can she trust any of them as her future husband? Each question, in a neutral, non-accusatory manner, should attempt to elicit clear, interpretable responses that are typical of truth or deception.

For instance, Jenn can ask, "Have you ever cheated on your partner?" Her subject's body language along with the actual content of his answer will reveal his level of trustworthiness. Does he hesitate? Press his lips together? Reposition on the loveseat? Feign confusion? Does he answer indirectly or avoid answering—and instead say something about finding a "ferocious love," like Sam M. says, over and over?

Jenn fed her guys this phrase, *ferocious love*, after first using it during her introduction as the next Bachelorette. Sam M. had latched onto it. An interviewer must be aware of when her subject is suggestible, such as children or people with low intelligence, or when he is simply echoing her words back to her, telling her what she wants to hear.

Another approach to interrogation entails starting with the person or persons most likely to be involved in the crime—in this case, of being there for the wrong reasons. This is the approach Jenn seems to have unwittingly taken when she gave Sam M. the First Impression Rose. One drawback of this approach is that the elite interviewer hasn't yet gathered information about her subject from other parties, before interrogating him. But an advantage is that, by gathering her suspect's version of events early on, Jenn can test it against subsequent versions.

For tonight's group date, Jenn and the guys visit the iHeart Radio station as guests on a talk show. "Today is all about communication," says Jenn, since a radio is made for listening. "Listening to your partner and communication is so important." Watching from our couch, my husband and I laugh. We have already seen how, on their one-on-one date in Australia, Sam M. was a bad listener. He had pressured Jenn—who cried, insisting she was terrified of heights and didn't want to go through with it—into bungee jumping off a skyscraper.

Now Jenn tells the camera that she's noticed her connection with Sam M. is "more physical than emotional." She wants to break through that barrier with him today, to build an emotional connection. She says there are "red flags" and that there's "something missing there."

"I'm someone who's gonna keep the main thing the main thing," Sam tells the camera. An elite interviewer needs to be alert to whether a subject is providing scripted answers, especially on *The Bachelor* franchise.

Sam is seated next to Jenn before a microphone. Everyone is on the air. The hosts play a game of rapid-fire association with the guys, starting with Spencer Conley, thirty, a pet portrait entrepreneur from Dallas. "*Rose*," one of the hosts says to him. "Me," says Spencer.

"*Shower*," they say to Grant Ellis, a thirty-year-old day trader from New Jersey.

"Every day," he says. Everyone laughs.

"*Fantasy suite*," they say to Sam M.

Sam chuckles to discharge his discomfort and buy time.

Devin Strader, twenty-eight, a freight company owner from Houston, urges him on. "It's rapid-fire."

"Aggressive," says Sam.

Everyone gets quiet.

"What did you say?" says one host, visibly horrified. "*Aggressive*?"

"What the hell?" says Jenn, under her breath.

"Is that what he said?" says another host.

"Aggressive," says another one.

Some of the guys cover their faces in embarrassment.

"Okay," says a host, moving on. They ask each of the guys for three words to describe Jenn. Grant says she's witty, charming, and intellectual. Devin says she's exhilarating, breathtaking, and spontaneous. Jonathon Johnson, twenty-seven, a creative director from Los Angeles, says she's driven, exciting, and open-minded. These guys' clear, spontaneous answers convey sincerity.

"Sam," says one of the hosts. "How do you feel about Jenn?"

Sam M. clears his throat. It is uncomfortable to deceive, and the body will show signs of it; our body will tell the truth even when we don't. An untruthful person will often display a pattern of behavior, such as a verbal tic, exhibiting discomfort. Jenn might notice her subject fidgeting or creating a "job" for his hands, like adjusting his suit jacket.

"Um," says Sam, stalling to formulate an answer. "I would say..." He looks at Jenn and shakes his head—communicating with his body that, regardless of whether his mouth is saying yes, deep down his heart is saying no. "Just, fire," he says. "And like, strong passion. So, uh...yeah, to say that..."—a long pause—"I've been doing nothing but falling in love with you from the—from the first time that we had a conversation would be uh...that would be a lie."

Devin smirks and raises his eyebrows. Jenn, who just a moment before had been laughing, now stares down at the table, seeming to disassociate.

"I didn't know if you would be able to show love the way that I knew how to," Sam continues. "And it literally took you giving a toast to all of us, saying, 'Cheers to a ferocious love,' um...for that to be so unorthodox... um, and I describe my love as *reckless*..."

Other signs of discomfort include sentences that trail off or that fail to answer the question and instead focus on something irrelevant—something other than Jenn altogether.

We cut to Devin rubbing his forehead and looking perplexed. "I have been saying this since he got here," Devin says to the camera. "Sam, he talks for the life of him, but nothing ever comes out of his mouth."

The radio hosts ask all the guys to leave except for Sam. This is Jenn's chance to attempt a participatory accusation—an untainted narrative that she can lock him into and then probe for contradictions. To that end, she wisely poses an open-ended question: What was Sam's first impression of her and how has that changed?

Fabrication is the most logistically difficult kind of lie and the easiest to disprove. Jenn asks Sam to tell her a story about his feelings for her, but since he doesn't really have any, he has to make the whole thing up. He attempts it, but he's not very smart, and he panics. He can't think of anything real to say, so he falls back on an old script and tries to improvise. "It's a testament to this process," he begins. "I told you...I almost didn't make it—I almost didn't even come here. Then I was like, 'No, this is a chance to find my wife. That's what I'm going to do.'"

"Then I got out of the limo," he continues, "and I'm like, 'Okay, this girl is not my type.' Like there's this whole idea of the unknown right there."

"Bro," says Spencer, violently cringing in the next room, where the guys are watching on a screen.

"I thought the Bachelorette was going to be Daisy or Maria," says Sam.

Everyone in the studio is shocked. Sam has stumbled into confessing to Jenn that he's not here for her.

"Obviously, you're stunning," says Sam, knowing he messed up but trying to minimize it. "There's no doubt about that right there, but like, that's—I know that that fades, but...I think I trust the process."

Qualifying words like "I think" belie doubt.

"Sounds phony," says Devin.

Jenn eliminates Sam M. My husband and I are proud of her. Then he returns for the "Men Tell All" episode. Jesse props him up in the hot seat to be interrogated by all the other guys, sitting on the studio risers, and by the rest of the world. "Well let's just keep the main thing the main thing," says Jesse. We watch a playback of the love story of Jenn and Sam M., their ascent and crash. "It's not my fault," Sam's voice-over says as it finishes.

We watch him walking out to the limo with his suitcase. "I can walk away, really, with my chin up."

We cut to him onstage now with Jesse, smiling with his teeth while he watches himself—then quickly shutting off the smile, assuming a somber expression.

"So how does it feel watching that back?" Jesse asks him.

"Yeah, it's tough," he says. "Um, it's so easy to see the—the areas where you wish you could have done something different. And I kind of have to live with it. It's something that I was trying to put a lot of stuff into words that I genuinely couldn't. And everything that came to mind, it just didn't feel like it was enough to truly define the way that I actually felt in that moment."

A deceptive person will often try to emphasize their own truthfulness with words like *truly*, *honestly*, *actually*, and *genuinely*.

"How strong did you feel for her?" says Jesse.

"Very strong," he says. But this contradicts what he said in his final episode when, as it was dawning on him that Jenn was breaking up with him, he had blurted out, "I love you."

"Truthfully, this is the first time that I've ever been really put in the position to have to explain why I love somebody," Sam says. "And I just fell extremely short in that moment right there." *Right there* is one of Sam M.'s verbal tics.

"I mean, you got put on the spot," says Jesse, of the iHeart Radio appearance. Jesse is offering Sam a rationalization to save face while confessing.

Sam takes the bait, saying, "One hundred percent."

Jesse presses on: "And I think Jenn, and I think a lot of people, just questioned your authenticity." A direct accusation.

"For sure," says Sam.

"With what you were saying."

"Yeah."

"You told Jenn that you loved her."

"For sure," says Sam, instead of saying yes. Jesse looks at him doubtfully. "Yeah, I stand—I really do—I stand by—"

"Sam, did you really love her?" Jesse interrupts him, reaccusing.

"One hundred percent," says Sam, while shaking his head.

"I think that to a lot of people watching that," says Jesse, "when you said that, it kind of felt like a Hail Mary."

"For sure," says Sam, "and I watch all this back on TV, and I think, 'I'm struggling.'"

Later in the episode, Jesse brings out Jenn. "I'm going to keep the main thing the main thing here," she says directly to Sam. She reminds him that he watched the season back on TV, just like she had—the same season.

But she says that, "Instead of taking accountability for your actions, you decided to blame it on the producers, the edit, the TV show, whatever it was."

"At the end of the day," she says, "the man that I saw on TV was exactly the man that I sat across from the entire journey." We cheer from our living room. She says that if Sam doesn't get honest with himself and learn from his actions, then she feels sorry for whoever he ends up with. She says, "This denial is not going to work for anybody."

Jenn proposes to Devin in the last episode, and he accepts. But, after the season ends, he starts to pull away. They break up before "After the Final Rose." Jenn is once again single.

So, above are some introductory techniques for her to take with her on her continued quest for the *ferocious love* she deserves. They'll help with fact-gathering, suspect identification, behavioral and discourse analysis, recognizing deception, making effective accusations, eliciting confessions, and conducting interviews in the field—such as when she and her date are bungee jumping off a building.

Or maybe, when she goes on dates closer to the ground. Such as on *Dancing with the Stars*, season 33, where she went after *The Bachelorette*. And where she met a much smarter, and seemingly more deserving boyfriend, Sasha Farber.

Sarah Gerard is an award-winning author of four fiction and nonfiction books, including *Binary Star*, *True Love*, *Sunshine State: Essays*, and, most recently, *Carrie Carolyn Coco: My Friend, Her Murder, and an Obsession with the Unthinkable*. She is a private investigator in Denver.

26

An Outsider's Perspective

AN

In today's interconnected world, media has a way of crossing borders, inviting viewers from all corners to engage with stories far removed from their own experiences. One show that has managed to transcend these boundaries is *The Bachelor*. Coming from India, where reality TV tends to revolve around family dynamics or talent competitions, I found myself captivated by this Western spectacle of romance, competition, and high-stakes drama. Shows like *Indian Idol*, *India's Best Dancer*, or even *India's Next Top Model* primarily showcase talent, while *MTV Splitsvilla*, a dating reality show, attempts to blend love and competition in a more casual, youth-oriented format. In contrast, *The Bachelor* unfolds as an entirely different universe, with its public declarations of love and emotional vulnerability laid bare for the world to see.

I first stumbled upon *The Bachelor* during one of those late-night internet rabbit holes, unexpectedly finding myself engrossed in clips of dramatic rose ceremonies and emotional breakdowns. I don't usually watch dating reality shows, preferring content in the comedy or drama genre, so this discovery was far from planned. It wasn't the love stories that pulled me in, but the cultural differences. As an outsider looking in, I've engaged with the show not as a fan but as a curious observer, analyzing how this global phenomenon reflects Western ideals—but also recognizing the universal themes that connect us all.

The entire setup—from lavish dates to emotionally charged eliminations—was unlike anything I'd seen on television before. While platforms like Amazon Prime make it accessible, *The Bachelor* isn't particularly popular in India. Shows like *MTV Splitsvilla* flirt with similar concepts, but they feel less about genuine connections and more about winning the game and amplifying the drama. It's not that emotional arcs are absent, but the focus leans toward strategic alliances and theatrical confrontations. The emotional depth and public vulnerability of *The Bachelor* felt unfamiliar. Seeing contestants openly discuss their relationships, share intimate moments, and express raw emotions in front of millions wasn't just intriguing—it was, at times, disorienting.

For instance, Hannah Brown's tearful confrontation during her season's finale or Clayton Echard's raw and unfiltered admissions of love to multiple contestants were particularly jarring. Watching the emotional weight of these moments, conveyed through trembling voices and tear-streaked faces, felt almost intrusive, as if I was witnessing something too intimate to be shared with millions. It wasn't just their words but the sheer vulnerability in their affect—quivering tones, extended silences, and conflicted expressions—that made these moments feel deeply personal and, at times, overwhelming.

For me, coming from a deep-rooted cultural background where matters of the heart, especially intimate ones, are often seen as private, it was both fascinating and uncomfortable. In my upbringing, personal emotions—especially those tied to love and relationships—are typically shared with someone you feel comfortable enough to confide in. This could be a close friend or a trusted family member, but it's rarely a large network of people. I remember during high school, like many teenagers, being overwhelmed by new feelings—some I couldn't even name. It was confusing and, at times, isolating. Coming from a conservative family, discussing such emotions at home wasn't an option. Instead, I turned to my friends. They didn't necessarily have the answers or perfect advice, but they offered a safe, nonjudgmental space to talk. That sense of comfort made it easier to navigate the uncertainty of those emotions, even if it was just through sharing and being heard. In many traditional families, particularly with elders, the topic of romantic relationships is not openly discussed, adding another layer of discretion.

Seeing people openly express their heartbreak or profess their love on camera felt both genuine and foreign to me. The moments that stood out the most were the scenes of deep emotional transparency during rose ceremonies, particularly during Becca Kufrin's season when Jason Tartick was sent home. Watching him hold back tears and sincerely express gratitude for their time together while grappling with rejection was both heartbreaking and memorable. The vulnerability in his words and demeanor stuck with me, making the scene feel deeply personal despite the public setting. It left me wondering: Does this openness make the connections more authentic, or does the setting amplify emotions for dramatic effect? Personally, I think it's a bit of both. The intensity of the environment—cameras rolling, dramatic lighting, and the high stakes—likely amplifies emotions, but the moments of raw honesty suggest a level of authenticity that can't be entirely staged.

It's this mix of authenticity and spectacle that continues to captivate me, even as I remain unsure of how to fully interpret it. At times, the show feels like a performance, designed to entertain and evoke reactions from the audience. Yet, one aspect doesn't feel staged to me: the genuine desire for a meaningful connection. Both the Bachelor and the contestants often seem earnest in their search for a compatible partner, which resonates beyond the theatrics of the format. I find myself questioning, can love be real when it unfolds in such an artificial setting? Colton Underwood, who famously jumped the fence for love, left me wondering whether his dramatic actions reflected true emotions, or were heightened by the show's pressure. At the same time, there are moments when I want to believe it. Clare Crawley's abrupt decision to leave her season early to pursue a connection with Dale Moss felt like an act of genuine conviction, as though love could transcend the constructed environment of the show. These moments leave me suspended between skepticism and belief, grappling with whether the shows' structures bring out deeper truths or simply magnifies fleeting emotions for the camera. Perhaps it's this uncertainty—the tension between doubt and faith—that makes it so compelling.

What I find most fascinating is how this show mirrors certain cultural values, particularly the emphasis on self-expression and individualism. On *The Bachelor*, it's all about fighting for personal happiness, even at the cost of exposing raw emotions on national television. Romance is portrayed as a high-stakes game where vulnerability is a strategy and confrontation is expected.

One of the most striking aspects of the game is its portrayal of group dating, where multiple people vie for the affection of one person. This setup seems deeply rooted in Western ideals of individualism and competition. It's not just about finding love; it's about proving your worth in a competitive environment. While this dynamic isn't entirely absent from the shows I'm familiar with, it takes on a different tone. In *MTV Splitsvilla*, the primary focus is on strategy and gameplay, with romance secondary. Displays of affection are less emotionally vulnerable and more tactical, often heightened by dramatic confrontations. What fascinates me about *The Bachelor* is how it shifts this dynamic. The openness, the intensity of emotional moments, and the willingness to confront issues head-on reveal values that are distinctly different from where I come from, but not entirely foreign. Personal stakes and individual expression take center stage, with participants openly exploring deep connections and addressing heartbreak in a way that feels much more personal. This level of emotional transparency, set against the backdrop of competition, offers an intriguing glimpse into how Western culture navigates the intersection of love and rivalry.

Initially, I was intrigued by how love could become such a public affair. As I continued watching, my interest deepened. I reflected on Western ideals and revisited the way I've always understood love and relationships in my own context. The way contestants share their stories, confront their feelings, and navigate relationships in such a transparent manner was unlike anything I had experienced or expected.

The show's portrayal of romance as a public spectacle is evident not just in its concept, but also in its visual execution. From grandiose settings like candlelit mansions and exotic vacations to elaborately planned dates that seem cinematic, every element is designed to amplify the drama. The visual excess—the glittering gowns, extravagant rose ceremonies, and even the dramatic camera angles during emotional confrontations—adds to the sense of a performance being played out for the audience.

Also amplifying drama are the archetypal characters—*villains* and *heroes*—who emerge as seasons progress. These tropes feel universal; they appear in most reality TV formats, though they're framed differently depending on cultural context. In *The Bachelor*, the villain is often someone who unapologetically prioritizes their own ambition or stirs up drama to stand out. This reflects a society where individualism is highly valued and personal goals take precedence over group dynamics—which I don't feel is inherently wrong. It's fascinating to see how these characters often justify their actions by expressing confidence in their pursuit of love, even if it comes at the expense of others. The emphasis on personal ambition contrasts sharply with the collective focus seen in many Indian shows I'm familiar with, highlighting another cultural difference.

Villains in the shows that I'm more culturally familiar with often disrupt group harmony or challenge deeply held social expectations. For example, in a family-focused reality show, a villain might be someone who openly disrespects elders or undermines traditional norms of respect and decorum. On the surface, their behavior—causing conflict or defying norms—may appear similar to villains in *The Bachelor*. However, the reasons they're considered disruptive differ. In the context of Indian reality

TV, such as *Bigg Boss*, villains are often framed as rebelling against traditional values, rather than embodying Western ideals of individualism. Their actions threaten the balance and hierarchy that are culturally prioritized, which is why they provoke such strong reactions.

To illustrate, a contestant in *Bigg Boss* might draw criticism for refusing to participate in household tasks or speaking out against an elder's judgment, acts that signify independence but clash with societal norms of respect and collective duty. While their behavior could be seen as empowering in a Western context, it's portrayed as disruptive in Indian media. This parallel highlights how similar archetypes take on different meanings depending on cultural values. It leaves me reflecting on whether these portrayals subtly introduce or resist Western ideals, creating a fascinating tension between rebellion and disruption. On *The Bachelor*, a "villain" might intentionally stir up jealousy among contestants by monopolizing time with the lead and frame it as part of their personal strategy to win. In contrast, in a talent competition I've seen, someone might earn the "villain" label by refusing to help a struggling teammate or calling out judges in an unfiltered way, actions that upset the group dynamic or defy expected humility. Both types of villains reflect their respective cultural values, offering a fascinating lens through which to examine how societies navigate conflict and ambition.

Despite the cultural distance, one thing that *The Bachelor* and other reality shows highlight is that love, rejection, and heartbreak are universal. Watching the contestants experience intense emotional highs and lows—the excitement of forming connections, the sting of rejection—reminds me that no matter where we come from, these feelings are shared. It resonates with me on a personal level because, like everyone else, I've experienced moments of vulnerability and the fear of not being enough, albeit in more private settings.

There are moments in *The Bachelor* where the veneer of competition falls away, and what's left is raw human vulnerability—someone opening up about their insecurities or facing the heartbreak of being sent home.

One such moment from season 24 is when Peter Weber sent Kelley Flanagan home. Her emotional reaction, feeling blindsided and heartbroken, was a powerful reminder of how deeply vulnerable the experience can make someone. Another was during season 13 when Jason Mesnick regretted his decision to eliminate Melissa Rycroft and publicly apologized to her later, showing a rawness rarely seen on the show.

These moments transcend cultural boundaries, making it easy to empathize, even if the setting or circumstances feel distant from my own. They remind me of the emotional arcs I resonate with most: the tension of love, the heartbreak of vulnerability, and the longing for connection. This emotional familiarity isn't necessarily tied to the shows I grew up with or my cultural background, but to my preference for stories that focus on human relationships and personal growth. I naturally gravitate toward narratives that emphasize the emotional journeys of individuals over overt competition.

Ultimately, *The Bachelor* may be steeped in Western ideals, but it speaks to shared human experiences that resonate with people everywhere, especially those who connect with the love stories portrayed on the show. By engaging with it through a cultural lens, I've come to appreciate how the media can both highlight our differences and underscore our shared human experiences. While the way love is expressed may vary across cultures, the emotions behind it—hope, desire, vulnerability, and heartbreak—are deeply universal. These moments, whether set in the heart of a Western reality show or within the bounds of any culture, remind us that, despite the different packages we wrap them in, the core of human emotion remains the same. This reflection not only connects me to the franchise but also affirms the power of love as a cross-cultural thread.

<u>AN</u> is a freelance writer passionate about storytelling in all its forms. As a growing writer, she's building a diverse portfolio, with some of her work

currently in the editing process. Rather than limiting herself to a single niche, she enjoys exploring a wide range of topics, pushing creative boundaries, and experimenting with different styles of narrative. Writing is her way of connecting with the world—whether through in-depth analysis, cultural essays, or human interest stories.

27

Everything Gold Can Stay

Samantha Paige Rosen

When I lived at home during the summers between semesters of college, I actively avoided the family room on Monday nights from eight to ten. I knew what I'd find once I descended the stairs: my mom and my teenage sister curled into mustard-tinted couch cushions, taking turns babbling over the television and shushing one another. It was *Bachelorette* time. While the romantic excursions played out onscreen, my mom was rapt, but if I made the mistake of being within earshot during a commercial, she might turn around and tell me why any given twentysomething's romantic trials "reminds me so much of you!" It was enough to make me wonder if ABC aired the show between May and August to torment me specifically, subjecting my dating life to comparisons and suggestions whenever I was back in Philadelphia.

At the time, I considered myself "unlucky in love," and the people in my life appeared to agree. In high school, I had been more focused on academics and music performance than on dating, with a grand total of one crush and one boyfriend (not the crush). I dated him because he asked, and he called it off after three weeks over my reluctance to spend time with him. I gave dating another try while attending Smith College, a space I sought out because I felt freer and more secure in my day-to-day environment surrounded only by other women. I made an OkCupid profile on my laptop, pre-mobile app, and went on dates with men I hoped I'd become comfortable with but never did. I held my breath as they walked me back to my dorm, praying both that they'd kiss me and I'd actually like it, and that they wouldn't even try because I already sensed I wouldn't. I'm not sure they noticed, but I never enjoyed myself; the whole experience was awkward and painful for me, although I couldn't understand why.

By the summer after my junior year, I was known by my loved ones as an intellectual go-getter who just couldn't catch a break on dates—and who was perhaps a little too picky. At the ripe old age of twenty-one, I felt behind. I felt like it was my fault that my romantic life was so far from the years-long relationships I observed my peers engaging in or the exciting trysts my mom and my sister were glued to on *The Bachelorette.*

Enter Ashley Hebert, the chestnut-haired lead of season 7. There was something about twenty-seven-year-old Ashley's search for love that made my mom wildly hopeful about my dating life. We were alike, she was convinced, in ways beyond our side-swept bangs. In the summer of 2011, despite trying to make myself scarce on Monday nights at home, I'd usually get an earful of: "Ashley is smart and down to earth, just like you!" "Ashley lived not far from us when she went to Penn dental school!" "Ashley also doesn't like one-night stands, but she's finding love, and so will you!" "See? There are guys out there for people like you and Ashley!"

The house never felt big enough in these moments. I didn't want to hear about or watch Ashley take risks for love, and probably find it, when my own efforts never worked out. And even though I talked openly about my dating trials, the pressure I felt coming from my mom to secure the relationship that would supposedly turn my life around was overwhelming. Her persistent comments gave me anxiety, as did the entire premise of *The Bachelor* franchise for that matter. How could one person date twenty people on national television when going on *one* date with *one* man made me nauseous? I wanted nothing to do with it, and I've spent much of my adult life trying to tiptoe around all things *The Bachelor*.

Nearly fifteen years later, a few things have changed: It turns out I'm gay, for starters. That realization certainly helped me enjoy dates more. I also fall somewhere on the asexual spectrum, and I'm still navigating what that means for me. Am I hopeful about encountering romantic love after all this time? Not really. I'm tired of messaging strangers and sometimes meeting up to introduce our lives to each other before the interactions peter out. I'm tired of striving for love and waiting for it. But embracing an adult life I didn't anticipate has turned out to be valuable. I get to choose my own balance of independence and community. Fun hobbies like pottery and singing in an a cappella group make up my time. And, oddly enough, my lesbian ace thirties have turned out to be fertile ground for me to get reeled in by *The Golden Bachelor*.

I first discovered *The Golden Bachelor* series from, appropriately, my mom. My intrigue over this evolution of the show annoyed me given my past hostility, but I couldn't help it. I was curious to see a romantic narrative that centered different kinds of people. I wanted a glimpse—with as much realism as heavily-produced reality TV can allow—into how people in their sixties and seventies spend time together: what they talk about and how they navigate aging, bodies, fun, desire, grief, money, work, and family. I wanted their wisdom.

When I told my mom, red-faced, that I was interested in this version of the show, she replied, "Let's watch it together." On the same mustard couch where she and my sister once screened *The Bachelorette*, my mom and I continued *The Golden Bachelor*. From the first few shots where seventy-two-year-old Gerry Turner looked in the mirror with genuine vulnerability in his eyes before recounting his decision to search for romantic love again after his wife suddenly died, I was hooked. When twenty-five-year-olds complain on TV about their harrowing search for love, I want to miniaturize a violin, but hearing seniors talk about their lives not going according to plan, as Gerry did, was more relatable, even though I'm half his age. I know what it's like for life to branch off in an unpredictable direction. Growing up, I always imagined I'd marry a man before thirty, then have two or three kids. What actually happened? That's the age I realized I was queer, and now, as a single thirty-four-year-old, I'm not entirely sure where I stand on being a parent.

While in Gerry's story I was attentive to the ways our lives diverge from our expectations, the women of *The Golden Bachelor* introduced me to possibilities for how to approach my own future. In that first episode, Sandra Mason, seventy-five, expressed how energetic and embodied she felt. April Kirkwood, sixty-five, said her participation was a chance to remember who she was before becoming a caretaker. Faith Martin, sixty, remarked that it has taken time for women in her generation to figure out what they want, but now they are more intentional in their choices. Some of these women are retired, some have second or third careers, and some still work well into their seventies—one as a pro-aging coach. Marina Perera, sixty, has three master's degrees. April, a therapist, hopes to write a bestselling book (same, girl). Seventy-year-old Theresa Nist hula hoops and taught herself about the stock market. Multiple *Golden Bachelor* contestants have dived with sharks. We don't usually hear about any of this in a culture that tends to lose interest in people over fifty, particularly women. What I observed in the first episode of *The Golden Bachelor*, as well as the internet rabbit hole I jumped into afterward, made me hopeful about aging and the different paths my life could go down.

In subsequent episodes, new layers of recognition emerged for me. Having had chronic pain since my twenties, I've often been isolated from my peers, especially on dates, where I'd awkwardly decline long walks and kayaking adventures—or worse, do these things despite my discomfort. I deeply related to Sandra's rejection of the top bunk because of her bad knees, to sixty-year-old Natascha Hardee's comment that the women should be allowed to sit during rose ceremonies, and to sixty-year-old Nancy Hulkower getting a stress fracture playing a game of pickleball.

I know my thirty-one-year-old sister, who has worn hearing aids since childhood, felt validated by Nancy flaunting her "ear candy," and by Gerry and Leslie Fhima, sixty-four, voicing their concerns over being considered less desirable because of them. In the uncommon representation of these *Golden* women, we both saw familiar pieces of ourselves.

Watching alongside my mom, I wasn't as afraid of judgment as I used to be; instead, I could talk more openly about my recent feelings around romantic partnership and what I might want out of them. After some of the women ate ice cream while playing "Never Have I Ever" and held hands in the pool while singing the Jewish folk song "Hava Nagila," I remarked that nurturing strong and joyful friendships was as important to me as romance. She understood and told me how life-changing it was to start meeting with her weekly canasta group once my youngest sister left for college. When Susan Vuocolo Noles, sixty-six, turned to Gerry on a date and told him that she'd been farting all day, I took note of how playful most of the women were—despite, or even because of, serious losses—and how liberating a lack of self-consciousness can be. My mom shared that she became more confident and lighthearted in her forties. Self-love arrived with time and experience.

I also identified with the admission of many *Golden Bachelor* participants that they hadn't felt hopeful about love for decades before coming on the show, which was echoed in the next iteration of the *Golden* series, *The Golden Bachelorette*. Early on in that season, Joan Vassos, sixty-one, somberly told her suitors that at first she felt like she didn't deserve another great love. She, as well as many of the contestants, took a risk anyway, and their hope was reignited: "I didn't know that I could feel like this again," was a frequent refrain. While I'm thrilled for them, I do feel that equating hopelessness over romantic love with sadness or dissatisfaction is, perhaps, harmful; it's why I felt inferior and dejected for much of my twenties. Were the contestants unhappy for all the years in which they didn't have a romantic partner? What else is out there for the two-dozen suitors who don't end up with the one Golden Bachelor or Bachelorette? Could they achieve a sort of radical acceptance, as I'm working on: "Although this could be great, and I'll remain open to it, I don't necessarily feel like something is missing"? Could they replace the kind of love they're searching for with something different but equally fulfilling?

The highlight of *The Golden Bachelorette* was exactly this: It depicted deeply close platonic connections that offered love and security, adding another dimension to what my future could entail. My mom and I were mesmerized seeing these adult men smoothing on face masks and meditating together, circling up and hugging as they jumped for joy, and crying—really, genuinely—when one of them wasn't given a rose and had to leave. We weren't the only ones. During the "Men Tell All" episode, where contestants who've left reconvene to reflect on their time in the house, audience members crafted "Here for the *Golden* bromance!" signs and the men were asked about the "camaraderie, love, and support" they offered each other. Gregg Lassen, sixty-four, explained that, at his age, "You've lost the opportunity to meet men on your own who are like yourself," but that the show allowed him to do just that. Fighting tears, Jonathan Rone, sixty-one, held up sticky notes that Mark Anderson, fifty-seven, left at the bottom of his empty coffee cup one morning. The first note instructed Jonathan to place the second one on his mirror, which said: "I am STRONG. I am INTERESTING. I am HANDSOME. I am DESERVING. I am ENOUGH." While I haven't had too much trouble making friends in adulthood, I aspire to give and receive this level of care and affection in my friendships. To me, this feels as comforting as the idea of romantic love.

In a way that neither the network nor viewers could have predicted, the series illustrates the forms that true love can take beyond the nuclear family. We've been sold an idea that there's one lid for every pot and only a handful of ways to have a family. But what happens to people like me who haven't fit into those boxes, or to the many people who once fit but are on the outside again? Romantic partnership is not guaranteed or everlasting the way our culture makes it out to be, but we all still deserve family, care, and security—and we can uncover it in a variety of relationships. Over the course of *The Golden Bachelorette* season, we watched the men come to this realization. After just four episodes, Dan Roemer, sixty-four, remarked, "I live alone, and to have a group of brothers is pretty cool." Gregg revealed in an interview that while his connection with Joan wasn't strong, he didn't care because he was "in love with half of the guys in the house." And as Charles Ling, sixty-six, who was still mourning his wife, left the show, he exclaimed, "It's a different form of love. I did find it." The remaining suitors then gathered to say goodbye to him, which is unprecedented in *The Bachelor* history (or so my mom told me). Only one of these men walked away with a romantic partner, but maybe it would be as life-changing if the rest became the kind of friends who are regularly and reliably in one another's lives. I hope they do.

I used to think I was "unlucky in love," and therefore unlucky in life, but I regret the time I wasted worrying. Getting hooked on *The Golden Bachelor* and *The Golden Bachelorette* has made me consider more deeply the different ways we can take care of each other as we get older—or anytime—whether as romantic partners, family, or friends. It has demonstrated fresh approaches to prioritizing love of all kinds—and fun too. How ironic that this franchise I'd deliberately avoided for so long has confirmed what I truly want out of life, thanks to the *Golden* group: love and community, self-determination, playfulness, openness about aging, and hope about the future. Imagine my surprise to discover that I could find everything that set me apart from my peers all these years in my elders—a small, even satisfying reminder that life, indeed, does not turn out the way we expect.

Samantha Paige Rosen writes about identity, arts, and culture for outlets including *Harper's Bazaar*, *Washington Post*, *Slate*, *Them*, *BOMB*, and *Literary Hub*. Her first book, *Living, Together: Reimagining Community*

in the Age of Disconnection, will be published in July 2026. Sam earned her MFA from Sarah Lawrence College and lives outside of Philadelphia, where she is a freelance writer, editor, writing tutor, and writing coach. After a lifetime of resisting *The Bachelor* franchise, she's glad she finally became a fan.

28

A Fantasy

Ilana Masad

I fill out a long form, list my age and height and weight. I attach a carefully curated collection of photos that show a lot of skin and capitalize on the thinness I "earned" (read: self-harmed myself into) via a years-long, relapse-filled bout of anorexia and (ongoing) recovery. A producer decides that my application is interesting; after all, how often do they see applicants with wholesome bookish tattoo sleeves, tasteful piercings, no apparent dreams of an influencer career, and a sincere desire to find love with a heterosexual hunk? I probably look more like a SuicideGirl[1] than the usual applicant, and that makes me unique enough to be considered for a spot as a contestant on *The Bachelor*.

(Of course, I don't *know* what the producers are looking for. I'm speculating, or perhaps it's more exact to say that I'm extrapolating from the data available to me in the near-decade I've been watching this franchise and making reasonable deductions.)

I get an email or maybe a call. The producers want to meet me! I

1 From the SuicideGirls website: "She's a girl that doesn't fit in with regular beauty standards. She often has piercings and tattoos and more. But really, it's about the attitude of creating her own definition of beauty and sharing that with the world. As for the name…the girls all commit 'social suicide' for not wanting to fit in."

undergo a lengthy interview—several, most likely—in which I attempt to seem like someone I am not: straight, cis, feminine, apolitical, a person of faith (i.e., Christian). They ask about my former relationships, and I tell them about the first high school boyfriend, then the second; I tell them about the whirlwind summer romance with the one I call Soldier Boy (they'll like that story); and the many disappointing dates and hookups with men that came in the couple years that followed. I omit the high school girlfriend, obviously, and the one in college, and the two I had (not simultaneously) in grad school.

They ask about my family, and I tell them I come from an unbroken home, which is to say, my parents were together for decades. My closest family are my mom; my brother, who is married and has a daughter; and my aunts. My aunts are gay and married, but contestants are allowed to have queers in their family these days, as long as they're not *too* out there. They're all so loving and supportive, and I tell the producers that family means everything to me. I'm telling the truth about this part.

Actually, outright lying makes me incredibly anxious, so I'm telling some version of the truth throughout, lying by omission. I'm not *saying* I'm straight, for instance, just not telling them I'm queer; I imagine this can be a fun admission to make once I'm on the show. Yes, I'm dressed in some kind of acceptable femme outfit, but they needn't know that it feels like I'm in drag. I'm not claiming I'm Christian, just not sharing that I'm Jewish; if they ask if I believe in a higher power, I can comfortably say I do, and they'll assume I mean god.

When asked about any hardships I've endured, I have plenty of palatable trauma to conveniently exploit (my dad died when I was sixteen; the aforementioned eating disorder). As a once (and thus, always) theater kid, I perform well enough to charm my interlocutors.

They want me. I can tell. I flush with pleasure. Part of me is forever a bullied seven-year-old kid, a tween getting left out of the cool kids' circle, a college student always being asked whether my hot friend is single. My nonconformist streak grew, at least in part, out of my desire to give the middle finger to the normative people and spaces that rejected me. *The Bachelor* is nothing if not the height of normcore, and the producers letting me into the club is thrilling. Yes, they know and *I* know that I'm never going to win, but I might make it surprisingly far on the *not like other girls* brand that my physical appearance could signal, and if nothing else, the producers think, there will be some viewers who will love to hate me and my whole vibe.

Next up: the background check.

This is where the fantasy always falls apart. Even if I scrubbed all my social media, the internet is forever, and I've written personal essays, articles, and reviews that publicize my political leanings, mental and chronic illnesses, and queer and polyamorous "lifestyle." All this would instantly disqualify me from one of the straightest dating shows on television. (Never mind that multiple men who've had restraining orders filed against them have passed their background checks unscathed.)

Long forms and applications are normally not a part of my fantasy life, but I've never stopped thinking about the *what if* of it all. Once, I even asked my partner if he'd be willing to remove our relationship status on Facebook, since I knew that if I had an obviously public one, I would automatically be out of the running. (He refused, not because he particularly cared about the status; he just didn't want to deal with the flood of "omg what happened?!" messages from friends and family if they noticed the change.)

I never expected to become a fan of any reality TV, let alone *The Bachelor* franchise, but once I firmly joined the ranks of avid viewers, I started wondering what it would be like to be contractually stuck in a house with a couple dozen women. No phones, no books, no TV, no internet. Instead, a rigorous filming schedule that requires them to stir up drama, do their hair and makeup every day (potentially multiple times), dress well for each outing (frequent outfit changes are part of the gig), and always (always!) be *on*.

While I'm an introvert, I give good social face, and I'm able to act the part of the extrovert when needed. Is that true for some of the women contestants? Might they, too, be acting out a version of themselves on-screen?

How much does the act of observation—the presence of cameras, the scrutiny from other contestants—influence their behavior? How different is real life, actually, in an age where we are always performing on social media which surveilles us in return?

Believe it or not, these existential questions fuel my enjoyment of the show. I'm endlessly curious about the tension between what is real and what is fake; what is pretend and what is sincere; what feels like truth in a moment of high intensity and what truths can last. I want to know what narratives the contestants tell themselves about their behavior while filming, and how those change when they're watching the show back, and how their viewpoint might morph again in ten or twenty or thirty years when their time on *The Bachelor* is long behind them. Most of what I want to know, I'll probably never learn; even the contestants who publish memoirs (likely ghostwritten) are still selling a version of themselves to go with their public persona and brand. I want to know how they share their experiences with their therapists, their moms, their children. I want to know what nightmares they wake up from years later.

Sometimes, when I'm watching a contestant having a meltdown over a man she's known for two weeks or proclaiming she's found the love of her life only to get over it by the time the next season of *Bachelor in Paradise* starts filming, I wonder what they must be feeling and thinking in that moment. How many of the crying fits are due to exhaustion, the lack of privacy, the constant camera lenses, the interview upon interview that last for hours? How often do people genuinely fall in love on the show but only because of the situationally heightened emotions, the whirlwind romantic dates, and the fantasy of a happy ending? And what does it really mean, ultimately, that people *choose* to go on these particular dating shows, known for humiliation and conflict?

In my fantasy, if I ended up on the show, I would be prepared because of how much time and energy I've spent on the franchise. I would plan to be as nice as possible, so as to make friends and not get a villain edit, but would pick sides in other people's drama (not that I would ever bring it up to the Bachelor), so as to get more screen time. I would ask the Bachelor a lot of questions about himself, and I would "be myself," by which I mean I'd be forward and honest, which will charm him because he likes a "strong woman" and, anyway, he's secretly always had a bit of a thing for bad girls and that's obviously what I am, what with all the skin I've deliberately inflicted needles on. I'd try to make it to the point of free international travel. I'd vow to use a little journal to write not about myself, but about everyone else; I'm a fiction writer, after all.

All right. Time to be honest with myself. First, there's simply no way I could ever—and I do mean *ever*—keep up with the hair and makeup and dressing routines of the other women. When I try to put eyeliner on these days, I end up looking more like my emo-kid self from 2005 than a thirty-five-year-old adult. Most of my clothes I've had for at least a decade (except for socks, which I seem to wear out faster than reasonable), some so old that they're falling apart, but they're comfortable. I haven't worn a dress in years, and while jumpsuits occasionally make an appearance on *The Bachelor*, they're rare at rose ceremonies; overalls and an old band T-shirt would probably get me preemptively kicked out of the Mansion by producers. Even if I could keep up my social facade, I'm not enough of a method actor to pull off the kind of femininity the franchise requires.

Second, I know that no matter how cynical my intentions, how armored and guarded I'd be, there would be real moments. Friendships I'd make, embarrassments I'd agonize over when trying to sleep, moments of conflict and shaking rage, and the haunting fear (present enough in my real life) that the others didn't like me. No matter how ready I'd think I was, I suspect things would get messy very quickly. I'd catch feelings (maybe even for one of the other contestants) or I'd end up crying both on- and off-camera or I'd just lose it and start yelling at people about heteronormativity and demanding to know how they can be comfortable wearing heels all the time.

No matter how curated, packaged, and scripted the narratives on our screens are, the process of creating *The Bachelor* and its offshoots is, truly, a social experiment—the shows are shockingly legal, incredibly well-financed, unambiguously exploitative, qualitative social experiments. A host of people are thrown together into luxurious-looking but realistically uncomfortable situations that might overwhelm, disgust, or trigger them. All the while, at their best—and mostly their worst—they're being filmed. The producers poke and prod at the contestants' emotions, inflame their insecurities, inflate their egos, encourage their impulses and outrages. Some contestants are chosen to deliberately dislike each other, whether organically due to personality clashes or pushed into those feelings by producer-leaked gossip. It's an experiment with no control group—unless that's us, the audience.

That's what gets me: Despite all the fakery, the women ostensibly vying for the lead's heart are also real people. They share bathrooms at the Mansion, snore or lie awake in their bunk beds, get drunk and silly or drunk and maudlin or drunk and unaware. They catch colds, feel the stirrings of desire between their legs, hunger for their favorite foods, miss their pets.

Yes, they know what they're getting into, at least theoretically. But honestly, how many of them have no idea how to deal with the intensity of the situation once they're in it? When I fantasize about joining them, it's always as a dispassionate observer, which I don't think anyone could ever be when put under this kind of microscope.

Ultimately, despite the fantasy, I don't envy these women one bit. The amount of pressure they're under, the constant need to look and sound and act palatable (or, often deliberately, otherwise) sounds utterly, devastatingly exhausting. I feel lucky, really, that I am who I am, that I cannot fathom giving this much of a shit about clothes or makeup or a man. It's not that I'm better than them—I'm not—but simply that I think being who I am is so much more comfortable. Instead of spending hours on my hair, I get to sit at home with a joint and a bowl of corn chips, a passive viewer in the ride of someone else's life.

Ilana Masad is a writer of fiction, nonfiction, and criticism whose work has appeared in *The New Yorker*, *The New York Times*, *The Los Angeles Times*, *The Washington Post*, *NPR*, *The Atlantic*, and many more. She holds a doctorate from the University of Nebraska-Lincoln and is the author of the novels *All My Mother's Lovers* and, most recently, *Beings*.

29

Birding in Paradise

Julia Moser

When Yellow-crowned Night Herons are courting, they show off their flying and display their neck-stretching skills to potential suitors. According to the Cornell Lab of Ornithology, the male Yellow-crowned Night Heron "slowly raises and then quickly retracts his head while fanning his long shoulder plumes," and "the female will sometimes reciprocate." Yellow-crowned Night Herons are mostly monogamous, sometimes maintaining their bonds from year to year. These couples nest near each other, and when the breeding season is over, they disperse to the north and the west.[1]

Doesn't that basically sound like your typical season of *Bachelor in Paradise*?

When I started bullying my boyfriend into watching *Bachelor in Paradise* with me in 2021, my pitch was: "A bunch of hot people dating each other and fighting on a beach. It's really humid, and half of them seem to lose their minds and end up leaving thinking they've found their soulmates after only four weeks—and some of them really do!" What sold him on it, however, were the birds.

1 "Yellow-crowned Night Heron Life History," CornellLab, All About Birds, accessed September 29, 2024, https://www.allaboutbirds.org/guide/Yellow-crowned_Night_Heron/lifehistory.

I joined Bachelor Nation during Emily Maynard's season of *The Bachelorette*, which aired the summer of 2012, when I was home from college between my freshman and sophomore year. As a *Jezebel*-reading nineteen-year-old who'd taken exactly one (1) Feminist and Gender Studies class, I struggled to justify this "guilty pleasure" viewing of a show that pits women against each other over a man—which is why my entrée into the franchise was *The Bachelorette*. You see, it's retrograde and misogynist to make thirty of the most beautiful dental hygienists in the country compete for the attention of a cardboard cutout who works in "medical sales" (whatever that means), but it actually makes me a feminist hero to watch a bunch of former college athletes reduced to tears as they try to win over a nice lady. I am essentially Gloria Steinem.

So I only watched *The Bachelorette*. I simply opted out of the love stories of Sean Lowe, Juan Pablo Galavis, and whoever "Ben Flajnik" is. But…I really liked Ben Higgins on Kaitlyn Bristowe's season, and then he became the Bachelor…so I broke my rule, and soon I was watching it all. I told myself that I wasn't really *enjoying* it; I was like a cultural anthropologist, observing how American attitudes towards gender, sexuality, dating, and relationships were changing. The show was getting more diverse and addressing thornier social issues, and more contestants were having frank conversations about their desires. Didn't that mean that America was changing for the better more broadly?

And then 2016 happened. Here's how Rachel Lindsay later described the experience of being on Nick's season of *The Bachelor* during that election: "We were in Finland for our Fantasy Suite episode. I made my producer take me to Victoria's Secret. I had this whole thing about being Mrs. Claus because we were going to Finland. I had red lingerie. I bought a mink hat. The day before had been the 2016 presidential election—I stayed up all night and watched Trump win. I ended up getting drunk on the date because I was so upset. Meanwhile, the producers were pressuring me to say 'I love you' to Nick. I liked him, but I was not ready to express it in that way. I thought, *Shit, I'm just going to say it, so they leave me alone.* That's how you start to feel."[2]

Anyway, it's safe to say my relationship with the franchise didn't become easier for me to grapple with after Donald Trump became president in 2016. The political environment and context around the show had changed for me, as had my understanding of what it was actually like to be a person on the show.

In 2016, I was working as the audience coordinator for *Good Morning America*, and because of corporate synergy, that meant we did a lot of promotion for *The Bachelor*. As the audience coordinator, I was responsible for gathering fans to cheer for the leads and notable contestants as they graced Times Square Studios with their presence and to get shots of their entrances and tease their interviews. Interestingly enough, the higher-ups also asked me to set up that classic *Bachelor* "Loading Dock Shot" the first time Trump himself came on the show as a candidate during the primaries. Even though the people there were not fans of his, that's what it looked like to viewers at home. Don't believe everything you see on TV folks…a good lesson for any fan of reality TV to learn.

This job also meant that I was in pretty close proximity to the contestants or leads themselves, and I was able to really understand how much hotter Nick Viall is in person than on-screen. And I started to see the contestants as more human (horrible to admit that I hadn't really thought of them as human before, but alas).

These experiences made me curious about how the *Bachelor* sausage was made. I read Amy Kaufman's incredible book, *Bachelor Nation: Inside the World of America's Favorite Guilty Pleasure*. I watched the show *UnREAL*, about a fictionalized *Bachelor*-type show loosely based on a former producer's experience. I started listening to the podcast *Love To See It* (formerly *Here to Make Friends*) which recaps the show through a feminist lens.

Director Penny Lane released a short film called *Normal Appearances*

---

2 Rachel Lindsay, "Rachel Lindsay Has No Roses Left to Burn," *Vulture*, as told by Allison P. Davis, June 21, 2021, https://www.vulture.com/article/rachel-lindsay-the-bachelor-franchise.html.

in 2018 which captures a lot of the cognitive dissonance that *The Bachelor* requires. The film takes clips from *The Bachelor* of the women on the show doing seemingly mundane things like adjusting their outfits, fixing their hair, or walking down a set of stairs. Lane removes the music and native sound from the show and replaces it with rerecorded sound effects of those actions—so you get just a woman fixing her bikini and hear the noise that would make turned all the way up. It highlights both the performed femininity that the show demands of its cast and puts the viewer in the position of these women: forcing us to imagine how cold they are and how uncomfortable their shoes feel.

In an interview with *Slate*, Lane was asked if she's a fan of *The Bachelor*, and she answered, "Yes." Then she went on: "I don't like the idea of a *guilty pleasure*. I've never really liked this phrase. But certainly, most people I know who like *The Bachelor* might categorize their love of *The Bachelor* in that way. Love-hate, love to hate, hate to love, I don't know. But the short answer is yes. I've been watching the entire franchise obsessively for many years."[3] I think I may have said exactly that several times.

So my viewing of the show has become more nuanced over time, and though I watch critically, I still watch. At a certain point I have to admit to myself that this isn't some grand noble academic project. I like the show! I'm a fan! Why is that so hard to admit? Why do I have to do so much *thinking* about it?

But recently, I found a new way to watch which feels delightfully uncomplicated: watching for the birds.

I have always liked *Bachelor in Paradise* the most out of all the shows. It's the fun drunk one. With its self-aware schlocky jokes and theme song that proclaims it "almost paradise," *Bachelor in Paradise* allows me to actually shut my brain off and enjoy the silly drama. The fraught gender and racial dynamics are, of course, still present in this iteration of the franchise,

3 Christina Cauterucci, "An Interview with Penny Lane, the Filmmaker behind *The Bachelor* Supercut *Normal Appearances*," August 14, 2018, https://slate.com/human-interest/2018/08/an-interview-with-penny-lane-the-filmmaker-behind-the-bachelor-supercut-normal-appearances.html.

but with an even number of men and women, not only can couples actually form in a manner that more closely resembles real life, but also that soul-crushing pressure on the lead is spread around. Everyone's on an equal playing field. *Bachelor in Paradise* gives the show's "villains" a chance to redeem themselves, or not, and a chance for fan favorites to show their darker sides. Plus, at this point in their reality television journeys, all the contestants pretty much know what they're signing up for! They've done it before! That makes it slightly easier to not get bogged down in the ethics of it all, the reality of reality TV.

And of course, one of the best parts of *Bachelor in Paradise* is the cutaways to all the critters crawling the beaches of Sayulita: the crabs, the bugs, the birds. And there are SO many birds! There are, of course, seagulls, crows, and pelicans, but there are also Lilac Crowned Parrots, Elegant Terns, Snowy Egrets, Cormorants, and so many more. It seems like the Yellow-crowned Night Herons are the producers' favorite though. They get just about as much screen time as bartender Wells Adams.

I was never really a nature gal growing up, but over the last couple of years, I've gotten really into birding. First of all, birds are fun little guys! They're goofy and filled with personality. Like, did you know that Corvids, like crows and ravens, can imitate human voices even better than parrots? Crows also hold grudges and remember faces. And hummingbirds are *MEAN.* I put a hummingbird feeder out on my balcony, and they're not only territorial with each other, but they also angrily chirp at you if you don't refill the feeder in what they consider a timely manner! Falcons are more closely related to parrots than they are to hawks, and all of them apparently live in my neighborhood of Koreatown, Los Angeles. I love to open up my Merlin Bird ID app and discover that the little yellow-and-black-striped dude staring at me through the window is a Yellow-rumped Warbler (who, I'm told, are often called "Butter Butts").

My boyfriend, Kenny, has been a birder for most of his life. He grew up camping and whatnot, and as an Eagle Scout, he earned a precious Bird Study Merit Badge. He can sometimes even identify birds without the app.

Not long after Kenny and I started dating, I felt like it was time to introduce him to this huge part of my life—this franchise to which I have devoted so many hours of viewing. I sat him down for the start of a new season of *Bachelor in Paradise* and told him to buckle up. He enjoyed the drama and the silliness (this was the season that Lil Jon and David Spade hosted), but it was really the Yellow-crowned Night Heron that got him excited. As we watched, we took out our Merlin Bird ID apps, set the locations to Sayulita and the date to the previous May, and identified the birds step-by-step. Birding in Paradise became a little show within the show, a fun side-game we played while the contestants did their thing.

I know we are not the only people paying attention to the avian characters on the beach—there is an entire Twitter account devoted to identifying all the birds shown in the cutaways: @bachelorbirds. They tweet things like "The Magnificent Frigatebird, it is truly magnificent to behold. I doubt the audio @BachParadise used was accurate so I looked up its actual call and I'm glad to know that they make NIGHT SCREAMS."[4] I am also glad to know that the Magnificent Frigatebird makes NIGHT SCREAMS.

I'm also glad to know about a conspiracy theory that one of the producers of *The Bachelor* is himself a birder. In 2021, Twitter user @RyanF-Mandelbaum found the eBird list of Playa Escondida, the resort where they filmed *Bachelor in Paradise*, and discovered that the birder spotting and recording the most birds at the resort shares a name with someone who works on the show...[5] Is that the reason that there are so many shots of Brown Boobies? We may never know.

More than anything, birding in Paradise made me realize that my interest in birding is not actually that different from my interest in *The Bachelor*. Both help me understand the world around me. Birding forces

4 Birds of the Bachelor (@BachelorBirds), "The Magnificent Frigatebird, It Is Truly Magnificent to Behold. '" Twitter (now X), October 11, 2022, https://x.com/BachelorBirds/status/1579970673489096704.

5 ryan (@RyanFMandelbaum), "Folks... This Might Be a Conspiracy But...the Birder with the Most Birds at the Resort Has the Same Name as a Bachelor Executive Producer/BiP Editor...," Twitter (now X), September 8, 2021, https://x.com/RyanFMandelbaum/status/1435418757304918019.

me to pay attention to my physical surroundings in a way I hardly ever did when I spent most of my time just looking down at my phone, doomscrolling about the state of the world. It sounds so corny, but I notice pretty sunsets now because I'm looking up at the sky to see if that big thing perched on top of the church in my neighborhood is a Peregrine Falcon or a Red-Tailed Hawk. I recognize my neighbors and smile at them. I feel more connected to my community just because I started observing it more. And it's fun! Is human-watching really so different from bird-watching? *The Bachelor* is like this funhouse mirror of society—a perverted modern twist on *Pride and Prejudice* where a single man in possession of a good fortune must be in want of a wife. People are also weird territorial creatures motivated by often primitive desires. We are goofy and mean and sweet, and we wear colorful sparkly outfits and partake in elaborate mating rituals. And who among us has not made a NIGHT SCREAM like the Magnificent Frigatebird?

Julia Moser is a writer and Emmy-winning producer who's worked on shows including *Good Morning America* and *AM to DM* from *BuzzFeed News*. She holds an MFA in screenwriting from UCLA, and her writing has appeared in *The Washington Post*, Betches, and elsewhere. Julia is perhaps best known for going viral in the spring of 2020 for getting dumped on Zoom, prompting *The Guardian* to coin the term "zumped." Julia lives in Los Angeles with her partner, dog, cat, and so many plants.

Editors' Conclusion: After the Final Rose

What an unimaginable journey this project has been! When we put out the call for pitches, we figured that we would get a mixed bag: people who believe in the love stories of the show, those who hate-watch, those who see the show as racist, sexist, and/or homophobic. We also suspected that we would hear from folks like us who found the community surrounding the show to be the most worthwhile thing about it. But we could not have imagined all the unique ways that Bachelor Nation thinks about and engages with the franchise. We squealed when we received proposals about birding and *Bachelor in Paradise*. We were incredibly curious to know more about a psychic live-posting her energetic reactions to contestants. And when we watched *The Golden Bachelor*, we knew it was likely to inspire plenty of reactions from potential contributors—and it did.

A lot has changed in Bachelor Nation since we were in grad school. Shit, a lot has changed since we conceptualized this anthology in 2020. Looking back at our old documents, our eyes mist over. We had dreams of Kareem Abdul-Jabbar (who is apparently a viewer!) writing for us; we looked at huge glossy anthologies for visual inspiration; we spent years meeting every week and slowly chipping away at the huge piece of marble from which we knew, eventually, a beautiful proposal would emerge; we shopped around for an agent who believed in us (and found the incredible Amy Bishop-Wycisk at Trellis Literary Management!); we bit our nails waiting to hear back from editors (and were so excited to find an enthusiastic editor in Amanda Chiu Krohn at Turner Publishing); we spent months and months meeting weekly (across time zones and through the illnesses and deaths of family and pets, pregnancy and birth, an ongoing pandemic, cross-country moves, and new jobs) and talking through logistics, methodically creating spreadsheets, inviting contributors, reading pitches and accepted pieces, and corresponding with the incredible roster of writers who joined us on this journey. In a sense, we went through a reverse *Bachelor* process: When we started, it was just us two, dreaming big. By the time we finished, our roses were accepted by nearly thirty beautiful, talented, thoughtful writers—instead of them all angling to get one final rose, we're all nestled close together in the pages of this book.

It's cliché and cringey to admit how optimistic we felt about the shows' trajectory back at the start of all that—but we did. Who doesn't think back to the turmoil of 2020 and wonder what *could've* been? In terms of the franchise, we thought that production was finally listening to its increasingly outspoken former contestants and leads, and maybe even to its fans. We thought there were glimmers of true attempts to do better in terms of diverse casting and addressing issues like mental health and sexual violence. In hindsight, the bar was so low, it was basically an underground speakeasy; we—the viewers—deserve far more than the little we thought to hope for.

We know that the shows' flaws—ones that mirror the larger shortcomings and inequities of our US American culture—are deal-breakers for many would-be and former viewers. Our contributors who write of leaving Bachelor Nation raise valid concerns and we respect their decisions. As has been pointed out: The franchise's follower-pull across various social media platforms has plummeted, and viewer numbers (with the added layer of streaming) are down too. There have long been fan discussions about the relevancy of the show. And some of the writers that we reached out to as potential contributors declined our offer because they couldn't see the value in supporting the franchise, even with a healthy dose of criticism.

That's fair! At the same time, our own contributors prove that there is still something worthwhile in sharing a monoculture. Whether it's finding representation and hope in a specific lead, maintaining friendships across distance and years via discussion of the drama, recognizing one's traumas reflected by the people on-screen, or being able to gain perspective about our own stage in life, Bachelor Nation continues to find both personal and collective value in its experience of the franchise.

We know that the discourse will and should continue. Even with our best efforts and eager interest in hearing from as many perspectives as possible, we know that not every viewpoint or identity in Bachelor Nation is represented in this anthology. This project was always going to be a sampling—interesting, insightful, and deeply human—and it was also going to be tied to a specific time and context. As discussed in a 2025 hottest Bachelor bracket on Reddit, recency bias is real—many of our contributors wrote about seasons from the last five years or so (or, because nostalgia is real too, about their first exposures to the show). Our call for pitches was only going to reach as far as our networks and the networks of those who passed it on. And plenty of people who have strong (and/or funny, profound, controversial) opinions about the franchise have no interest in committing those thoughts to paper. That this has become a book—a physical cultural artifact—was important to us as writers, readers, and academics. *The Bachelor* franchise is perceived as lowbrow, trashy, and unimportant, and it might be those things, but it is also, unintentionally perhaps, the center of a vast and diverse community that is worthy of documentation and preservation in the annals of history.

In closing, we're reminded of some memorable After the Final Rose episodes, when the engagement ended before airing. On-screen, when that happens, there's a weird mix of feelings on display: love (what could've been), heartbreak (the disappointment), and a sense of possibility (a turn toward the future, reinvention). Many of the shows' leads, even when having to face public dissolutions of relationships just barely launched, put on a strong face. We hear about it all being a part of their journey to discover their inner resolve, realizing that the love they found was self-love or even friendship—and ultimately, there's a feeling that life goes on.

For better or worse, we—Stevie and Ilana—are here to stay. Don't misunderstand us, we're not advocating for the show to live on in perpetuity. We are, instead, committed to taking pop culture seriously (while also enjoying it). More importantly, though, we're here for each other.

Acknowledgments

Thank you, first of all, to Bachelor Nation, to all the fellow fans, critics, Redditors, podcasters, writers, enthusiasts, meme-makers, etc. who have kept us company throughout the journey. Thank you, thank you, thank you to our contributors for trusting us with your words. We literally couldn't have done it without you.

Thank you to our OG shared watch party: Katie "Bones" McWain, Natalie O'Neal, Jessica Masterson, and Emily Dowdle. And thank you to our friends and family who humored us and joined for an episode here or there—we appreciated the company.

Thank you to our inimitable team: Amy Bishop-Wycisk at Trellis Literary, Amanda Chiu Krohn and Ashlyn Inman at Turner Publishing, Kelli McAdams for the cover of our dreams, Aric Dutelle for the line editing, Jacequlyn Leann Mills for the copy editing, Claire Ong for proofreading, and Jane Flautt for the marketing.

Stevie would like to thank Drs. Amelia Montes, Stacey Waite, Maureen Honey, and Gwendolyn Audrey Foster for mentorship in feminist pop culture studies. Thank you also to my chosen family: Sarrah and Kyle, Nicole, Jenny, Mitch and Dan, Emily and Katie, Anna, Bekki, Amy, Todd, Clay and Taylor, and so many more who support me in my daily life. Thank you to my parents for everything. Thank you to James for EVERYTHING.

Ilana would like to thank the friends and colleagues who listened patiently—you know who you are—during enthusiastic monologues about why an anthology like this matters. Thank you to my family for always being supportive of my many weird endeavors. And thank you to my partner, Mike, for always giving me the time and space to watch these silly shows both before and after Micha. Thank you to every stranger who, when they heard the line in my bio about this anthology, expressed their enthusiasm.

www.ingramcontent.com/pod-product-compliance
Lightning Source LLC
Chambersburg PA
CBHW021139090426
42740CB00008B/856

* 9 7 8 1 6 8 4 4 2 6 1 1 9 *